The Complete Australian Barbecue Kettle Cookbook

Ross McDonald • Margaret Kirkwood

Publisher: McDonald-Kirkwood Pty. Ltd.
Consultant Editor: Peter Battye
Design: Peter Watt
Home Economist: Margaret Kirkwood
Photography: Phil Wymant
Food Stylist: Anne Creber
Finished Artwork: Hank Byker
Consultant: Jim Sutton
Consulting Agency: Clemenger, Adelaide, South Australia
Editorial Co-ordinator: Ross McDonald

Printed in Australia by Custom Press
Adelaide, South Australia

First Printed 1988
Second Printing 1989
Third Printing 1990
Fourth Printing 1991
Fifth Printing 1992
Sixth Printing 1993
Seventh Printing 1994
Eighth Printing 1995
Ninth Printing 1996 (Revised edition) 1997
Tenth Printing 1998
Eleventh Printing 1999
Twelfth Printing 2000
Thirteenth Printing 2001 (Revised edition) 2002
Fourteenth Printing 2003
Fifteenth Printing 2004
Sixteenth Printing 2005
Seventeenth Printing 2006
Eighteenth Printing 2006
Nineteenth Printing 2007
Twentieth Printing 2007

ISBN 0 7316 3925 1

Published by McDonald-Kirkwood Pty. Ltd.
P.O. Box 5069 Halifax Street P.O. Adelaide SA 5000. 1300 301 290
© McDonald-Kirkwood Pty. Ltd.

Weber®, the Weber® and silhouette® are trademarks of the
Weber-Stephen Products Co.

Acknowledgements

So many people have contributed to the publication of this book that we have found it impractical to thank everyone, individually, for their contribution.

The character and personality of this cookbook has come, not from the authors alone, but from our many friends who have readily given advice, assistance and professional expertise.

We are indebted and grateful to the staff at Bottomline and particularly Pete Watt. Pete was an inspiration to both of us throughout the many months that it took to put this book together. His organisational ability, creativity, energy and enthusiasm during this time will never be forgotten.

We thank Peter Battye, Jane Blacket, Ross Magor, Chris Bowering and all the other staff from McDonald Co. for their help, effort and dedication.

We had so much fun working with Phil Wymant, Ann Creber and "Bruce". Their creative ability and endurance is reflected in the beautiful photographs throughout this book. We sincerely thank them.

We also thank John and Margaret Brammy and Tony and Paul, from High Street Meat Service. They provided us with all the magnificent meat that was used in recipe testing. The knowledge that they were able to pass on to us has been a major contribution to this book.

We thank Jim Sutton for his assistance in co-ordinating printing.

Finally, we thank the late George Stephen who invented the barbecue kettle, for without him this book would have never been written.

Margaret
Ross

Contents

Beef Tenderloin with Orange and Ginger (page 66)

Foreword

Ross McDonald and Margaret Kirkwood

The origins of this book date back to 1977. It was in that year that a brash young barbecue salesman approached Margaret Kirkwood intent on selling her a barbecue kettle.

The salesman was Ross McDonald and he had done his homework. Margaret's reputation as a magnificent cook was well known by the public in South Australia and the professional cooking fraternity in the other states of Australia. It would be a great advantage to him if she liked his barbecue kettles and was prepared to endorse them for him. Ross decided a magnificent roast of lamb would be just the taste sensation he needed to convince her.

He arrived in a van with his barbecue kettle and a specially selected leg of lamb. After introducing himself, he began lighting a cooking fire.

"Oh", she said, "you've got a barbecue kettle too!". So much for his homework. Margaret had purchased a barbecue kettle in America two or three years earlier. The sale was lost, but the seeds for an authoritative barbecue kettle cookbook had been sown.

Over the next ten years Margaret continued teaching people the art of gourmet cooking by conducting cooking schools, appearing on television segments, radio programs and writing regularly in the daily press.

During that time, Ross went on to help transform Australian backyards and patios with the now familiar barbecue kettle.

In 1988 Ross again approached Margaret. He was aware that there had been a few books written on barbecue kettle cooking, but there had never been an authoritative publication written for Australians. Ross had spent the last eleven years perfecting barbecue kettle cooking techniques but did not have the detailed cooking knowledge needed to produce a complete manual.

To his delight Margaret agreed to unlock many of her cooking secrets and join with him in the production of this book.

Margaret and Ross soon became very good friends. They worked tirelessly at testing and re-testing the recipes that Margaret knew so well. Many of these had never been cooked in a barbecue kettle before.

The result is a unique book which is a combination of barbecue kettle know-how and gourmet cooking expertise.

Joy McDonald

Choosing and Using Your Barbecue Kettle

The barbecue kettle - a masterpiece of cooking supremacy. When cooked in a barbecue kettle, meat, poultry and seafood have a magnificent taste and appearance, and they remain naturally juicy. Because the round kettle is really a very sophisticated convection oven, food is cooked quickly and evenly on all sides. Beautiful flavours are created by small amounts of smoke. These occur naturally in the kettle.

The secret of this remarkable cooking lies in the shape and design of these barbecues. When properly vented, they allow cold air to enter through the bottom vents. This cold air is drawn by convection, to the glowing coals, where it provides oxygen to keep them burning. Here the air becomes heated. It rises up and around the food being cooked, and finally passes out through the top vent. This flow of air continues in, around and out of the cooking chamber for as long as the fuel lasts, or until the vents are closed.

The temperature of the air is determined by the amount of fuel which is burning inside the kettle. The more fuel you have burning inside, the higher the temperature will be. The less fuel you have burning, the lower the temperature.

No matter how much fuel is being used, the temperature is always higher at the commencement of cooking. As the fuel gradually burns away, the temperature inside the kettle begins to fall. It continues falling gradually until the fuel is finally exhausted. This whole process can take as long as nine hours, depending on the quantity and type of fuel being used. At any time the temperature may be dropped abruptly by closing off the top and bottom vents. This deprives the coals of oxygen, causing them to go out.

Conventional barbecues can only grill or fry the food; kettles are able to do this, but they are also able to roast and bake. The picture shows a cross section of a barbecue kettle which is ready to roast or bake. You will notice that the coals providing

the heat are placed out to the sides. When roasting or baking, the food is placed on the upper grill between the two fires, directly above a foil tray. This method of cooking is called indirect cooking. It will be used for the majority of recipes in this book.

Cross-section of a complete barbecue kettle

Contents

Choosing a Barbecue Kettle

The first thing you should do is to make sure that you get a real barbecue kettle. Barbecue kettles are round, not rectangular. It is this "roundness" that provides the near perfect air circulation which gives them such a huge cooking advantage.

Over the past 20 years, there have been somewhere between 30 and 40 different brands of barbecue kettles sold in Australia (interestingly only 2 or 3 of these brands still survive).

Barbecue kettles vary greatly in price and quality. Often the essentials needed for barbecue kettle cooking are not included as standard equipment with your purchase. For these reasons we thought it would be helpful to examine the component parts of a barbecue kettle, and identify the essentials required for successful cooking.

Handles

The handles on barbecue kettles are normally of two types; they are either welded to the bowl or bolted through it. If the handles are welded to the barbecue, they are much stronger. Bolted handles inevitably work loose. This means enormous leverage is placed on the body of the barbecue resulting in chipped enamel or damaged paint work.

Vents

The vents are very important because they control the amount of air which can flow through the barbecue. They create the natural convection necessary for this type of cooking. Both top and bottom vents should be large enough to allow a good flow of air to enter and exit the cooking chamber.

In our opinion the One-Touch™ system as found on some of the Weber® models is superior to all others. It allows the user to remove accumulated ashes without having to remove the internal grills. It also allows the 3 bottom vents to be closed with one simple movement.

Enamel or Paint

One thing is certain - all barbecue kettles should be coated inside and out with vitreous or porcelain enamel.

Painted barbecues inevitably deteriorate for two reasons. They are usually unable to withstand the fierce heat generated by cooking fires, and they cannot withstand cleaning with caustic-based oven cleaners. Perhaps this is why kitchen ovens have always had an enamel surface.

Leg Attachment

For safety reasons, the legs should be firmly attached to the barbecue bowl. They should be capable of being locked into place, rather than merely held by thumb screws. This will avoid possible serious accidents.

Inside the Barbecue

There should be two grills. The top grill (cooking grill), which is usually chromed or nickel plated, supports the food. The bottom grill (charcoal grill) supports the barbecue fuel.

If you intend to roast or bake in your barbecue kettle, charcoal rails or baskets are essential. They hold the hot coals to the sides and prevent them from collapsing and falling under the food. If these were not included as standard equipment with your barbecue kettle, they can be acquired as an accessory. Some type of tray placed between the coals on the bottom grill will be required to catch fats falling from the meat being cooked above. We recommend the use of foil trays, rather than baking dishes or steel trays which may become too hot, causing the fats to smoke excessively or even ignite

The Size of Your Barbecue Kettle

Most barbecue kettles are 57 cm (22$\frac{1}{2}$") in diameter. This is an excellent working size for the average family. (We always use two barbecues when entertaining friends with a menu of several courses.) For instance, you could smoke food or use the wok on one barbecue while cooking a large roast on the other. Barbecue kettles with a smaller diameter than 57 cm usually have limitations with respect to the size and variety of food that can be cooked on them.

Barbecue Kettle Accessories

There is an extensive range of barbecue kettle accessories, many of which are excellent value and of great aid to the outdoor chef.

The Charcoal Basket Lighting System.

Developed during the 1990s this system is a must for people who bought their kettle for the purpose of roasting outdoors.

They make lighting preparation much quicker and easier.

This system comprises two accessories; the first, metal baskets that hold just the right amount of fuel for indirect cooking and the second, a specially shaped charcoal grill, with cavities designed to hold firelighters directly below the baskets.

Barbecue Tongs

We recommend that the barbecue kettle chef has at least three sets of household tongs for use with the kettle. One pair we always leave with our barbecues. It is a long pair, and is used solely for moving hot coals, or left over fuel around from one side to the other in the barbecue. This long set is not used to pick up or turn food. The two other sets of tongs are shorter, and are used for picking up small or large roasts, steaks, chops and the like. They soon become an extension of your hand.

Gas Conversions

Many people have such a busy lifestyle that they simply don't have time available for lighting briquettes. These are the people who love to use their barbecue kettle with gas. Remember when purchasing a gas conversion kit to select one that is designed to cook by the indirect method. The best of them have two heat settings so that you can easily produce a flavour that almost perfectly matches that of briquettes.

The Weber Gas Kit

The Weber Gas System is the only gas burner system we have found to meet these requirements. It has been specifically designed for indirect cooking.

Weber provides lighting instructions with the Gas Kit which are simple to follow. Once the barbecue is alight place the drip pan(s) on the bottom grill between the burners. Replace the top grill. The food should be positioned on the top grill over the drip pan(s). Commence cooking by replacing the lid.

Following are instructions on how to use the Weber Gas System with the recipes from this book. Each recipe details the type of fire to be used.

Hot Fire: Set the control knob to High and cook for 50-60 minutes, then turn to Low for the remainder of the cooking time.

Normal Fire: Set the control knob to High and cook for 25-30 minutes then turn to Low for the remainder of the cooking time.

Low Fire: Set the control knob to Low for the entire cooking time.

Follow these directions and in nearly all cases you'll find that cooking times are the same as shown in the recipes in this book.

Meat Thermometer

The meat thermometer takes the guesswork out of barbecue cooking. You can estimate when your food will be ready, but the meat thermometer confirms it for you by indicating the internal temperature of the meat being cooked.

Cooking Chart

Meat	Final Temperature	
Beef, Lamb (rare)	140° F	60° C
Beef, Lamb (medium)	160° F	71° C
Beef, Lamb (well done)	170° F	77° C
Pork	170° F	77° C
Ham, fully cooked	140° F	60° C
Ham, uncooked	160° F	71° C
Turkey, unstuffed	185° F	85° C
All other fowl	185° F	85° C
Venison roasts	140° F	60° C

The thermometer should be inserted into the thickest part of the meat. Wait a few minutes and you can then read the temperature. This indicates how well the meat is cooked. We have found it is better not to leave the thermometer in the meat during the cooking process. Meat thermometers may shatter under the fierce heat generated inside the barbecue kettle. They also tend to brown over

and become difficult to read. Using the thermometer when you think the meat is cooked is a much better idea. When inserting the thermometer take care not to touch any bone as this will give you a false reading.

The very latest in meat thermometers is the digital/remote version. It beeps to let you know when your roast is cooked to your liking. It doesn't even need to be near the barbecue, you can carry it around on your belt or leave it somewhere handy.

Weber Barbecue Beeper.

Portable digital receiver

The portable digital receiver displays the type of roast, the cooking options, the target temperature and the current temperature in the centre of the meat.

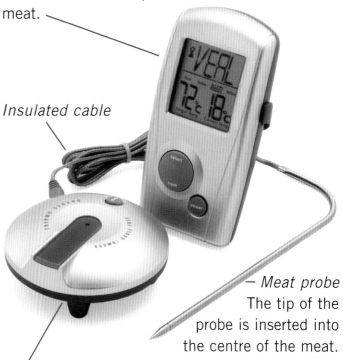

Insulated cable

— Meat probe
The tip of the probe is inserted into the centre of the meat.

Digital transmitter

The Digital Transmitter is connected to the probe by the insulated cable so that it can be located outside the barbecue.

Oven Mittens or Cloth

An insulated mitten or cloth can be a great help. Some barbecues have bottom vents located near the coals and they can become extremely hot to touch. Avoid closing any of the vents on the barbecue with your bare hands.

Skewers

For kebabs we like to use the cane variety. These require no washing up. They are fully disposable, and do an adequate job on the barbecue. If you are going to place wooden skewers directly over the coals, it pays to soak them in water for some time prior to cooking. It is important, however, to use stainless steel skewers when cooking foods which take a long time.

Chinese Wok

Wok cooking on the barbecue adds a delightful variety to outdoor entertaining. Woks are exciting to watch when being used, and they add a lot of atmosphere to outdoor cooking.

Woks are available at barbecue shops and the barbecue departments in most major retail stores. They are designed to fit both 57 cm (22½") and 47 cm (18½") barbecue kettles.

Cast Iron Cooking Grill

A cast iron grill, like the one pictured, fits on top of the cooking grill. When pre-heated, the iron becomes very hot. Cooking a steak on this surface brands the meat, giving it a magnificent appearance and flavour.

Hotplate

To complete your barbecue kettle equipment you really should have a hotplate. This will enable you to cook old favourites like onion rings, eggs, bacon, hamburgers and pancakes.

The Indirect Cooking Method

Preparing Your Barbecue for Indirect Cooking

It is the indirect cooking method that distinguishes the barbecue kettle from other barbecues. When roasting or baking, the food is placed on the upper grill between the two fires, directly above a foil tray. This method of cooking is called indirect cooking. It will be used for the majority of recipes in this book (see photograph on page 2).

If your barbecue is equipped with a Charcoal Basket lighting system go directly to **Indirect Cooking using a Charcoal basket lighting system** on page 9.

1. Open the top and bottom vents on the barbecue, and remove the lid.

2. Position the bottom grill so that its steel rungs run across the bottom of the barbecue from front handle to back handle, and set the charcoal rails in place.

3. When positioning the charcoal rails, make sure that the hooks on the rails hook over the outside straight rungs of the bottom grill. The front of the charcoal rails will then slip over the third rung of the bottom grill and click into place.

Lighting the Indirect Fire

1. Having positioned the charcoal rails correctly, place two fire-lighters on each side so that they are about 80-100 mm apart.

2. Add the required number of barbecue briquettes (for quantities see table on page 11) so that they completely cover the fire-lighters.

7

3. Light the fire-lighters by passing a lighted match or taper through the charcoal rails, and touching the lighters with the flame. Make sure that all of the fire-lighters are burning well before leaving the barbecue (sometimes a strong wind can blow them out if they are not burning well).

4. The barbecue may now be left until the coals are ready to cook. It will take about 45 minutes for the fire to establish itself. During this time, make sure that the lid is left off the barbecue. This allows more oxygen to reach the coals. ***On no account should you place the lid on the barbecue while the fire is getting ready to cook.***

The fire will now progress through the following stages.

Stage 1. The firelighters burn with a yellow flame for about 10 minutes. Do not attempt to cook in this time. The temperature will not be hot enough, and the food will absorb kerosene fumes giving it an unpleasant taste.

Stage 2. After the fire-lighters cease burning, the fire will appear to go out. This is not so, the coals are in fact burning below, and the fire will continue to grow. There is insufficient temperature to cook at this stage.

Stage 3. 20-25 minutes after lighting, some of the coals will be glowing and coated with a brownish ash. To achieve the correct cooking temperature, all of the briquettes should be ashed over, so don't attempt to cook yet.

Stage 4. 40-45 minutes after lighting, all the coals will be ashed over and ready for cooking,

This completes the fire preparation for indirect cooking.

Indirect Cooking Fire - Quick Method

The time taken to establish the fire can be shortened from 45 minutes to about 30 minutes. This is done by using 4 fire-lighters on each side instead of 2. This "quick method" should only be used in emergencies, due to the increased cost of fire-lighters involved.

Indirect Cooking using a Charcoal Basket Lighting System.

1. Open the top and bottom vents on the barbecue, and remove the lid.
2. Position the bottom grill so that its steel rungs run across the barbecue rather than from front to back, this ensures that the hot baskets are not located under the handles when your fires are alight.
3. Place 4 fire-lighters (2 on each side) in the cavities provided in your Charcoal grill.
4. Place the metal baskets on the Charcoal grill and fill them with the required number of briquettes. (For quantities, see table on page 11).

The inside of your barbecue kettle should now look like this.

Lighting the Indirect Fire using a Charcoal Basket Lighting System.

1. Light the fire-lighters using a lighted match or taper. Make sure that all of the fire-lighters are burning well before leaving the barbecue (sometimes a strong wind can blow them out if they are not burning well).

2. Once the fire-lighters are alight move the metal baskets to the centre of the Charcoal grill over the flames.

Stage 1. The fire-lighters burn with a yellow flame for about 10 minutes. Do not attempt to cook at this time. The temperature will not be hot enough and the food may absorb kerosene fumes, giving it an unpleasant taste

Stage 2. After the fire-lighters cease burning, the fire will appear to go out. This is not so, the coals are in fact burning below, and the fire will continue to grow. There is insufficient temperature to cook at this stage.

3. The barbecue may now be left until the coals are ready to cook. It will take about 35 minutes for the fire to establish itself. During this time, make sure that the lid is left off the barbecue and all vents are open. This allows more oxygen to reach the coals which helps establish the fire faster. **On no account should you place the lid on the barbecue or close the vents while the fire is getting ready to cook. (Your barbecue is not the same as an oven.)**

The fire will now progress through the following stages.

Stage 3. 20-25 minutes after lighting, some of the coals will be glowing and coated with a brownish ash. To achieve the correct cooking temperature, all of the briquettes should be ashed over, so don't attempt to cook yet.

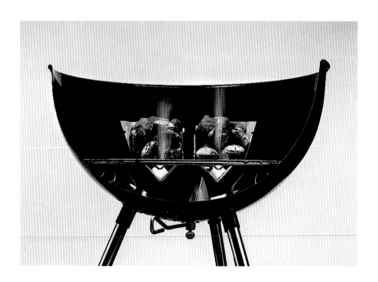

4. About 35-40 minutes after lighting, all the coals will be ashed over and ready for cooking. It's now time to separate the metal baskets. Using long handled tongs and mittens, move them as far as possible out to the sides.

This completes the fire preparation for indirect cooking.

Controlling the Temperature - Indirect Cooking

The temperature inside the barbecue is determined by the number of barbecue briquettes burning inside. In Australia there are two sizes of barbecue briquettes available to consumers. If you are using the smaller size briquettes you will need more of them to achieve the correct cooking temperature than the larger size briquettes. Originally all barbecue briquettes were about golf ball size or a little smaller. More recently larger barbecue briquettes (about twice that size) have been introduced to the Australian market.

In this book, cooking temperatures are described for the various recipes in the following way:

Hot fire
Normal fire
Low fire
Low smoke fire

In a 57 cm (22 ½") barbecue kettle these temperatures are achieved by using the following barbecue briquette quantities:

Large Briquette Quantities (Heatbead® Brand).

Hot fire	64 barbecue briquettes - 32 on each side
Normal fire	50 barbecue briquettes - 25 on each side
Low fire	36 barbecue briquettes - 18 on each side
Low smoke fire	12 barbecue briquettes - 6 on each side

Small Briquette Quantities (Other Brands).

Hot fire	90 barbecue briquettes - 45 on each side
Normal fire	70 barbecue briquettes - 35 on each side
Low fire	56 barbecue briquettes - 28 on each side
Low smoke fire	16 barbecue briquettes - 8 on each side

We suggest that you actually count the briquettes when preparing your first few indirect cooking fires. After a while, you will become familiar with the various quantities required and you will be able to judge them visually.

As we mentioned earlier, the temperature is always higher at the commencement of cooking, and as the fuel gradually burns away, the temperature falls. As a rule of thumb, after approximately 2 hours of cooking with the lid on, a hot fire will become the equivalent of a normal fire, and a normal fire will become the equivalent of a low fire after the same period of time. Knowing this can be very useful when planning to cook a second course.

11

Cooking Using the Indirect Method
Use of Foil Drip Trays

When the fire is ready for cooking, a drip tray or trays will need to be placed on the bottom grill between the two fires. These trays will catch any fats, juices and bastes which fall from the food during cooking. When selecting a drip tray, it is important that the tray be large enough to catch all of the drippings from the food above. In this book, we have suggested two configurations for the use of drip trays.

A single drip tray is used for smaller roasts, and is adequate for most meals. For larger meals 1½ drip trays should be used by placing one large and one small tray on the bottom grill as shown in the illustration.

1 drip tray

1½ drip trays

Positioning the Cooking Grill

Place the cooking grill on the barbecue with the grill handles directly over the fires. You will notice that there are holes in the grill located beneath the handles. These are to facilitate the addition of either smoking wood chunks or, should the need arise, extra barbecue fuel. A wonderful innovation in the design of cooking grills was the introduction of hinged doors in the grill for this purpose. These hinged cooking grills can now be purchased as accessories.

The Hinged cooking grill in action.

Indirect Smoke-Cooking

Smoke-cooking adds a beautiful change to the aroma and flavour of many foods. Throughout this book, we have provided many recipe suggestions using smoke-cooking. Smoke-cooked foods are particularly delicious when combined with sweet glazes. The great advantage of this type of cooking is that it is so simple.

Normal indirect fires are transformed into smoke-cooking fires by adding just 1 or 2 chunks of hickory wood (or other smoking material) to the coals on each side of the barbecue. The more smoke flavour you require, the more hickory chunks you add. It is a good idea to leave the lid off for a little while when adding the hickory. This allows it to catch fire. Once it is burning, replace the barbecue lid, and it will begin smoking quite intensely. It is important to use chunks of smoking wood rather than chips or sawdust. The chunks smoke longer and require less attention, resulting in a far superior smoke flavour.

Lower temperatures are created inside the barbecue by using less fuel. We have found "The Low Smoke Fire" (see page 11 for briquette quantities) creates an excellent temperature for smoking small fish.

Preparing a Low Smoke Fire

1. For this type of fire, only 1 fire-lighter is used. Place the fire-lighter behind a charcoal rail on one side of the barbecue.

2. Count out the required number of barbecue briquettes and carefully pile them over the firelighter. Ignite the fire-lighter in the normal manner.
3. Allow all of the barbecue briquettes to ash over (about 40 minutes), then use tongs to transfer half of the briquettes to the other side of the barbecue.

4. Position the drip tray on the bottom grill and add 1 dry hickory chunk to the coals on each side. Leave the lid off until the hickory is smoking well.
5. Place the cooking grill in position, and commence cooking as the recipe directs.

The Direct Cooking Method

This method of cooking differs from the indirect cooking method because the coals which provide the heat are placed on the bottom grill directly under the food being cooked. In barbecue kettles, direct cooking is used for grilling steaks, either on the wire grill provided or a cast iron cooking grill. Foods containing lots of fat, such as chops and sausages, should never be cooked using this method. The fats dripping from such foods cause excessive smoking and grease build-up inside the barbecue. They should be cooked using the indirect method. The direct cooking fire is also used for hotplate and wok cooking. We never use a direct cooking fire for any application other than steaks, toast, hotplate or wok cooking.

Preparing the Barbecue for Direct Cooking

1. Open the top and bottom vents on the barbecue and remove the lid.

2. Position the bottom grill so that its steel rungs run across the barbecue from front handle to back handle, and set the charcoal rails in place.

3. When positioning the charcoal rails, make sure that the hooks on the rails hook over the outside straight rungs of the bottom grill. The front of the charcoal rails will then slip over the third rung of the bottom grill, and click into place. In the case of direct cooking the charcoal rails keep the coals centrally located on the bottom grill.

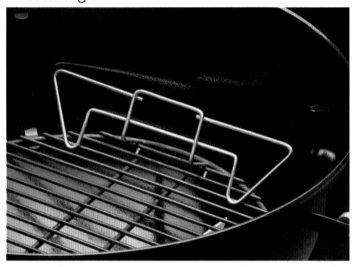

Lighting the Direct Fire

1. Having positioned the charcoal rails correctly, place 3 or 4 fire-lighters on the bottom grill between the charcoal rails, and add the barbecue briquettes (not heating briquettes).

2. Light the fire-lighters with a match or taper, and using a pair of tongs, cover them with barbecue briquettes. Make sure that all of the fire-lighters

are burning well before leaving the barbecue (sometimes a strong wind can blow them out if they are not burning well).

3. The barbecue may now be left until the coals are ready to cook. It will take about 45 minutes for the fire to establish itself. During this time, make sure that the lid is left off the barbecue. This allows more oxygen to reach the coals. **On no account should you place the lid on the barbecue while the fire is getting ready for cooking.**

The fire will now progress through the 4 stages previously described under the section dealing with lighting the indirect fire (see pages 8-9).

40-45 minutes after lighting, all the coals will be ashed over and ready for cooking. This completes the fire preparation for direct cooking.

Controlling the Temperature - Direct Cooking

The temperature of a direct cooking fire is determined by the number of barbecue briquettes used. In this book, direct cooking fires are described in two ways:

Direct fire
Low direct fire

In a 57 cm (22½") barbecue kettle, these temperatures are achieved by using the following barbecue briquette quantities:

Large Briquette Quantities (Heatbead® Brand)

Direct fire	40 barbecue briquettes
Low direct fire	25 barbecue briquettes

Small Briquette Quantities (Other Brands).

Direct fire	70 barbecue briquettes
Low direct fire	45 barbecue briquettes

We suggest that you actually count the briquettes when preparing your first few direct or low direct cooking fires. After a while, you will become familiar with the quantities required and you will be able to judge them visually.

Positioning the Cooking Grills, Hotplate or Wok

Place the wire cooking grill on the barbecue so that the handles are directly over the charcoal rails. If you are using a cast iron cooking grill or hotplate, it is placed centrally on top of the wire grill - see photograph page 6.

When cooking with the wok, the wire cooking grill is not required. Position the wok on the barbecue so that the base of the wok is just above the hot coals. Make sure that the wok is level, and that it rests on the 4 internal lugs inside the kettle.

How to Test the Temperature of the Oil when Deep Frying

When deep frying in the wok, always test the temperature of the oil before adding your food. This is best done by using the handle of a wooden spoon. To do this heat the oil for a short time. Place the handle of the spoon in the oil so that it is pressing against the bottom of the wok in the centre. If bubbles rise freely from the wood at the bottom, the oil is hot enough for cooking.

Warning!

Do not leave the wok unattended. A hot wok containing 1-2 litres of cooking oil should always be under adult supervision. After cooking always remove the wok from the barbecue and put it in a safe place out of the reach of children. If the wok is left on the barbecue, the oil may overheat and even ignite. Because the wok becomes very hot,

very quickly, never preheat the wok for more than 20 or 30 seconds before adding your oil. If the wok becomes too hot the oil will spontaneously ignite.

Use of Weights and Measures in this Book

Australian Standard metric measuring cups and spoons are used throughout this book. All spoon measurements are level.

1 cup	250mls
1 tablespoon	20mls
1 teaspoon	5 mls

We suggest that you purchase a set of plastic metric measures bearing the seal of approval of the Standards Association of Australia. These form the basis of all metric cookery and will be invaluable for future use. They consist of:

1. A set of four measuring cups based on the 250ml cup.
2. A set of four spoons - 1 tablespoon, 1 teaspoon, $1/2$ teaspoon and $1/4$ teaspoon.
3. A one litre measuring jug with both cup & millilitre graduations.

It is also a good idea to invest in a set of metric scales for measurement of ingredients where a weight rather than a cup measurement is required e.g. 500 g Topside Steak.

When testing the recipes for this book, we used Weber® 57 cm (22$1/2$") One-touch™ barbecues and accessories, Heat Beads® barbecue fuel and Jiffy® fire-lighters. All barbecue fuel quantities, lighting times and cooking times have been determined using these products.

Tempura

16

Guide to Meat and Poultry Cooking times.

Measuring the thickness of meat will normally give a better indication of how long it needs to cook, rather than weighing it.

Although nearly all cookbooks suggest that you cook meat for so many minutes per kilo (or pound), we believe that the cooking time of roasts has surprisingly little to do with the weight of meat. It has more to do with its thickness and temperature.

The steak (above), 2.5cm (1 inch) thick takes approximately 20-25 minutes to cook in a barbecue kettle using the indirect cooking method. Yet exactly the same piece of meat rolled into a round roast (below) will take about 2 hours to cook.

This is because meat cooks by absorbing heat from the outer surface to its middle. Consequently, the thicker the meat the longer it takes to cook.

When cooking two or more roasts simultaneously, you will need to allow more cooking time. Extra roasts absorb a surprisingly high amount of heat from the coals.

In addition to the factors that affect cooking times (on pages 20-21) the temperature of the meat when you start cooking is important. Obviously if the meat is icy-cold it will take much longer to cook. Try and start off with meat that is at or near room temperature and use a meat thermometer to confirm that the meat is cooked properly, see page 5.

Meat Roasting.

How to estimate the cooking times of lamb, beef and pork roasts.

A good guide to the time needed to cook roasts in this book is to measure the thickness of the meat and allow 1 minute of cooking time per millimetre of thickness. If done correctly, this should produce a roast that is cooked to medium. For example, a leg of lamb 90 mm thick should cook to medium in approximately 90 minutes or $1\frac{1}{2}$ hours. If you want your lamb to be well done, you will need to add 20% (or 18 minutes) to the cooking time. On the other hand, if you want it rare you deduct 20% (or 18 minutes).

The procedure for estimating the cooking time of meat is as follows:-

1. Lie the roast on a workbench with its broadest side at the bottom.

2. By holding a skewer like a pencil, measure the depth of the meat to its highest point from the base.

3. Using a ruler, measure from the skewer the thickness of the roast in millimetres. This will represent the approximate cooking time in minutes needed to cook the roast.

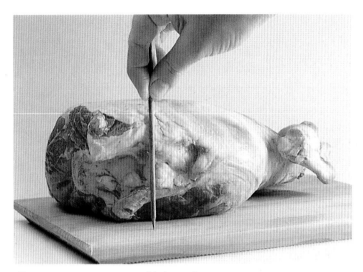

How to measure roast with bone in.

How to measure boneless roast (roll).

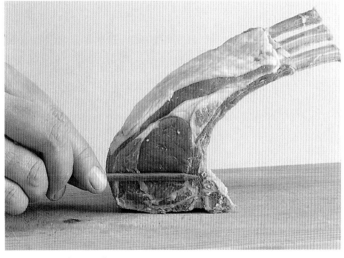

How to measure rib on the bone.

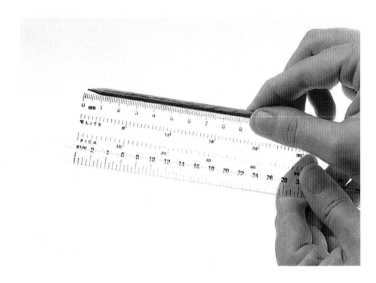

Poultry roasting.

Using the fuel quantities recommended in this book the following estimated cooking times are a good guide for all roasting birds including chicken, turkeys, ducks and geese.

All poultry should be at refridgerated temperature before being cooked. If the bird has been frozen, place your hand in the cavity of the bird to check that it has thawed completely. If there is still ice in the centre you'll need to immerse the bird in warm to hot water until completely thawed. Always pat the bird dry and drain the cavity before coating it with cooking oil.

It's easy to estimate the cooking time for poultry. You simply select the Number or Weight of the bird that you want to cook, find this on the table on the opposite page and read off the cooking time.

Size of bird	Metric Weight	USA/UK Weight	Cooking time	Size of bird	Metric Weight	USA/UK Weight	Cooking time
Number 4	400g	0.9 lb	40 mins	Number 56	5.6kg	12.3 lbs	2 hours 24 mins
Number 5	500g	1.1 lbs	42 mins	Number 57	5.7kg	12.5 lbs	2 hours 26 mins
Number 6	600g	1.3 lbs	44 mins	Number 58	5.8kg	12.8 lbs	2 hours 28 mins
Number 7	700g	1.5 lbs	46 mins	Number 59	5.9kg	13.0 lbs	2 hours 30 mins
Number 8	800g	1.8 lbs	48 mins	Number 60	6.0kg	13.2 lbs	2 hours 32 mins
Number 9	900g	2.0 lbs	50 mins	Number 61	6.1kg	13.4 lbs	2 hours 34 mins
Number 10	1.0kg	2.2 lbs	52 mins	Number 62	6.2kg	13.6 lbs	2 hours 36 mins
Number 11	1.1kg	2.4 lbs	54 mins	Number 63	6.3kg	13.9 lbs	2 hours 38 mins
Number 12	1.2kg	2.6 lbs	56 mins	Number 64	6.4kg	14.0 lbs	2 hours 40 mins
Number 13	1.3kg	2.9 lbs	58 mins	Number 65	6.5kg	14.3 lbs	2 hours 42 mins
Number 14	1.4kg	3.0 lbs	1 hour	Number 66	6.6kg	14.5 lbs	2 hours 44 mins
Number 15	1.5kg	3.3 lbs	1 hour 2 mins	Number 67	6.7kg	14.7 lbs	2 hours 46 mins
Number 16	1.6kg	3.5 lbs	1 hour 4 mins	Number 68	6.8kg	15.0 lbs	2 hours 48 mins
Number 17	1.7kg	3.7 lbs	1 hour 6 mins	Number 69	6.9kg	15.2 lbs	2 hours 50 mins
Number 18	1.8kg	4.0 lbs	1 hour 8 mins	Number 70	7.0kg	15.4 lbs	2 hours 52 mins
Number 19	1.9kg	4.2 lbs	1 hour 10 mins	Number 71	7.1kg	15.6 lbs	2 hours 54 mins
Number 20	2.0kg	4.4 lbs	1 hour 12 mins	Number 72	7.2kg	15.8 lbs	2 hours 56 mins
Number 21	2.1kg	4.6 lbs	1 hour 14 min	Number 73	7.3kg	16.0 lbs	2 hours 58 mins
Number 22	2.2kg	4.8 lbs	1 hour 16 mins	Number 74	7.4kg	16.3 lbs	3 hours
Number 23	2.3kg	5.0 lbs	1 hour 18 mins	Number 75	7.5kg	16.5 lbs	3 hours 2 mins
Number 24	2.4kg	5.3 lbs	1 hour 20 mins	Number 76	7.6kg	16.7 lbs	3 hours 4 mins
Number 25	2.5kg	5.5 lbs	1 hour 22 mins	Number 77	7.7kg	16.9 lbs	3 hours 6 mins
Number 26	2.6kg	5.7 lbs	1 hour 24 mins	Number 78	7.8kg	17.2 lbs	3 hours 8 mins
Number 27	2.7kg	5.9 lbs	1 hour 26 mins	Number 79	7.9kg	17.4 lbs	3 hours 10 mins
Number 28	2.8kg	6.2 lbs	1 hour 28 mins	Number 80	8.0kg	17.6 lbs	3 hours 12 mins
Number 29	2.9kg	6.4 lbs	1 hour 30 mins	Number 81	8.1kg	17.8 lbs	3 hours 14 mins
Number 30	3.0kg	6.6 lbs	1 hour 32 mins	Number 82	8.2kg	18.0 lbs	3 hours 16 mins
Number 31	3.1kg	6.8 lbs	1 hour 34 mins	Number 83	8.3kg	18.3 lbs	3 hours 18 mins
Number 32	3.2kg	7.0 lbs	1 hour 36 mins	Number 84	8.4kg	18.5 lbs	3 hours 20 mins
Number 33	3.3kg	7.3 lbs	1 hour 38 mins	Number 85	8.5kg	18.7 lbs	3 hours 22 mins
Number 34	3.4kg	7.5 lbs	1 hour 40 mins	Number 86	8.6kg	18.9 lbs	3 hours 24 mins
Number 35	3.5kg	7.7 lbs	1 hour 42 mins	Number 87	8.7kg	19.1 lbs	3 hours 26 mins
Number 36	3.6kg	7.9 lbs	1 hour 44 mins	Number 88	8.8kg	19.4 lbs	3 hours 28 mins
Number 37	3.7kg	8.1 lbs	1 hour 46 mins	Number 89	8.9kg	19.6 lbs	3 hours 30 mins
Number 38	3.8kg	8.4 lbs	1 hour 48 mins	Number 90	9.0kg	19.8 lbs	3 hours 32 mins
Number 39	3.9kg	8.6 lbs	1 hour 50 mins				
Number 40	4.0kg	8.8 lbs	1 hour 52 mins				
Number 41	4.1kg	9.0 lbs	1 hour 54 mins				
Number 42	4.2kg	9.2 lbs	1 hour 56 mins				
Number 43	4.3kg	9.5 lbs	1 hour 58 mins				
Number 44	4.4kg	9.7 lbs	2 hours				
Number 45	4.5kg	9.9 lbs	2 hours 2 mins				
Number 46	4.6kg	10.1 lbs	2 hours 4 mins				
Number 47	4.7kg	10.3 lbs	2 hours 6 mins				
Number 48	4.8kg	10.6 lbs	2 hours 8 mins				
Number 49	4.9kg	10.8 lbs	2 hours 10 mins				
Number 50	5.0kg	11.0 lbs	2 hours 12 mins				
Number 51	5.1kg	11.2 lbs	2 hours 14 mins				
Number 52	5.2kg	11.4 lbs	2 hours 16 mins				
Number 53	5.3kg	11.7 lbs	2 hours 18 mins				
Number 54	5.4kg	11.9 lbs	2 hours 20 mins				
Number 55	5.5kg	12.0 lbs	2 hours 22 mins				

Use foil to shield the edges of larger birds.

Using our Easy Recipe Guide

Each recipe in this book is headed with a recipe key. For example:

GINGER PRAWNS

Normal fire, indirect, 8-15 minutes, with lid on. Serves 8-10

Normal fire indicates the type of fire you should use - either hot, normal, low, low smoke, direct, or low direct.

Indirect indicates the cooking method - either direct or indirect.

8-15 minutes indicates the total cooking time for the recipes.

With lid on, all recipes with the exception of some wok, toast and hotplate recipes are cooked with the lid on.

Serves 8-10 indicates the number of people who may be served with the quantities given in the recipe.

This recipe key enables you to look at any recipe in the book, and at a glance, determine the type of fire required, the cooking time, and the number of people the recipe ingredients will cater for.

Useful Tips

1. When using the indirect cooking method, always make sure that the fires are located to the sides of the barbecue bowl and not adjacent to the bowl handles. This will help keep the handles cool and produce a more even air-flow through the bottom vents.

2. When moving your barbecue, always remove the lid. This will prevent the lid from falling off the barbecue and becoming damaged. Do not place a hot lid on a lawn or any other surface which could be damaged by heat.

3. When lighting your barbecue for indirect cooking, make use of any breeze or wind. This will help fan the fires, resulting in a faster light up time. The barbecue should be placed in a position so that either the front or back handle is facing into the direction of the wind. This will allow the wind to fan both fires evenly, rather than having one side catch faster than the other.

4. Make sure that the top and all the bottom vents are fully open before placing the lid on the barbecue to commence cooking. If this is not done, the fire will go out.

5. Before lighting your barbecue, make sure that the vents at the bottom are not obstructed by ash or left-over briquettes from previous cooking.

6. Heating briquettes available for slow combustion stoves are **not suitable** for cooking in barbecue kettles. These briquettes contain quite large quantities of toxic volatiles.

7. When lighting the fire there will initially be fumes generated by the fire-lighters. Do not stand over the barbecue inhaling these fumes.

8. When using the indirect cooking method, always make sure that both fires are burning evenly. If one fire is burning faster than the other more oxygen will be drawn to it. This may cause the other fire to go out due to lack of air. You may use tongs to transfer coals from one fire to the other in order to balance them.

9. Before cooking, it is necessary to wait until all of the coals are coated with ash. Any coals which are not burning properly will reduce the temperature inside your barbecue.

10. When preparing a hot fire for your kettle barbecue the lighting time may extend from the normal 40-45 minutes to approximately

1 hour. You should take this into account for timing purposes.

11. All meats should be thawed and at room temperature before cooking.

12. Wind cools the surface of the barbecue kettle. On a windy day this will considerably lengthen the cooking time. It is advisable to carefully move the barbecue to a sheltered place.

13. When indirect cooking, if the food is too close to the coals, burning may occur on the edges nearest the fires. This can be avoided by shielding the edges of the food with some foil, see page 27.

14. When you are glazing and smoking food, only apply the glaze during the last 30-40 minutes of cooking time. If applied too early, the sugar in the glaze will caramelise and turn black. If the meat has been smoked prior to glazing, the glaze will not adhere. Always glaze before adding smoking wood.

15. When preparing egg wash, mix equal quantities of beaten egg and water if you want your pastry nice and crisp. For softer pastry, mix equal quantities of beaten egg and milk.

16. Do not continually lift the lid to check the food while cooking. This will cause considerable heat loss and lengthen the cooking time.

17. Hickory wood is generally regarded as the world's best smoking wood, but dried mallee root, red-gum or acacia pieces also work reasonably well. *For health reasons, only use recognised smoking hard-woods, and make sure that they have not been treated or painted in any way.*

18. When using the wok, the barbecue lid can be used as a wok lid. The lid vent may be open or closed as needed.

19. Always use tongs when removing meats from the barbecue. Piercing the meat with a fork allows the juices to escape.

20. We have mentioned earlier that a hot fire will become a normal fire, and a normal fire a low fire after about 2 hours of cooking. If you intend using either of these fires for a second course, you should remove the barbecue lid for about 10 minutes before cooking the second time. This allows a flood of oxygen to reach the coals and revitalise them.

21. If you need to add more barbecue briquettes to the fire to cook a second course, you must leave the lid off the barbecue until the additional briquettes are ashed over before you continue cooking. This will take about 20-30 minutes. These additional briquettes will ignite without the use of fire-lighters.

22. If a breeze is blowing ash on you or your guests while you are cooking, carefully move the barbecue down wind, or move your guests up wind.

23. When you have finished cooking, remember to close the top and bottom vents to extinguish the fire. Any left-over fuel may be used as part of your cooking fire the next time your barbecue is used. By doing this quite large savings will result.

24. Store your unused fire-lighters in a plastic bag secured with a twist tie or rubber band. If they are left unsealed for any length of time, the flammable ingredients will evaporate and reduce their effectiveness.

25. Always store your barbecue briquettes in a dry place. Never try to use damp or wet barbecue fuel for cooking.

26. When cooking a roast and your guests are late, do not over-cook the food. Remove the roast from the barbecue when it is properly cooked. The meat will retain its heat for a remarkably long time provided that it has not been carved.

27. When cooking large roasts which take 2 hours or more to cook, allow up to twice as much time as normal for the vegetables to cook.

Carving Tips

The art of carving meat was once considered an essential refinement in table service. In days gone by the head of the family would carve the meat at the dinner table for all to see. In this way children learnt the skills of carving by merely being at the table.

The advent of fast foods, snacks and casual eating habits has meant that many of these skills have been lost to the average Australian household.

The barbecue kettle is used to cook so many beautiful roasts. These often need to be carved and served in the presence of your family and friends. There is nothing worse than to see a lordly roast or noble bird hacked and butchered until it becomes an untidy mess.

With this in mind, we thought it would be helpful to illustrate some carving techniques for the basic cuts of meat and poultry.

Carving Equipment

Truly successful carving requires a very sharp knife with a perfect edge. If you have difficulty sharpening your knives, ask your butcher for help. Most butchers are more than happy to show you the sharpening techniques. If requested, some will even create and maintain a perfect edge for you.

Traditional carving has always involved the use of a fork. We have found that with careful use, short-handled tongs do a better job. They enable you to hold a roast without piercing it. Furthermore they make it easier to transfer the carved slices of meat from the carving dish to the dinner plate.

The Jam Roll Cut

This is used for rolled roasts of beef, Beef Wellington, roasts of scotch fillet and other similar cuts.

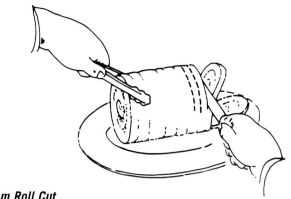

Jam Roll Cut

Rib Roasts and Loins on the Bone

Remove the meat from the bone as shown. Cut the meat into steaks, one for each person.

Legs of Lamb, Pork and Ham

Always carve these vertically as illustrated, starting at the shank end and working towards the cushion.

Carving in this way means that less of the uncarved meat is exposed to the air. The roast will not dry out as readily. Furthermore, if the leg has been smoked or glazed, this carving method ensures that everybody receives a taste of the smoked or glazed surface.

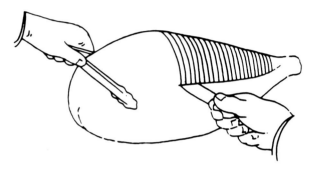

Crown Roast

Slice the roast downwards between the ribs.

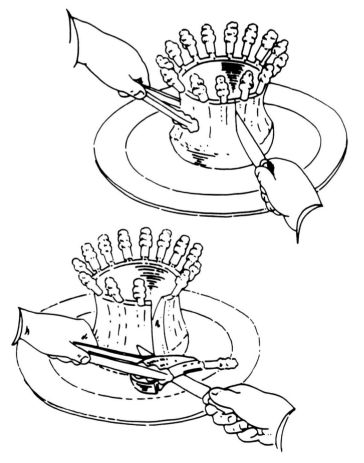

Chicken

1. Remove the thigh and drumstick from the chicken by cutting between the thigh and the body of the chicken to expose the thigh joint. Using tongs, prise the thigh away from the body and cut through the joint with your knife. Repeat this for the other drumstick and thigh.

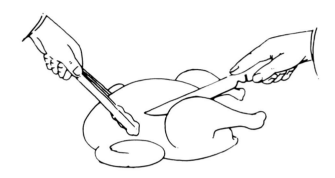

2. Remove the wing by slicing the breast meat slightly above it and cutting down until the joint is exposed. Cut through the joint to remove the wing with part of the breast meat attached. Repeat this process on the other side of the bird.

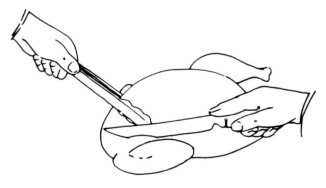

3. Carving the breast is now simple. Slice from top to bottom as illustrated.

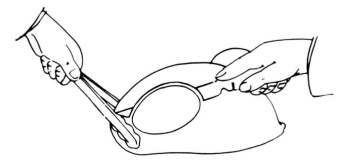

Turkey

1. Lay the turkey on its side with its back facing toward you. Hold the end of the leg with one hand. Apply pressure to straighten the leg while cutting through the joint to remove the drumstick.

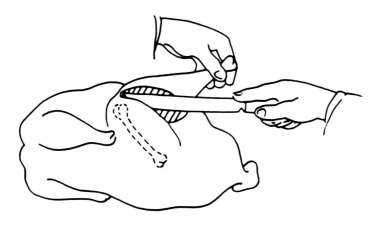

2. The drumstick may be served whole, or the meat carved from it as illustrated.

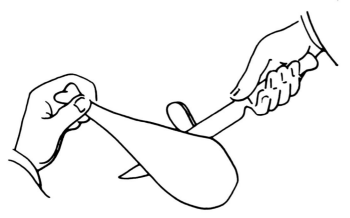

3. To carve the thigh, take some slices from it until the thigh bone is showing.

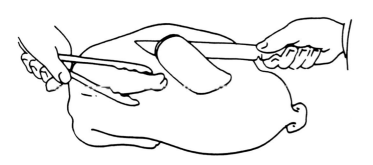

4. Remove the thigh bone with tongs after cutting around it with a knife to loosen it from the meat. Continue taking slices of meat from the thigh.

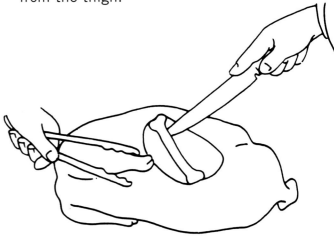

5. Take some slices lengthways from the breast so that the joint attaching the wing to the body is exposed. Using tongs and your knife, remove the wing.

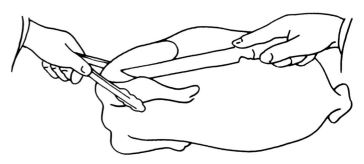

6. Now slice the remaining breast meat until this side of the turkey is completely carved.

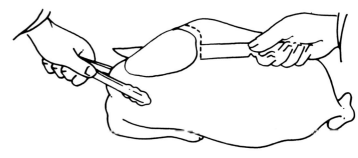

7. Turn the turkey over and repeat the above procedures on the other side.

Trouble Shooting

Problem	Remedy
Food tastes like kerosene Food has been placed on the barbecue while the fire-lighters are still burning, or before the barbecue briquettes have completely ashed over.	Discard food. Next time you cook ensure that the fire-lighters have completely burnt away and that the coals are completely ashed over before you commence cooking.
Food takes too long to cook Insufficient fuel being used to create adequate cooking temperature.	Use correct fuel quantities as detailed on pages 11 and 15. Add the additional fuel required and leave the lid off the barbecue until all the coals are ashed over before recommencing cooking.
Fire not properly established.	Remove the lid from the barbecue and allow all the coals to ash over before recommencing cooking.
One or more vents are not properly opened or are partially blocked by ash or briquettes.	Check ventilation. Carefully clear any blockages and remove the barbecue lid until the fire is burning freely and all the coals are ashed over before recommencing cooking.
Barbecue is cooking in windy conditions resulting in lower cooking temperatures.	Carefully move the barbecue to a sheltered position and continue cooking.
Wrong fuel being used. Wood, charcoal or poor quality briquettes may smoke, go out or not produce the required cooking temperatures.	Remove this fuel and replace it with Heat Beads® barbecue fuel. Fully establish the new fire with the lid off and continue cooking.
Fat dripping into ash catcher No drip tray on the bottom grill or the drip tray is too small to catch all the drips.	Carefully remove the meat and cooking grill (use oven mittens for the grill). Add a tray or trays large enough to catch all the drips. Replace the cooking grill and food and continue cooking. Allow the ash catcher to completely cool before cleaning it.
Drip tray or foil has melted under the heat or has a hole in it.	Remove food and cooking grill and add a good quality barbecue drip tray.
Fatty food such as chops and sausages are being cooked by the direct method.	Remove the food and trim off all the fat. Next time you cook this type of food use the indirect cooking method.

Problem	Remedy
Fire goes out on one side when indirect cooking The fires were not equally established when the lid was placed on the barbecue. This may cause more air to be drawn to the stronger fire resulting in suffocation of the weaker fire.	Remove the lid and using tongs, exchange coals from one side to the other to balance the heat generated by both fires. Leave the lid off until both fires are completely ashed over before resuming cooking.
Fire-lighters burn but do not successfully ignite briquettes Fire-lighters may have lost their potency due to the evaporation of the flammable ingredients. Barbecue briquettes may be damp.	Reset the fire with fresh fire-lighters. Be careful, some briquettes may be very hot. Use tongs to do this. Keep unused fire-lighters in an air-tight container until required. Remove the briquettes with tongs and replace them with dry briquettes. Allow damp briquettes to dry before attempting to re-use them.
Bitter tasting steak or chops Grease builds up on the cooking grill in a dark oily film. This is transferred to the meat giving it a bitter taste.	Clean the cooking grill to remove the oily film before you use the barbecue again.
Meat thermometer glass shatters over food Due to the high temperatures attained in the barbecue kettle, the glass may shatter if the thermometer is placed in the meat at the commencement of cooking. The thermometer may also shatter if the hook located under the lid of the barbecue accidentally hits it.	Do not eat the food. Fine fragments of glass may be consumed. In future use your meat thermometer in the manner described on page 5. Always remove the thermometer from the meat before replacing the barbecue lid.

Problem	Remedy
Vegetables have not cooked in the suggested cooking time but the meat is cooked This problem occurs when cooking a large roast e.g. pork or turkey. The reason for this is that the barbecue loses heat over a period of time. Potatoes, for example, added in the last hour of a $3\frac{1}{2}$ hour cook will not cook in the suggested cooking time. This is because the temperature in the barbecue has dropped well below the normal cooking fire temperature.	Remove the vegetables and finish cooking in another appliance e.g. microwave or electric frypan. While doing this the roast may be removed from the barbecue and allowed to stand. Provided it has not been carved the roast will stand for a remarkably long time without losing its heat. When cooking large roasts which take more than 2 hours to cook, allow up to twice as much time as normal for the vegetables to cook.
Food has scorched on the bottom or edges when using the indirect cooking method This is caused by the food being cooked too close to the coals, either directly over them or so close that it becomes scorched by radiated heat.	If badly affected, cut away the offending food before serving. In future be careful not to place food over, or too close to the coals when cooking for any length of time. Foil may be used to shield the edges.

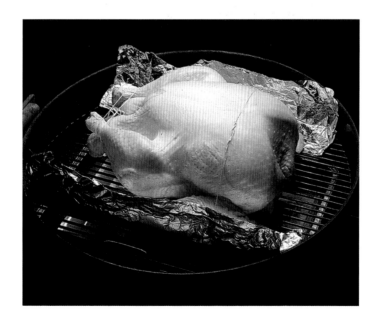

Snacks and Breakfasts

When enjoying drinks in the garden, what could be nicer than to have your host pop around with a lovely selection of hot barbecued snacks? With a little forethought, a whole range of tasty treats may be cooked to cater for almost everybodys' taste. Try a selection of Pork Crackling and Apple Dip, Oysters with Herbed Butter, Mini Fillet Mignons and Kofta Kebabs with Yogurt Dip.

In this section we provide a multitude of ideas for nibbles with drinks.

Perhaps the way you will use this chapter is to select a favourite, and serve it as an entree to your main course. These entrees may be served as finger food in the garden, but they are equally at home in a formal dinner or lunch setting. Ginger Prawns, Smoked Chicken Wings, Kidneys and Bacon or Skewered Quail would be excellent for this purpose.

If the morning is just right, it's lovely to enjoy a Sunday breakfast by the pool, or on the patio. A bottle of champers and some bacon and eggs served with our Yukon Pancakes would be perfect; or perhaps Grilled Grapefruit with Scrambled Eggs and Mushrooms, served with a selection of Barbecued Toasts.

This chapter is exciting because it is new and different, and we know that you will enjoy the almost endless ways you can use our recipes.

Contents

GINGER PRAWNS

Normal fire, indirect, 8-15 minutes, with lid on. Serves 8-10.

1¹/₂ kg fresh green prawns in shell

MARINADE

¹/₂ cup olive oil

¹/₃ cup lemon juice

1 onion, peeled and quartered

6 cloves garlic, peeled

5cm piece fresh ginger, peeled

1 teaspoon chilli powder

Salt and pepper to taste

Shell the prawns, leaving the tails intact. Blend all the marinade ingredients in a food processor until they are smooth. Dip the prawns in this mixture and marinate them, covered, in the refrigerator for 1 hour or more. Thread them on to bamboo skewers. Cook them on the barbecue, with the lid on, for 8-15 minutes depending on size. The prawns will turn pink when they are cooked. This recipe is also excellent for yabbies or Moreton Bay bugs.

SESAME PRAWNS

Normal fire, indirect, 8-15 minutes, with lid on. Serves 6-8.

1 kg fresh green prawns in shell

MARINADE

¹/₂ cup soy sauce

¹/₃ cup spring onions, chopped

¹/₄ cup sesame oil

¹/₄ cup water

3 cloves garlic, pressed

1¹/₂ teaspoons ground ginger

¹/₂ teaspoon freshly grated nutmeg

Shell the prawns leaving the tails intact. To make the marinade, combine all the ingredients, mixing them well. Marinate the prawns, covered, in the refrigerator for 1-2 hours. Remove the prawns and thread them on to bamboo skewers. Cook them on the barbecue, with the lid on, for 8-15 minutes depending on size.

Ginger Prawns, Sesame Prawns and Oysters in Shell

OYSTERS IN SHELL

Normal fire, indirect, 5-10 minutes, with lid on. Serves 3-4.

1 dozen oysters, in shell

Place the oysters in their shells in a drip tray, each topped with ¹/₂ teaspoon of your chosen topping. Cook them on the barbecue, for 5-10 minutes, with the lid on, until they are hot. Some of our favourite toppings are:

CHEESY OYSTER TOPPING

Mix equal quantities of sour cream or natural yogurt and grated cheddar cheese.

SMOKED SALMON CREAM

Equal quantities of chopped smoked salmon mixed with sour cream or natural yogurt, and a touch of horseradish.

BACON AND TOMATO

Equal quantities of chopped, cooked bacon, tomato sauce and Worcestershire sauce.

HERBED GARLIC BUTTER

Mix 2 tablespoons of butter, 1 tablespoon of chopped parsley, 1 teaspoon of snipped chives, 1 teaspoon of chopped spring onion, 1 teaspoon of lemon juice and 1 pressed clove of garlic.

KILPATRICK

A mixture of chopped, cooked bacon and Worcestershire sauce.

FRESH SMOKED OYSTERS

Normal fire, indirect, 8-10 minutes, with lid on. Serves 6-8.

2 dozen oysters

6 bacon rashers, cut into 2.5cm squares

60g butter, melted

1 clove garlic, pressed

1 teaspoon chopped fresh coriander

Thread the oysters and the squares of bacon alternately on to bamboo skewers. Brush them with a mixture of the butter, garlic and coriander. Place 2 chunks of hickory on the coals on each side of the barbecue and allow them to smoke. Place the skewers on the barbecue. Smoke-cook them, with the lid on, for 8-10 minutes.

SKEWERED QUAIL

Normal fire, indirect, 20-30 minutes, with lid on. Serves 6-8.

4 quail

60g butter, softened

1-2 cloves garlic, pressed

Salt and pepper to taste

To prepare the quail, cut them in half and remove the backbones. Place each ¹/₂ quail on a bamboo skewer. Combine the butter, garlic, salt and pepper to make a baste. Brush this on to the quail. Place them on the barbecue and cook them, with the lid on, for 20-30 minutes.

SKEWERED KIDNEYS AND BACON

Normal fire, indirect, 8-12 minutes, with lid on. Serves 6-8.

6 lamb kidneys, skin removed, cut into halves and trimmed

4 bacon rashers

60g butter, melted

1 teaspoon Worcestershire sauce

Thread the lamb kidneys on to bamboo skewers alternately with rolled strips of the bacon. Brush them with a mixture of the melted butter and Worcestershire sauce. Cook them on the barbecue, with the lid on, for 8-12 minutes.

MUSHROOM KEBABS

Normal fire, indirect, 3-5 minutes, with lid on. Serves 6-8.

500g button mushrooms

MARINADE

2 cloves garlic, pressed

¹/₄ cup olive oil

¹/₄ cup lemon juice

1 tablespoon finely chopped parsley

Salt and pepper to taste

¹/₂ teaspoon dry mixed herbs

To make the marinade, combine all the marinade ingredients in a bowl and mix them well. Add the mushrooms to the marinade, cover and marinate them for 3-4 hours. Remove the mushrooms and thread them on to bamboo skewers. Cook them on the barbecue, with the lid on, for 3-5 minutes.

SKEWERED BRAINS AND BACON

Normal fire, indirect, 10-12 minutes, with lid on. Serves 6-8.

2 sets lamb brains

4 bacon rashers

MARINADE

¹/₄ cup lemon juice

1 tablespoon chopped fresh thyme, or ¹/₂ teaspoon dried thyme

¹/₂ cup olive oil

White pepper to taste

Soak the brains in cold, salted water for 30 minutes, and then drain them well. In a small saucepan, with enough water to cover them, poach the brains for 8-10 minutes on the stove. Drain and refresh them with cold water. Allow them to cool, and drain them well. Place the brains between sheets of plastic wrap. Press them with a 1kg weight overnight in the refrigerator. To make the marinade, combine all the marinade ingredients in a bowl and mix them well. Cut the brains into cubes, and add them to the marinade. Allow them to marinate for about 1 hour, turning them occasionally. Cut the

bacon into 5 cm pieces. Roll them up and alternate them with the brain cubes on bamboo skewers. Cook them on the barbecue, with the lid on, for 10-12 minutes.

PORK CRACKLING

Normal fire, indirect, 10-20 minutes, with lid on.

White pork skin with some fat attached

Oil

Salt

Ask your butcher for a piece of white pork skin, and have him score it through the rind. Oil and salt the rind and place it on the barbecue. Cook the rind, with the lid on, for 10-20 minutes, or until the skin blisters and crackles. Break the crackling into pieces, and serve as nibbles with apple dip.

APPLE DIP OR SAUCE

Normal fire, indirect, 15-20 minutes, with lid on.

2 apples

¹/₄ cup water

2 tablespoons sugar

Peel the apples and cut them into quarters. Remove the cores and slice the apples. Place them in a Glad oven bag or a small pan with water and sugar. Cook them on the barbecue, with the lid on, for 15-20 minutes. Mash the apples and serve them as a dip with the pork crackling.

CRACKLING BACON RINDS

Normal fire, indirect, 8-12 minutes, with lid on. Serves 6-8.

125g bacon rinds

Quite often, when bacon has been trimmed the rind is thrown away. The rind is delicious roasted on the barbecue, and served as nibbles. Place the bacon rinds on the barbecue. Cook them, with the lid on, for 8-12 minutes or until they are crisp. Serve them hot or cold as nibbles with drinks.

Skewered Quail, Skewered Kidney and Bacon and Mushroom Kebabs

BANANAS IN BACON

Normal fire, indirect, 8-10 minutes, with lid on. Serves 6-8.

1-2 large firm bananas

2 tablespoons lemon juice

7-8 bacon strips

Hot pepper sauce

Peel the banana and cut it diagonally into thick slices. Toss the banana slices in the lemon juice and place 1 slice of banana on each bacon strip. Season them with a drop of hot pepper sauce and wrap the bacon around the banana. Secure the bacon with toothpicks. Cook them on the barbecue, with the lid on, for 8-10 minutes.

DEVILS ON HORSEBACK

Normal fire, indirect, 8-10 minutes, with lid on. Serves 6-8.

250g pitted prunes

250g bacon rashers

Trim the rind from the bacon and cut the rashers into 5 cm lengths. Wrap the prunes in the bacon and secure them with toothpicks. Cook them on the barbecue, with the lid on, for 8-10 minutes. For a change, the prunes may be filled with anchovies curled around almonds, chopped mango chutney or stuffed olives.

MINI FILLET MIGNONS

Normal fire, indirect, 8-15 minutes, with lid on. Serves 6-8.

500g fillet steak, cut into 2.5cm cubes

6 bacon rashers

Wrap the bacon around the small pieces of fillet steak, and secure it with toothpicks. Cook the mini fillet mignons on the barbecue with the lid on for 8 minutes (rare) or 12-15 minutes (well done). For improved appearance turn them over to show the grill bar marks when serving.

CHICKEN WING DRUMS

Normal fire, indirect, 20-30 minutes, with lid on. Serves 6-8.

18-20 chicken wings

MARINADE

Salt and pepper to taste

2 teaspoons ground ginger

1 tablespoon brown sugar

3 tablespoons soy sauce

1 tablespoon lemon juice

3 tablespoons sweet sherry

2 tablespoons oil

Tabasco or chilli sauce to taste

Disjoint the chicken wings. Set the wing tips aside for another use. Carefully loosen the flesh around the lower joints of the remaining wing portions. Push the flesh from the loosened end up over the joint so that it resembles a small chicken drumstick. To make the marinade, combine all of the marinade ingredients in a bowl. Place the chicken wing drums in the marinade for about 1 hour, turning them occasionally. Cook them on the barbecue, with the lid on, for 20-30 minutes.

SKEWERED CHICKEN LIVERS

Normal fire, indirect, 8-10 minutes, with lid on. Serves 6-8.

500g chicken livers

250g bacon rashers

MARINADE

1 teaspoon soy sauce

2 teaspoons lemon juice

1 clove garlic, pressed

1 tablespoon olive oil

To make the marinade, combine the soy sauce, lemon juice, garlic and oil in a bowl. Marinate the chicken livers for 1-2 hours. Trim the rind from the bacon and cut the rashers into 10 cm lengths. Remove the chicken livers from the marinade, and cut them in half lengthways. Wrap the bacon rashers around the halved livers and secure them with toothpicks. Place them on the barbecue, and cook with the lid on, for 8-10 minutes.

PARMESAN CHICKEN WINGS

Normal fire, indirect, 20-30 minutes, with lid on. Serves 6-8.

1kg chicken wings

Crumb Mixture

1 cup dry breadcrumbs

$^1/_2$ cup freshly grated Parmesan cheese

1 tablespoon chopped parsley

$^1/_4$ teaspoon chilli powder

Salt and pepper to taste

1 clove garlic, pressed

125g butter, melted

To make the crumb mixture combine the breadcrumbs, cheese, parsley, chilli powder, salt, pepper and garlic. Dip the wings in melted butter, allowing any excess butter to drip off. Coat the wings well with the crumb mixture. Cook them on the barbecue, with the lid on, for 20-30 minutes.

SMOKED CHICKEN WINGS

Normal fire, indirect, 20-30 minutes, with lid on. Serves 4-6.

12 chicken wings

1 cup oil

Salt and pepper to taste

Dip the chicken wings, 1 at a time in the oil. Place them on a paper towel and allow them to drain for 2-3 minutes. Season them with salt and pepper. Place 2 hickory chunks on the coals on each side of the barbecue, and allow them to smoke. Place the chicken wings on the barbecue, leaving a little space between them to allow the smoke to circulate. Smoke-cook them with the lid on, for 20-30 minutes.

Kofta Kebabs

KOFTA KEBABS

Normal fire, indirect, 15-20 minutes, with lid on. Serves 6-8.

1kg minced lamb or beef

2 onions, finely chopped

2 cloves garlic, pressed

Salt and pepper to taste

³/₄ teaspoon ground cumin

1 teaspoon chopped fresh coriander

2 eggs

Olive oil

2-3 tablespoons plain flour

1 cup natural yogurt

Combine the meat with the onion, garlic, salt, pepper, cumin and coriander. Mix these well, and then add the eggs and continue mixing until they are well combined. Form the mixture into small sausage shapes around the ends of bamboo skewers. Brush them with the olive oil, and roll them in flour. Cook them on the barbecue, with the lid on, for 15-20 minutes. They should be crusty on the outside and pink in the centre. Serve with natural yogurt as a dip.

SAVOURY PITA SNACKS

Low fire, indirect, 5-10 minutes, with lid on.

3 small pita breads

125g butter, melted

1 packet French onion soup mix

1 teaspoon lemon pepper

1 teaspoon powdered garlic

Split open the pita breads and brush the rough side with the melted butter. Sprinkle with the French onion soup, lemon pepper and garlic. Place the pita breads on the barbecue and cook them, with the lid on, for 5-10 minutes, or until they are golden brown and crisp. Break them into small pieces to eat as nibbles with a dip. When cool, these savoury pita snacks may be stored in air-tight containers.

SATAYS OF LAMB, CHICKEN OR BEEF

Normal fire, indirect, 10-15 minutes, with lid on. Serves 6-8.

500 g lamb, chicken or beef, cut into 2cm cubes

MARINADE

¹/₂ teaspoon ginger

¹/₂ teaspoon mustard powder

1 teaspoon sugar

1 teaspoon sesame oil

1 tablespoon soy sauce

1 clove garlic, pressed

Thread the meat on to bamboo skewers, pressing it close together at one end of the skewer, so that the other end may be used as a handle. Combine all the marinade ingredients and brush the marinade on the prepared satays. Cover the satays in a bowl, and refrigerate them for 2 hours or so. Place them on the barbecue and cook them, with the lid on, for 10-15 minutes. These satays are delicious served plain or with the peanut sauce on page 81.

MELBA TOAST

Low fire, indirect, 8-12 minutes, with lid on. Serves 6-8.

6-8 very thin slices white bread, crusts removed

Halve the bread slices diagonally to form triangles. Cook them on the barbecue, with the lid on, for 8-12 minutes, or until they are golden brown.

PLAIN TOAST ON THE BARBECUE

Direct fire, lid off.

Sandwich bread

Place the bread on the cooking grill over the direct fire and turn it until it is golden brown.

RAISIN TOAST

Direct fire, lid off.

Raisin bread

Place the raisin bread on the cooking grill over the direct fire, and turn it until it is golden brown.

ANDREWS' RIVER TOAST

Direct fire, lid off.

Sandwich bread

Butter

Butter the bread on each side and cook on the cooking grill over the direct fire, and turn it until it is golden brown.

CINNAMON TOAST

Direct fire, lid off.

Sandwich bread

Butter

Cinnamon

Sugar

Cook the bread on the grill over the direct fire. Butter the toast and sprinkle it with a mixture of cinnamon and sugar.

Variety of Toasts

FRENCH TOAST

Direct fire, lid off, hotplate on.

1 egg

¼ cup milk

Salt and pepper to taste

2 slices of bread

2 tablespoons butter

Beat the egg, add the milk and seasoning, mixing it well. Dip the bread in the egg mixture. Heat the hotplate, add the butter, and cook the French Toast on each side until it is golden brown. Serve it topped with grilled bacon if desired.

FRANKFURT AND CHEESE SAVOURIES

Normal fire, indirect, 8-10 minutes, with lid on. Serves 6-8.

500g cocktail frankfurts

250g Edam cheese, sliced

250g bacon rashers

Slit the frankfurts and insert strips of the sliced cheese. Wrap the frankfurts in the bacon, and secure them with toothpicks. Cook them on the barbecue, with the lid on, for 8-10 minutes.

Breakfast on the Patio

BREAKFAST ON THE PATIO

GRILLED GRAPEFRUIT
Direct fire, hotplate on, with lid on.

¹/₂ **grapefruit per person**

1 teaspoon soft brown sugar per person

1 teaspoon sweet sherry per person

¹/₂ **glace cherry per person**

Cut the grapefruit in half and remove the membrane from between the segments, or just loosen it to make it easy to eat. Sprinkle the top with sugar and sherry. Place ¹/₂ a cherry in the centre.

Place the grapefruit on the barbecue and cook them with the lid on for 4-5 minutes. Serve them immediately.

SCRAMBLED EGGS WITH MUSHROOMS
Direct fire, lid off, hotplate on.

4 eggs

3 tablespoons milk

Salt and pepper to taste

125g button mushrooms

Snipped chives

1 tablespoon butter

3 slices buttered toast

Beat the eggs and milk together. Season them with salt and pepper. Melt the butter on the hotplate and pour on the eggs. Stir them gently until they are creamy.

Make the toast on the side over the direct coals, turning it until it is golden brown.

Cook the mushrooms in butter on the hotplate, while the eggs are cooking. Serve the scrambled eggs on toast accompanied with the mushrooms, and garnished with chives.

Roast Chestnuts

ROAST CHESTNUTS

Normal fire, indirect, 15-20 minutes, with lid on.

1kg chestnuts

Butter

Salt to taste

Prepare the chestnuts by cutting a small slit in their skins. Place the chestnuts in a drip tray, and roast them on the barbecue, with the lid on, for 15-20 minutes until the skin splits open. Serve them hot before or after a meal, dobbed with butter and a sprinkle of salt.

BREAKFAST IN THE BUSH

Direct fire, lid off, hotplate on.

Eggs

Bacon

Sausages

Tomato Halves

Bread

Place the sausages on a heated and oiled hotplate. Cook them for a few

Breakfast in the Bush

minutes, turning them regularly. Place rashers of bacon on to the hotplate, break eggs into egg rings, and place tomato halves alongside. Cook with the lid on the barbecue for 4-5 minutes, until the eggs are glazed and set.

Make toast on the side over the direct coals, turning it until it is golden brown.

Hamburgers

HAMBURGERS

Direct fire, lid off, hotplate on

500g lean minced beef

1 tablespoon olive oil

3 spring onions, chopped

1 cup fresh breadcrumbs

1 teaspoon parsley, chopped

1 teaspoon oregano, chopped

1 egg beaten

salt and pepper to taste

1 tablespoon white wine or sherry

Combine all of the ingredients, mix them well and shape them into hamburger patties. Flatten them to the desired thickness and refrigerate them until they are ready to cook.

Heat the hotplate and grease it with a little oil. Fry the patties on the hotplate until golden brown-about 3 to 4 minutes each side or until cooked.
Serve in pre-heated hamburger buns with onion rings, salad, eggs and bacon, and your favourite relish and sauce.

SCOTCH EGGS

Direct fire, lid off, wok on. Serves 6.

1-2 litres oil for deep-frying

6 hard boiled eggs

1 tablespoon flour, seasoned with salt and pepper

500g sausage mince

1 tablespoon grated onion

1 tablespoon finely chopped parsley

1 tablespoon tomato sauce

1 egg beaten with 1 tablespoon milk

Dry breadcrumbs

Shell the eggs, coat them with the seasoned flour and set them aside. Combine the sausage mince, onion, parsley and tomato sauce. Divide this mixture into 6 portions. Shape each portion around the eggs, enclosing them completely. Brush them with the beaten egg, and coat them with the breadcrumbs. Heat the wok and add the oil. When the oil is hot and bubbles when tested with the handle of a wooden spoon, fry the eggs for 5-7 minutes. Serve them cold as a snack for picnics, or pack them in lunches.

YUKON PANCAKES

Direct fire, lid off, hotplate on.

1¹/₂ cups self raising flour

1 tablespoon sugar

1 egg

1 cup milk

1 tablespoon butter

Combine all the ingredients, and beat them well. Allow the mixture to stand for 15 minutes. Heat the hotplate and grease it well with butter. Put tablespoonfuls of this mixture on to the hotplate. Cook them until bubbles rise to the surface through them. Turn them over and cook on the other side. Pile them one upon the other in a cloth to keep warm. Serve them with butter, honey or Maple syrup.

ONION RINGS

Direct fire, lid off, hotplate on.

2 onions, peeled and sliced into rings

1 tablespoon butter

Salt and pepper to taste

Heat the hotplate, add the butter, and fry the onions until they are cooked. Season them with salt and pepper.

HOT PLATE TOASTED SANDWICHES

Direct fire, lid off, hotplate on.

Sandwich bread

Butter

FILLINGS

Pineapple and cheese

Ham and mustard

Ham, cheese and tomato

Chicken and mayonnaise

Make the sandwiches by buttering the outside of the bread instead of the inside. Fill them with your desired fillings.

Heat the hotplate. Place the sandwich on the hotplate, and cook it until it is golden underneath. Turn the sandwich and finish with the lid on for a few minutes.

Cut the sandwiches in half, and serve them with salad.

Yukon Pancakes

Hot Plate Toasted Sandwiches

Lamb

Australia has an abundance of beautiful lamb. This fine quality meat is relatively inexpensive and that is why it has always been our most popular barbecue tucker.

The arrival of the barbecue kettle has changed forever the way we think about barbecued lamb. The Aussie chop will always be a favourite, and rightfully so. However the barbecue kettle has expanded our barbecue recipes to include delicious meals. Roasted Lamb Shanks, Glazed Racks of Lamb, Butterflied Lamb Greek-style and Crown Roast can now be barbecue favourites.

A hint of rosemary smoke, a few cloves of garlic thrown onto the coals, or a splash of redcurrant glaze combined with the natural flavour that only comes from a barbecue kettle, provide exciting new taste sensations you will love.

So now it's time that you re-discovered lamb. Why not start with our Lamb & Fruit Kebabs and work your way through?

Contents

LAMB & FRUIT KEBABS

Normal fire, indirect, 15-20 minutes, with lid on. Serves 4.

500g boneless lamb (loin, forequarter or leg)

2 tablespoons butter

2 tablespoons brown sugar

2 teaspoons curry powder

2 tablespoons canned pineapple syrup

8 apricot halves, canned or fresh

3 canned pineapple slices, each cut into 4 pieces

2 bananas, each cut into 4 pieces

Cut the lamb into 2.5 cm cubes. In a saucepan melt the butter and blend in the brown sugar, curry powder and pineapple syrup. Heat this mixture until it is boiling and then allow it to cool. Thread the lamb on to 4 skewers and brush them with the butter mixture. Cook the kebabs on the barbecue, for 10-15 minutes, with the lid on. Place the fruit pieces on to another four skewers and brush them with the butter mixture. Cook the fruit for the last 5 minutes along with the meat. Serve the kebabs with hot boiled rice and salad.

LAMB MIGNON WITH MUSHROOMS

Normal fire, indirect, 20-30 minutes, with lid on. Serves 6-8.

Loin of lamb, boned and fat removed

250g bacon slices

SAUCE

150g mushrooms, sliced

$\frac{1}{2}$ cup chopped spring onions

2 tablespoons butter

1 cup undiluted tomato soup

$\frac{1}{4}$ cup red wine

Salt and pepper to taste

1 tablespoon Worcestershire sauce

Roll the meat and cut it into slices about 4 cm thick. Wrap a strip of bacon around the outside of each slice. Secure the bacon with toothpicks. Place the meat on the barbecue and cook it with the lid on for 20-30 minutes. To prepare the sauce, fry the mushrooms and spring onions in the butter and add the remaining ingredients. Simmer gently for 10-15 minutes. Serve the meat with the sauce and accompany it with vegetables or salad.

Lamb & Fruit Kebabs

Lamb Mignon with Mushrooms

Boned Lamb with Walnut Stuffing

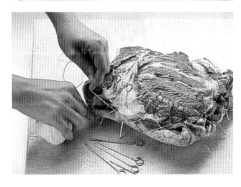

BONED LAMB WITH WALNUT STUFFING

Normal fire, indirect, 1-1½ hours, with lid on. Serves 6.

1 boned forequarter lamb

Salt and pepper to taste

STUFFING

125g walnuts, chopped

1 tablespoon butter

1 small onion, chopped

3 tablespoons fresh breadcrumbs

1 tablespoon chopped parsley

1 tablespoon chopped mint

Grated rind of ½ lemon egg

Salt and pepper to taste

Combine all the stuffing ingredients and place them on the inside of the meat. Roll up the meat and secure it with poultry pins and string. Score the fat surface of the meat with a knife and season it with salt and pepper. Place the meat on the barbecue and cook it for 1-1½ hours with the lid on. Slice the meat and serve it with selected garden vegetables.

ROASTED LAMB SHANKS

Normal fire, indirect, 50-60 minutes, with lid on. Serves 6.

6 lamb shanks

¼ cup oil

Salt and pepper to taste

1 clove garlic, pressed

Oil the lamb shanks and smear them with the garlic. Season them with salt and pepper. Cook them on the barbecue, with the lid on, for 50-60 minutes. 1-2 chunks of hickory added to the coals during cooking adds a superb flavour and aroma. Serve them plain or with the following barbecue sauce.

BARBECUE SAUCE

2 onions, sliced

1 clove garlic, pressed

1 cup celery, sliced

1 cup tomato sauce

1 tablespoon Worcestershire sauce

1 cup water

To make the sauce, place all the ingredients in a pan and simmer them gently for 5-10 minutes.

CROWN ROAST OF LAMB

Normal fire, indirect, 50-60 minutes, with lid on. Serves 6.

1 crown roast of lamb, 14-16 cutlets

Salt and freshly ground pepper, ground thyme and marjoram to taste

1 clove garlic, pressed

Juice of 1/2 lemon

Oil

Order a crown roast from your butcher a day or two before it is required. Ask him to trim some of the fat from the lamb racks before shaping them. If you wish to stuff the roast, ask him to sew a layer of lamb skin, skin side up, across the bottom to form a base to hold any stuffing. Brush the outside of the roast with oil. Rub the surfaces of the roast with salt, pepper and herbs. Combine the garlic with the lemon juice and brush this over the meat. The bone ends may be covered with pieces of foil to protect them. Cook the roast on the barbecue, with the lid on, for 30 minutes. Fill the roast with your favourite stuffing if desired and cook for 20-30 minutes longer. Alternatively, the centre may be filled with a combination of green peas and diced carrots, or mashed potatoes. Serve the roast with vegetables, or a salad of your choice.

ROAST LAMB WITH EGG AND LEMON SAUCE

Normal fire, indirect, 1 1/4-1 1/2 hours, with lid on. Serves 6.

1 leg of lamb

Salt and pepper to taste

3 cloves garlic

1/4 cup oil

1/4 cup lemon juice

1 teaspoon rosemary leaves

6 large potatoes, peeled

Paprika

Rub the surface of the lamb with salt and pepper. Peel the garlic and cut it into thin slivers. Cut slits in the lamb and insert the slivers of garlic. Brush the lamb with oil. Sprinkle lemon juice and rosemary over the lamb. Brush the potatoes with the remaining oil and sprinkle them with paprika. Place the meat and potatoes on the barbecue. Cook them with the lid on for 1 1/4-1 1/2 hours. Serve the meat sliced, with egg and lemon sauce.

EGG AND LEMON SAUCE

2 tablespoons butter

3 tablespoons flour

1 1/2 cups chicken stock

3 tablespoons lemon juice

Salt to taste

4 egg yolks

1 tablespoon chopped parsley

Melt the butter in a pan, add the flour and stir until it is smooth. Add the chicken stock, lemon juice and salt. Cook until boiling, stirring all the time. Beat in the egg yolks and add the parsley.

ORANGE BASTED LOIN OF LAMB

Normal fire, indirect, 35-45 minutes, with lid on. Serves 6.

1kg boned loin lamb

Grated rind of 1 orange

BASTE

1 teaspoon mustard powder

2 tablespoons brown sugar

1 cup orange juice

1/4 cup cider vinegar

2 tablespoons honey

1 tablespoon soy sauce

Salt and pepper to taste

Place the grated orange rind on the meat and roll it up. Tie the meat at regular intervals to secure it. Combine the baste ingredients and brush these over the meat. Cook the meat on the barbecue, for 35-45 minutes, with the lid on, basting occasionally during the last 10-15 minutes. Serve the meat sliced with the remaining baste heated to form a sauce.

SPICED FOREQUARTER OF LAMB

Normal fire, indirect, 1 1/2 hours, with lid on. Serves 6.

2kg forequarter lamb, boned and rolled

BASTE

1 large onion, chopped

1 clove garlic, pressed

1/2 cup apple cider

1/4 cup tomato sauce

1 tablespoon Worcestershire sauce

1 tablespoon fruit chutney

1 tablespoon brown sugar

Salt and pepper to taste

Place the lamb on the barbecue and cook it for 55 minutes, with the lid on. Combine all the remaining ingredients and use them to baste the lamb. Cook for 35 minutes longer, basting 3 or 4 times.

LAMB AND TAMARILLO

Normal fire, indirect, 30-40 minutes, with lid on. Serves 6-8.

1 whole loin lamb, boned and trimmed of fat

2 tablespoons oil

Salt and pepper to taste

Fresh herbs to garnish

SAUCE

1 cup red wine

1 cup tomato puree

4 tamarillos, peeled and chopped

Tie the lamb with string to form a roll. Brush it with the oil and season it with salt and pepper. Cook the meat on the barbecue, with the lid on for 30-40 minutes.

Make the sauce by boiling the wine to reduce it by half. Add the tomato puree and simmer for 5-10 minutes. Add the tamarillos and heat them through. Serve the meat sliced, spooning the sauce over it and garnishing it with the fresh herbs.

Roast Leg of Lamb

ROAST LEG OF LAMB

Normal fire, indirect, 1¼-1¾ hours, with lid on. Serves 6

Leg of lamb

Oil

Salt and pepper to taste

Brush the lamb with oil and season it with salt and pepper. Place the lamb on the barbecue and cook it with the lid on for 1¼-1¾ hours, or until done. Vegetables may be placed around the roast during cooking. Serve the meat sliced with mint sauce or jelly. (Recipe page 210). This is the traditional Australian way of cooking roast lamb. If you would like to try something a little different, some of our favourite variations are described below.

HICKORY OR ROSEMARY SMOKED ROAST LAMB

Normal fire, indirect, 1¼-1¾ hours, with lid on.

To smoke the roast lamb with hickory, add 1 hickory chunk to the coals on each side of the barbecue just before you put the lamb on.

or

For rosemary smoke, add a large sprig of fresh rosemary to the coals for the last 5 minutes of cooking. Be careful when smoking to make sure that any vegetables being cooked are wrapped in foil or placed in a Glad oven bag. This prevents the smoke taste penetrating them.

MARINATED ROAST LAMB

Normal fire, indirect, 1¼-1¾ hours, with lid on.

MARINADE

½ cup chicken stock

½ cup white wine

3 tablespoons chopped mint

1 small onion, chopped

1 clove garlic, pressed

Combine the marinade ingredients and mix them well. Place the leg of lamb in the marinade and allow it to stand for several hours, covered, in the refrigerator. Remove the meat from the marinade and cook it as previously described, basting the lamb with the marinade every 20 minutes or so. Warm the left over marinade and serve it with the meat as a sauce.

GLAZED ROAST LAMB

Normal fire, indirect, 1¼-1¾ hours, with lid on.

To glaze the roast lamb brush it liberally 3-4 times during the last 15-20 minutes of cooking time with a mint, redcurrant, or apricot glaze. (Recipes page 203).

SHASLICKS

Normal fire, indirect, 15-20 minutes, with lid on. Serves 4.

500g boneless lamb (loin, forequarter or leg)

1 red and 1 green pepper

MARINADE

1 small onion, finely chopped

1 clove garlic, pressed

1 tablespoon chopped parsley

½ teaspoon dried oregano

Freshly ground black pepper to taste

3 tablespoons oil

⅓ cup lemon juice

Cut the lamb into 2.5cm cubes. Combine the onion, garlic, parsley, oregano, ground pepper, oil and lemon juice, stirring well to form the marinade. Add the lamb cubes to the marinade and allow them to marinate for a few hours. Cut the red and green peppers into squares. Thread the lamb and pepper alternately on to 4 skewers leaving a little space between them. Brush them with the marinade and cook them on the barbecue for 15-20 minutes, with the lid on. Serve the shaslicks with rice and salad.

Mutton Ham or Corned Leg of Lamb

MUTTON HAM OR CORNED LEG OF LAMB

Normal fire, indirect, 1¹/₂-2 hours, with lid on. Serves 6-8.

1 corned leg of lamb, uncooked

1 onion, peeled

4 whole cloves

3 bay leaves

2 cups water

Soak the meat in a large bowl of cold water for several hours, changing the water once or twice to remove excess salt. Stud the peeled onion with cloves and place it in a Glad oven bag with the lamb, bay leaves and the 2 cups of water. Tie the bag with a twist tie and make a small hole in the top of it. Place it on the barbecue and cook with the lid on for 1¹/₂-2 hours. Corned lamb is delicious: hot with vegetables, cold with salad, or in a sandwich.

LAMB CUTLETS WITH MUSTARD BUTTER

Normal fire, indirect, 15-25 minutes, with lid on. Serves 8.

8 double-ribbed lamb cutlets

2 teaspoons olive oil

1 clove garlic, pressed

1 tablespoon lemon juice

Salt and pepper to taste

MUSTARD BUTTER

125g butter, softened

2 tablespoons Dijon mustard

1 teaspoon lemon juice

1 clove garlic, pressed

Salt and pepper to taste

Have your butcher trim the lamb cutlets by cutting away the meat from the ends of the bones. Brush the cutlets with oil and spread them with garlic. Sprinkle the meat with lemon juice, salt and pepper. Cook the cutlets on the barbecue with the lid on for 15-25 minutes. Serve them with the mustard butter; which is made by beating all the ingredients together.

Lamb Cutlets with Mustard Butter
These Cutlets have been glazed (page 54)

Glazed Racks of Lamb

RACKS OF LAMB

Normal fire, indirect, 30-45 minutes, with lid on. Serves 6.

6 racks, 3-4 chops each

¹/₂ cup oil

Salt and pepper to taste

Rub the racks with oil and season them with salt and pepper. Wrap some foil around the bone ends of the chops to protect them. Place the racks in a standing position on the barbecue. Cook them with the lid on for 30 minutes (rare), 35 minutes (medium) or 45 minutes (well done). This is the usual method for cooking racks of lamb. However, we have found that most people love the following variations.

HICKORY OR ROSEMARY SMOKED

Normal fire, indirect, 30-45 minutes, with lid on. Serves 6.

Hickory wood chunks or large sprigs of rosemary are added to the coals at the commencement of cooking. This adds a magnificent flavour to the lamb.

GLAZED RACKS OF LAMB

Normal fire, indirect, 30-45 minutes, with lid on. Serves 6.

Grated rind of 1 orange

1 jar redcurrant jelly, warmed

Rub the fat surface of the racks with salt and pepper and then rub the grated orange rind into the fat and meat. To glaze, spread 1 tablespoon of redcurrant jelly over each rack of lamb 2-3 times during the last 15-20 minutes of cooking time.

HERBED CRUMBED RACKS

Normal fire, indirect, 30-45 minutes, with lid on. Serves 6.

¹/₄ cup Dijon mustard

1 cup dry breadcrumbs

2 cloves garlic, pressed

2 teaspoons chopped fresh herbs

60g butter, melted

During the last 15 minutes of cooking time, spread the mustard over the surface of the racks. Coat with the dry breadcrumbs, garlic and herbs mixed together. Carefully pour the melted butter over this crumb mixture and finish the cooking.

GARLIC AND ROSEMARY RACKS

Normal fire, indirect, 30-45 minutes, with lid on. Serves 6.

¹/₂ cup vegetable oil

Salt and pepper to taste

2 cloves garlic, pressed

1 teaspoon dried rosemary

Remove all the fat from the lamb racks. Brush them with oil and sprinkle them with salt and pepper. Smear them all over with the garlic and sprinkle them with the dried rosemary. Serve the racks with new potatoes, boiled in their jackets and with salad or vegetables.

Breast of Lamb with Lemon and Dill

BREAST OF LAMB WITH LEMON AND DILL

Normal fire, indirect, 45-60 minutes, with lid on. Serves 4.

Lamb flap, trimmed, with under-skin removed

MARINADE

¹/₃ cup lemon juice

¹/₃ cup chopped fresh dill

2 tablespoons Dijon mustard

Salt to taste

¹/₃ cup olive oil

Place the marinade ingredients in a bowl with the lamb. Cover and allow it to marinate for 6-8 hours, turning the meat occasionally. Remove the lamb and reserve the marinade. Cook the meat on the barbecue with the lid on, for 45-60 minutes, basting occasionally with the marinade. The meat should be crisp on the outside and no longer pink inside when served. Cut it into riblets and serve with sweetcorn and salad.

LAMB CHOPS WITH ORANGE MARINADE

Normal fire, indirect, 25-35 minutes, with lid on. Serves 6.

6 lamb chops, cut 4 cm thick

MARINADE

1 cup orange juice

1 tablespoon red pepper flakes

3 tablespoons soy sauce

I teaspoon sugar

1 teaspoon chopped rosemary

¹/₂ cup oil

Place the chops with the marinade ingredients in a bowl. Chill and marinate for 6-8 hours, turning the meat once or twice. Remove the chops and reserve the marinade for basting. Cook the chops on the barbecue with the lid on for 25-35 minutes, or until done. Baste them occasionally with the marinade during cooking. Serve with salad and crusty French bread.

LOIN OF LAMB WITH HAM AND SPINACH

Normal fire, indirect, 35-45 minutes, with lid on. Serves 6.

1kg boned loin lamb

Salt and pepper to taste

Stuffing

125g ham, cut into julienne strips (long match-like strips)

1 cup chopped cooked spinach

¹/₂ cup fresh breadcrumbs

2 tablespoons pine nuts

Salt and pepper to taste

Have your butcher skin, bone and prepare a loin of lamb ready for stuffing and rolling. Combine the stuffing ingredients and spread this over the meat. Roll up the meat and tie it with string at regular intervals to secure it. Season with salt and pepper. Cook the lamb on the barbecue, with the lid on for 35-45 minutes, or until done. Serve the meat sliced and accompany it with vegetables or a salad.

STUFFED BREAST OF LAMB

Normal fire, indirect, 45-60 minutes, with lid on. Serves 4.

1 lamb flap

Salt and pepper to taste

SAUSAGE FORCEMEAT

500g sausage meat

1/2 cup fresh breadcrumbs

1 small onion, finely chopped

2 tablespoons chopped parsley

To make the sausage forcemeat combine the forcemeat ingredients and mix them well. Trim some of the fat from the lamb, then turn it over and spread the forcemeat along the underside. Roll the lamb flap up into a neat roll, tying it with string. Rub the surface of the meat with salt and pepper. Place it on the barbecue and cook for 45-60 minutes with the lid on. Serve the meat cut into thick slices with vegetables.

BUTTERFLIED LAMB GREEK-STYLE

Normal fire, indirect, 45-60 minutes, with lid on. Serves 6.

1 leg of lamb, boned, trimmed and butterflied

MARINADE

2 cloves garlic, pressed

1/4 cup lemon juice

1/4 teaspoon ground black pepper

1/4 teaspoon ground anise

1 cup natural yogurt

Ask your butcher to bone, trim and butterfly a leg of lamb. Combine all the marinade ingredients and coat the lamb with this mixture. Marinate the lamb (skin side up) in a bowl, cover and refrigerate it for 3-4 hours. Place the lamb on the barbecue and cook with the lid on for 45-60 minutes, or until done. Baste it occasionally with the remaining marinade. Serve it sliced with vegetables of your choice.

MONGOLIAN LAMB

Direct fire, lid off, wok on. Serves 4-6.

750g boneless lamb, sliced thinly

2 tablespoons oil

MARINADE

1 teaspoon cornflour

1/2 teaspoon fresh grated ginger

1 teaspoon sugar

2 teaspoons sesame oil

2 tablespoons water

SAUCE

1 teaspoon cornflour

2 teaspoons soy sauce

3 tablespoons dry sherry

3 cloves garlic, pressed

1 bunch spring onions, sliced

To make the marinade, combine all of the marinade ingredients and mix well. Place the meat in the marinade and allow it to marinate for several hours. Heat the wok and add the oil. Remove the meat from the marinade and stir fry it in the wok until it is brown. Combine the remaining marinade with the sauce ingredients. Add this mixture to the meat and stir it well. Serve the lamb with fried rice and salad.

LEG OF LAMB IN PASTRY

Normal fire, indirect, 1 1/2-1 3/4 hours, with lid on. Serves 6.

2kg leg of lamb, boned

Salt and pepper to taste

4 slices ham

6 anchovies

1 tablespoon chopped mixed fresh herbs

1 tablespoon chopped spring onion

375g puff pastry

Egg wash

Open up the lamb and flatten it slightly with a mallet. Sprinkle it with salt and pepper. Lay the ham slices, anchovies, herbs and onion on top of the meat. Roll the meat up and tie it with string.

Sprinkle the meat generously with salt and pepper. Cook it on the barbecue with the lid on for 30-40 minutes. Allow it to cool slightly. Roll the pastry into a rectangle on a floured surface. Place the lamb on top of the pastry. Brush the edges of the pastry with the egg wash. Enclose the lamb in the pastry, overlapping all of the edges of the pastry. Trim off the excess pastry and reserve the trimmings. Use the pastry trimmings to decorate it. Brush the egg wash all over the top surface of the pastry. Place the meat on foil and cook it on the barbecue for 1 hour with the lid on, or until the pastry is golden brown.

SPICED LAMB

Direct fire, lid off, wok on. Serves 6.

750g lamb fillet, cut into 2.5 cm cubes

1/2 cup yogurt

1 cup tomato sauce

1 chilli, seeded and chopped

1 clove garlic, pressed

1 onion, chopped

1 tablespoon chopped mint or coriander

SPICE MIXTURE

1/4 cup oil

3 cardamom pods

2 cinnamon sticks

1 small onion, finely chopped

1 teaspoon ground ginger

1/2 teaspoon chilli powder

1 chilli, seeded and finely chopped

Marinate the lamb for 2 hours or so in the yogurt, tomato sauce, chilli, garlic, onion and mint or coriander. Heat the wok, add the oil and the remaining spice mixture ingredients. Quickly stir-fry. Add the lamb with the marinade to the spice mixture and cook it with the barbecue lid on the wok, for 5-10 minutes stirring occasionally. Serve the spiced lamb with hot boiled rice and salad.

LAMB CHOPS

Normal fire, indirect, 20-30 minutes, with lid on. Serves 4.

8 loin lamb chops, cut 2.5cm thick

Salt and pepper to taste

Lamb chops are normally cooked on the barbecue, flat on the grill, with the lid on and turned over half way through cooking. If you are feeding a crowd, the lamb chops may be cooked on the barbecue in an upright position joined together with a skewer. Make sure you leave enough space between each chop to allow the hot air to circulate. Chops are delicious plain, seasoned with salt and pepper, or smeared with garlic. If desired, they may be marinated with a marinade of your choice before cooking. If the chops are thinner than 2.5 cm, the cooking time will be less.

RACK OF LAMB WITH BLUEBERRY SAUCE

Normal fire, indirect, 30-40 minutes, with lid on. Serves 6-8.

6 racks lamb, 3-4 chops each

1 cup fresh or canned blueberries

¹/₂ cup redcurrant jelly

2 teaspoons Dijon mustard

1 tablespoon lemon juice

¹/₄ cup port wine

12 fresh rosemary sprigs

Trim all the fat from the meat. Reserve some of the blueberries for decoration and crush the remainder. To make the sauce, heat the jelly, mustard and lemon juice, stirring in the crushed blueberries. Boil the port in a saucepan and add the blueberry sauce. Continue boiling the sauce until it has thickened. Place the meat on the barbecue and cook with the lid on for 30-40 minutes, or until done. During the last 15-20 minutes of cooking time, the meat may be basted with the sauce 2-3 times. Serve the meat sliced, with the sauce and garnish it with the reserved blueberries and rosemary sprigs.

Lamb Chops

PERSIAN LAMB CHOPS

Normal fire, indirect, 20-30 minutes, with lid on. Serves 6-8.

6-12 thick loin lamb chops

2 tablespoons lemon juice

Paprika

Salt and pepper to taste

1 cup natural yogurt

¹/₂ cup finely chopped onion

1 clove garlic, pressed

Place the lamb chops in a bowl with the lemon juice and let them stand for 5 minutes. Sprinkle the chops with paprika, salt and pepper. Combine the yogurt with the onion and garlic. Pour this over the chops. Cover the bowl and refrigerate them until required. Cook the chops on the barbecue with the lid on for 20-30 minutes. Serve them with salad and potatoes.

BRAISED LAMB SHANKS

Low fire, indirect, 45-50 minutes, with lid on. Serves 6.

6 lamb shanks

2 large tomatoes, sliced

Salt to taste

1 teaspoon paprika

1¹/₂ cups beef stock

Place all the ingredients in a drip tray and cover with foil. Cook on the barbecue for 45-50 minutes, with the lid on.

BUTTERFLIED LAMB

Normal fire, indirect, 45-60 minutes, with lid on. Serves 6.

1 leg of lamb, boned and butterflied

MARINADE

¹/₂ cup olive oil

Thin strip of lemon peel

¹/₄ cup lemon juice

¹/₄ cup white wine

I large clove garlic, pressed

Few sprigs fresh rosemary

1 white onion, peeled and sliced

2 teaspoons soy sauce

Ask your butcher to butterfly the lamb. Place the marinade ingredients and the lamb in a bowl. Cover the bowl and marinate in the refrigerator for a few hours or overnight. Remove the meat and reserve the marinade to use as a sauce. Cook the meat on the barbecue for 45-60 minutes with the lid on. Boil the marinade for 5 minutes and spoon it over the sliced meat. Serve with Dinkum Damper (recipe page 199) and fresh salad.

Beef

Something we all know is that Australians love steak. However, some barbecue kettle owners may think it is hard to justify lighting their barbecue just to cook a few steaks. This chapter will probably change their thinking forever. After tasting just one steak cooked on a cast iron cooking grill inside your barbecue kettle, you'll never want to cook steak any other way again.

Sunday lunches, dinner parties or an outdoor feast - we've covered the lot. Olde English Roast Beef with Yorkshire Pudding, Beef Wellington, or Bushman's Corned Beef, all cooked to perfection on your barbecue kettle.

For something different, our Beer and Beef Casserole, Peppered Rolled Sirloin or Tournedos with Crayfish Bearnaise will make your parties an instant hit.

Contents

EASY CORNED BEEF AND CABBAGE

Low fire, indirect, 2 hours, with lid on. Serves 6-8.

2kg piece uncooked corned beef

1 large carrot, sliced

2 large onions stuck with 4 cloves

Cabbage

1 teaspoon mustard powder

1 sprig thyme or parsley

Pepper to taste

1 cup water

Place all the ingredients, except the cabbage, in a large Glad oven bag. Cook on the barbecue with the lid on for 1 hour. Add the cabbage cut into wedges and cook for a further hour. Serve the meat sliced with the cabbage.

GARLIC STEAKS

Direct fire, 4-5 minutes per side, with lid on.

Choose fillet, T-bone, porterhouse, sirloin or rump steaks, cut 2.5cm thick

2 cloves garlic, pressed

Salt and pepper to taste

Pre-heat a cast iron cooking grill (refer to page 7). Spread the steak with garlic and season it with salt and pepper to taste. Place the steak, garlic side down, onto the cast iron grill. Cook with the lid on for 4-5 minutes each side. Slice into serving portions and serve with salad.

T-BONE STEAK

Direct fire, 4-5 minutes per side, with lid on.

T-bone steak, cut 2.5cm thick

Salt and pepper to taste

Pre-heat a cast iron cooking grill (refer to page 7). Place the steak on the cast iron grill. Cook it on the barbecue with the lid on for 4-5 minutes each side. Serve the steak on a pre-heated steak plate, and add a dob of Maitre d'hotel butter - (recipe page 63) out of this world!

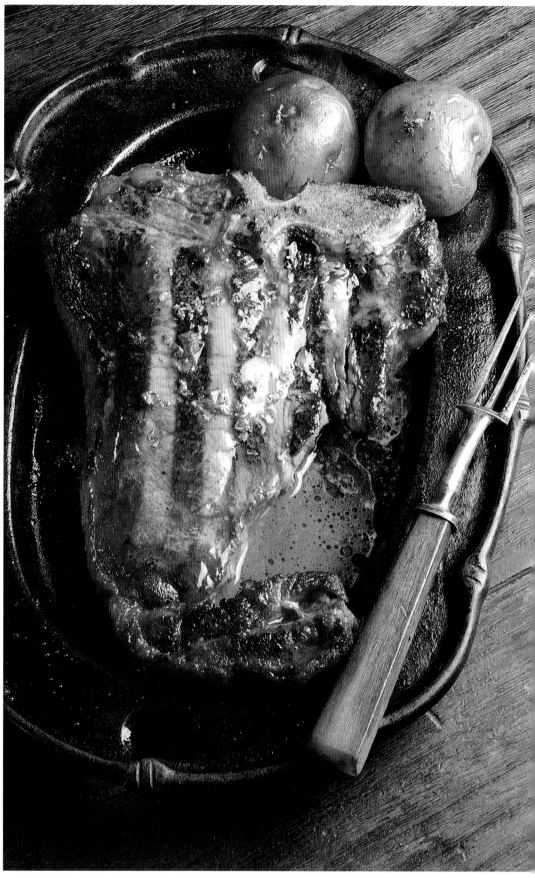

T-Bone Steak

61

Carpet-bag Roast Rump

PEPPERED ROLLED SIRLOIN

Normal fire, indirect, 40-45 minutes, with lid on. Serves 6.

1kg piece, butcher-prepared peppered sirloin, or peppered eye of fresh silverside

Place the meat on the barbecue and cook for 40-45 minutes with the lid on. This stunning meat is pale and tender inside and is surrounded by a black pepper crust. It is excellent carved and served hot or cold with vegetables or salad.

POCKET STEAK

Direct fire, 5 minutes per side, with lid on. Serves 3-4.

1 slice rump steak 2.5cm thick, pocketed

Salt and pepper to taste

FILLING

1 small onion, chopped

100g mushrooms, chopped

1 clove garlic, pressed

4 sprigs parsley, chopped

50g butter

In a saucepan cook the onion, garlic, mushrooms and parsley in butter for 2-3 minutes, while stirring. Allow it to cool. Place this mixture in the pocket of the steak and secure it with toothpicks. Season the steak with salt and pepper. Cook it on the barbecue for 5 minutes each side with the lid on. Serve with salad or vegetables in season.

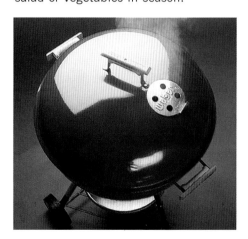

CARPET-BAG ROAST RUMP

Normal fire, indirect, 35-50 minutes, with lid on. Serves 4-6.

1 slice rump steak, cut 4cm thick

1 dozen oysters

Salt and pepper to taste

30g butter, cut up

Olive oil

Cut a pocket through the fat and into the steak . Season the oysters with salt and pepper and place them in the pocket with the butter pieces. Secure the pocket with poultry pins and tie with string. Brush the steak with oil and place it on the barbecue. Cook with the lid on for 35-50 minutes. Serve the steak cut into thick slices topped with Maitre d'hotel butter.

MAITRE D'HOTEL BUTTER

125g butter

1/2 cup chopped parsley

Juice of 1/2 a lemon

Beat the parsley and butter together; add the lemon juice and beat it in. Form this mixture into a roll and cut it into butter pats. Place 1 pat of butter on each serving of the steak.

Casserole of Beef with Beer

CASSEROLE OF BEEF WITH BEER

Low fire, indirect, 2 hours, with lid on. Serves 6-8.

1kg chuck steak, cut into serving portions

2 large onions, thinly sliced

250g mushrooms, sliced

1 clove garlic, pressed

Salt and pepper to taste

15 pitted prunes

$\frac{1}{2}$ teaspoon basil

$\frac{1}{2}$ teaspoon thyme

$\frac{1}{2}$ teaspoon mustard powder

$1\frac{1}{2}$ cups beer

Combine all the ingredients in a drip tray and cover it with foil. Cook the casserole on the barbecue with the lid on for 2 hours, or until it is tender. Thicken the juices if desired, with blended cornflour, before serving. The casserole may be stored in the freezer and reheated at some future time.

OLDE ENGLISH ROAST BEEF

Normal fire, indirect, 1¼-1¾ hours with lid on. Serves 6.

1.5kg whole piece scotch fillet or rolled roast

Salt and pepper to taste

2 tablespoons butter

Rub the beef well with salt, pepper and dab the butter over it. Place the roast on the barbecue and cook it with the lid on for 1¼ hours (rare), 1½ hours (medium) or 1¾ hours (well done). You may check the degree of cooking with a meat thermometer. Allow the meat to stand for 10-15 minutes before carving it. Serve with a gravy made from the pan drippings and Yorkshire Pudding.

GRAVY FOR YOUR ROAST

Pan juices or drippings

2 tablespoons flour

1 cup stock, water or wine

Salt and pepper to taste

Skim 2 tablespoons of fat from the pan drippings into a small saucepan. Drain off the remainder of the fat, leaving the pan juices in the drip tray. Add the stock to the drip tray to dissolve any sediment. Heat the fat in the saucepan, stir in the flour and allow it to brown. Pour in the liquid from the drip tray stirring it until it is boiling. Taste and then add salt and pepper to adjust the seasoning.

YORKSHIRE PUDDING

Serves 6.

1 cup plain flour

Salt to taste

2 eggs

1 cup milk

Beat all the ingredients until smooth. Cover and allow to stand for 30 minutes. Pour the mixture through the grill bars into the heated drip tray containing the hot drippings from the roast. Cook with the lid on for the last 30 minutes of cooking time, or until puffed and golden brown.

Olde English Roast Beef and Yorkshire Pudding

BEEF TENDERLOIN WITH ORANGE AND GINGER

Normal fire, indirect, 30-40 minutes, with lid on. Serves 6.

1 eye fillet of beef

2.5cm piece of fresh ginger, slivered

1 tablespoon butter, softened

MARINADE

Reserved ginger, chopped

Grated rind of 1 orange

Juice of 1 orange

2 tablespoons honey

1 teaspoon lemon pepper

Trim the meat, cutting away the silver skin. Tie it with string or use poultry pins to form a neat shape.

Make incisions in the meat and insert slivers of ginger all over it, reserving a little ginger for the marinade.

To make the marinade, combine all the ingredients and mix them well. Marinate the meat in this for a minimum of 2 hours.

When ready to cook, remove the meat from the marinade. Cook the meat on the barbecue with the lid on for 30-40 minutes.

When cooked, remove any poultry pins and string and serve the meat sliced accompanied with slices of orange and needleshreds of orange rind.

POCKET BOLAR STEAK

Normal fire, indirect, 1-1½ hours, with lid on. Serves 6-8.

2kg bolar beef, with pocket cut

STUFFING

1 large onion, peeled and sliced

4 rashers bacon, roughly chopped

1 tablespoon butter

1 red pepper, seeded and roughly chopped

2 cooking apples, roughly chopped, skin on

In a pan sauté the onion and bacon in butter for 2-3 minutes. Add the red pepper and apple, mixing it together. Cook for 5-10 minutes, stirring, until the apples are tender, then allow it to cool. Fill the pocket in the meat with this mixture. Secure it with toothpicks. Any remaining stuffing may be placed in a Glad oven bag and cooked alongside the meat for the last 30 minutes of cooking time. Place the meat on the barbecue and cook with the lid on for 1-1½ hours. Serve sliced with the stuffing and vegetables in season.

UNFORGETTABLE STANDING RIB ROAST

Normal fire, indirect, 1-1½ hours, with lid on. Serves 6-8.

Rib roast on bone, about 25cm long

Salt and pepper to taste

Place the meat in a standing position, fat side up, on the barbecue. Cook with the lid on for 1½-2 hours. Remove the meat from the bone in one piece. Slice it into thick, juicy steaks and serve it with baked potatoes and green vegetables, accompanied with horseradish sauce or mustard. If you choose good quality meat, this will be the best roast beef you've ever tasted!

BUSHMAN'S CORNED BEEF

Low fire, indirect, 1½ hours, with lid on. Serves 6-8.

2kg piece uncooked corned silverside

Place the corned meat in a dish of cold water and allow it to soak for 1-2 hours. Remove the meat and discard the water. Cook the meat on the barbecue fat side up for 1½ hours with the lid on. After 20 minutes of cooking time, pour ½ cups of water over the meat to remove any salt crust. Repeat this process every 20 minutes until the

meat is cooked.

15 minutes before the end of cooking time the meat can be glazed and a hint of smoke added.

GLAZE

½ cup marmalade

1 tablespoon brown sugar

Combine the ingredients and heat until the sugar dissolves. Brush the glaze over the meat during the last 15 minutes of the cooking time. Repeat glazing every 5 minutes, remembering to replace the lid after each application.

BEEF WITH BLACK BEAN SAUCE

Direct fire, lid off, wok on. Serves 6.

2 tablespoons oil

500g rump steak, trimmed and cut into thin strips

2 onions, peeled and cut into thin wedges

2 stalks celery, thinly sliced

1 red pepper, sliced

½ cup bottled black bean sauce

425g can Chinese mixed vegetables, well drained

2 tablespoons dry sherry

Heat the wok for 20-30 seconds and add the oil. Stir-fry the beef strips and onions. Add the celery and red pepper and cook for 1-2 minutes. Add the sauce, vegetables and sherry. Cook until they are heated through. Serve with hot boiled rice or noodles.

Beef Wellington

BEEF WELLINGTON

Normal fire, indirect, 40-45 minutes, with lid on. Serves 6-8.

375g packet puff pastry

Fillet of beef, about 20cm long, from the thick end

60g liver paté

2-3 mushrooms, sliced

Salt and pepper to taste

Egg wash

Roll the pastry until it is very thin. Place the meat on the top, spread it with the liver paté and dot it with the mushrooms. Season it with salt and pepper and roll it up securely, using the egg wash to seal the edges. Decorate the pastry as desired, brushing the eggwash over all. Place it on a sheet of foil and cook it on the barbecue with lid on for 40-45 minutes, or until the pastry is golden brown and crisp. Serve with vegetables or a salad.

STIR-FRY TERIYAKI STEAK

Direct fire, lid off, wok on. Serves 4.

500g topside or blade-bone steak

2 tablespoons oil

2 teaspoons cornflour

$1/2$ cup water or orange juice

MARINADE

1 tablespoon soy sauce

2 tablespoons sugar

$1/2$ teaspoon ground ginger

1 clove garlic, pressed

To make the marinade, combine all of the marinade ingredients and mix them well. Cut the meat into thin strips and place it in the marinade. Allow it to marinate for 30-60 minutes. Heat the wok for 20-30 seconds and add the oil. Stir-fry the meat until it is cooked. Blend the cornflour with the orange juice or water and add it to the mixture. Serve the Teriyaki Steak with fried rice and salad.

WHOLE FILLET OF BEEF

Normal fire, indirect, 30-40 minutes, with lid on. Serves 6.

2kg piece beef fillet

Brandy

Fresh cracked pepper

125g liverwurst

2-3 rashers bacon, rind removed

Chopped parsley

Trim the beef fillet to remove any fat and gristle. Brush it with the brandy and sprinkle it with pepper. Allow it to stand for I hour. Blend the liverwurst with a little brandy to soften it. Add a sprinkle of pepper and spread the liverwurst over the surface of the meat. Wrap the rashers of bacon around the meat and place it on foil. Shape the foil to hold in all the juices. Cook the meat on the barbecue, with the lid on for 30-40 minutes. Serve it sliced and sprinkled with parsley.

PEPPERED STEAKS

Direct fire, 5 minutes per side, with lid on. Serves 6.

6 porterhouse steaks, cut 2.5cm thick

MARINADE

1 tablespoon coarsely crushed peppercorns

$1/4$ cup olive oil

Salt to taste

1 teaspoon paprika

1 teaspoon dried rosemary

1 clove garlic, pressed

In a bowl combine the peppercorns, oil, salt, paprika, rosemary and garlic. Rub the steaks with this mixture and let them marinate, covered, in the refrigerator for 24 hours. Place the steaks on the barbecue and cook with the lid on for 5 minutes on each side. Serve the steaks with salad or vegetables in season.

CURRIED BEEF LOAF

Low fire, indirect, 45 minutes, with lid on. Serves 6.

750g finely minced beef

1 cup cooked rice

1 onion, finely chopped

2 small eggs, beaten

½ cup chopped raisins

3 teaspoons curry powder

Salt to taste

¼ cup oil

2 tablespoons fruit chutney

Combine the meat, rice, onion, eggs, raisins, curry powder and salt until they are thoroughly mixed. Shape this into a loaf. Brush a loaf pan with oil and place the meat into it. Brush the top of the loaf with oil. Cook on the barbecue with the lid on for 30-40 minutes. Spread the chutney on top of the loaf and cook for a further 5-10 minutes. Serve with vegetables or salad in season.

TOURNEDOS WITH CRAYFISH BEARNAISE

Direct fire, 5 minutes per side, with lid on. Serves 6.

6 pieces fillet steak, cut 2.5cm thick

6 rashers bacon

Cracked pepper to taste

200g cooked crayfish meat

Pat the steaks dry and wrap them with the bacon, mignon style. Season them generously with pepper, pressing it into both sides of the meat. Cook the steaks on the barbecue, with the lid on for 5 minutes each side. Serve the steaks topped with the crayfish meat and napped with Bearnaise sauce.

BEARNAISE SAUCE

¼ cup red wine

¼ cup tarragon vinegar

1 tablespoon chopped parsley

1 tablespoon chopped spring onion

1 tablespoon chopped tarragon

Tournedos with Crayfish Bearnaise

Cayenne pepper to taste

3 egg yolks, beaten

1 tablespoon water

1 teaspoon cornflour

180g butter

Salt and pepper to taste

In a saucepan combine the wine, vinegar, parsley, spring onion, tarragon and cayenne pepper. Boil and reduce the mixture to about one half, then allow it to cool slightly. Add the egg yolks, water and cornflour and whisk it well over a gentle heat, to thicken (for best results place the saucepan containing the sauce in a larger saucepan which contains gently boiling water). Add ⅓ of the butter to the sauce and stir until thick and smooth. Remove the saucepan containing the sauce from the heat, add the remaining butter and beat it in well. Season it with salt and pepper. Do not overheat this sauce as it may curdle. Serve at room temperature.

Meatloaf with Spicy Tomato Sauce

MEATLOAF WITH SPICY TOMATO SAUCE

Normal fire, indirect, 40-45 minutes, with lid on. Serves 6.

750g topside mince

³/₄ cup rolled oats

³/₄ cup evaporated milk

1 onion, finely chopped

1 tablespoon chopped parsley

Salt and pepper to taste

SAUCE

3 tablespoons tomato sauce

1 teaspoon Worcestershire sauce

1 teaspoon instant coffee powder

Combine all the ingredients for the meat loaf and pack the mixture in a buttered loaf pan. Cook it on the barbecue with the lid on for 30 minutes. Drain the liquid from the meatloaf into a saucepan containing the sauce ingredients. Bring this to the boil and pour it over the meatloaf. Return the meatloaf to the barbecue and continue cooking for 10-15 minutes, basting occasionally with the sauce mixture. Serve it hot or cold.

LEBANESE KEBABS

Normal fire, indirect, 6-8 minutes, with lid on. Serves 6-8.

500g topside mince

1 small onion, finely chopped

2 tablespoons natural yogurt

1 teaspoon curry powder

Salt to taste

1 clove garlic, pressed

1 tablespoon lemon juice

Extra natural yogurt to serve

Combine all the ingredients and mix them well. Divide the mixture into 8 equal portions. Mould each portion around the end of a bamboo skewer. Place the kebabs on the barbecue and cook with the lid on, for 6-8 minutes. Serve with a bowl of natural yogurt as a dip.

SAUERBRATEN

Low fire, indirect, 2 hours, with lid on. Serves 6-8.

2kg bolar or blade pot roast

2 tablespoons flour

2 tablespoons butter

1 onion, chopped

2 carrots, quartered

1¹/₂ tablespoons brown sugar

MARINADE

1 cup red wine

¹/₂ cup vinegar

¹/₂ cup water

Salt to taste

¹/₄ teaspoon whole peppercorns

1 large onion, sliced

1 large carrot, sliced

¹/₄ cup chopped celery

4 thin slices lemon

2 bay leaves

4 parsley stalks

¹/₄ teaspoon whole allspice

4 cloves

Pat the meat dry and place it in a bowl. Boil the marinade ingredients and then allow them to cool. Pour the marinade over the meat. Cover and leave it in the refrigerator for 3 days, turning the meat occasionally. Remove the meat from the marinade and pat it dry, strain the marinade to remove the solids. Sprinkle the meat with flour and place it in a Glad oven bag. Add the butter, onion, marinade, carrot and brown sugar. Tie the oven bag and make a hole in the top for any steam to escape. Cook on the barbecue for 2 hours, with the lid on. Use the marinade as a sauce and serve the meat hot and sliced. Spoon the sauce over the slices and accompany them with noodles and steamed red cabbage.

Barbecued Hamburgers (with Heroic Hot Dogs see page 134)

BARBECUED HAMBURGERS

Low direct fire, 4-5 minutes per side, with lid on. Serves 6.

1kg topside mince

1 onion, finely chopped

1 cup dry breadcrumbs

2 eggs

Salt and pepper to taste

2 tablespoons oil

1 tablespoon finely chopped parsley

Combine all the ingredients and mix them well. Shape the mixture into 12 patties, 2 cm thick and store them in the refrigerator, layered between plastic sheets, until required. Place the hamburgers on the barbecue and cook with the lid on for 4-5 minutes each side. Serve them topped with shredded lettuce, sliced tomatoes, dill cucumber, raw onion rings and tomato sauce on toasted buttered buns.

MOROCCAN SHISH KEBABS

Normal fire, indirect, 10-12 minutes, with lid on. Serves 6.

1kg round steak, cut into 2.5cm cubes

2 green peppers, cut, into squares

18 medium sized mushrooms

MARINADE

1 cup natural yogurt

2 tablespoons lemon juice

1 teaspoon olive oil

1 large onion, finely chopped

½ cup chopped fresh mint leaves

2 tablespoons chopped coriander or parsley

Salt and pepper to taste

¼ teaspoon cayenne pepper

In a bowl combine the yogurt, lemon juice, olive oil, onion, mint, coriander, salt, pepper and cayenne pepper. Add the meat to the marinade mixture.

Cover and store in the refrigerator for 6-8 hours. Arrange the meat on skewers, alternating with the green pepper and mushrooms. Cook the kebabs on the barbecue with the lid on for 10-12 minutes.

SMOKED STEAKS

Direct fire, 4-5 minutes per side, with lid on.

Choose sirloin, porterhouse, rump, fillet or T-bone steaks cut 2.5cm thick

Salt and pepper to taste

Smoke with either hickory or redgum chunks, or a whole knob of garlic, halved. Add 2 chunks of smoking wood or the garlic to the coals before cooking. Preheat a cast iron cooking grill (refer to page 7). Season the meat with salt and pepper. Place it on the barbecue and smoke-cook it with the lid on for 4-5 minutes each side. Serve with salad or vegetables in season.

Pork and Ham

There is something special about the aroma of pork cooking, sizzling and crackling outdoors on the barbecue kettle. The high temperature attained in the barbecue kettle virtually guarantees perfect pork crackling outside and delicious, moist meat inside.

Pre-cooked hams can be glazed and reheated. Raw hams, cured for you by your butcher, can be cooked and smoked on your own barbecue. They have a flavour and moistness you will have never experienced before.
Glazes add a new dimension to ham incorporating extra flavour, succulent sweetness and glossy appearance, and they are so simple to prepare.

We love American-style pork spare ribs. They are fun to eat and very easy to prepare. Outdoors is the best place to enjoy eating such a treat.

After trying our Old-Style Smokey Bacon, you'll probably never buy commercially prepared bacon again. If some of these ideas have whetted your appetite, you might as well know it's our favourite chapter too.

Contents

LOIN PORK ROAST WITH PRUNES AND MACADAMIA NUTS

Hot fire, indirect, 1¹/₄-1³/₄ hours, with lid on. Serves 6-8.

1.5kg loin of pork, boned, rind scored

1 teaspoon chicken seasoning

FILLING

Grated rind of 1 orange

¹/₂ teaspoon ground coriander

1 clove garlic, pressed

6 pitted prunes, cut in half

6 macadamia nuts, coarsely chopped

1 apple, cored and chopped with skin on

To make the filling combine all of the filling ingredients and mix them well. Open the pork and spread the filling over the meat. Roll the pork firmly and tie it with string. Rub the chicken seasoning into the scored rind. Place the pork on the barbecue and cook it for 1¹/₄-1³/₄ hours, with the lid on. Serve it sliced with roast potatoes and strawberry and spinach salad.

HAM PARCELS

Normal fire, indirect, 15-20 minutes, with lid on. Serves 6.

6 thick slices ham

6 slices canned pineapple

3 tablespoons chutney

3 tablespoons brown sugar

2 tablespoons mustard powder

60g butter

Place each slice of ham on a buttered square of foil. Arrange the pineapple slices on top. Add the chutney and sprinkle with brown sugar and mustard. Add dabs of butter to each. Gather the foil up around the sides to make a parcel. Cook the parcels on the barbecue with the lid on, for 15-20 minutes. Fold back the foil and serve them hot. These foil packages may be stacked one upon the other on the barbecue when feeding a crowd.

Loin Pork Roast with Prunes and Macadamia Nuts

JAMBALAYA

Direct fire, lid off, wok on. Serves 6-8.

1 tablespoon oil

2 rashers bacon, chopped

2 onions, chopped

2 cloves garlic, pressed

2 stalks celery, sliced

1 small red pepper, cut into strips

1 small green pepper, cut into strips

2 tomatoes, peeled and cut into strips

1 cup raw long grain rice

2 cups chicken stock

1 teaspoon fresh thyme or ¹/₂ teaspoon dried thyme

Dash of tabasco

250g ham, cut into strips

Salt and pepper to taste

Heat the wok and add the oil. Stir-fry the bacon, onion and garlic. Add the celery, red and green peppers, stirring well. Add the tomatoes, rice, 1¹/₂ cups of the chicken stock, thyme, tabasco, ham, salt and pepper. Bring to the boil, then place the barbecue lid on the wok and cook for 5-10 minutes. Check the mixture, stir and add extra chicken stock if the rice dries out before it is cooked. Cook with the barbecue lid on the wok for 5-10 minutes longer, or until the rice is tender.

Barbecued Pork Belly Spare Ribs

BARBECUED PORK BELLY SPARE RIBS

Normal fire, indirect, 25-30 minutes, with lid on. Serves 2-3.

6 lean pork belly spare ribs, cut about 2.5cm wide

MARINADE

1 tablespoon soy sauce

1 tablespoon sherry

1 teaspoon honey

2 cloves garlic, pressed

¼ teaspoon grated fresh ginger

To make the marinade, combine all of the marinade ingredients and mix them well. Marinate the ribs for several hours in the refrigerator, turning them once or twice. Remove the ribs and reserve the marinade for basting. Place them on the barbecue and cook with the lid on, for 25-30 minutes. Baste them with the marinade occasionally. Serve the ribs with hot boiled rice or potatoes and a salad.

LEG OF CRACKLING PORK

Hot fire, indirect, 3-3½ hours, with lid on. 1½-2 drip trays required.

5-6kg leg of pork

Oil

Salt and pepper to taste

If not already scored, the pork should be scored in a diamond pattern, ensuring you cut right through the rind, but not too deeply into the fat. Rub the oil and salt over the roast. Season it with pepper and place it on the barbecue. Cook it with the lid on, for 3-3½ hours, or until the meat is well cooked. Do not lift the lid during the first hour of cooking time as this may prevent the skin from crackling. Serve the pork sliced with vegetables or salad; and partner it with apple sauce, gravy, or baked fruit.

We have found that you can almost guarantee crackling on your pork by

Leg of Crackling Pork

following the 3 golden crackling rules.
1. Cook with a very hot fire.
2. When you buy the pork, make sure that it has white skin (not yellow or brown).
3. The pork should have a good layer of fat under the skin.

PORK AND OYSTER FILLETS

Normal fire, indirect, 15-25 minutes, with lid on. Serves 4.

750g pork fillet

105g smoked oysters

Salt and pepper to taste

1 teaspoon salad herbs

4 rashers bacon

Divide the pork fillet into 4 serving portions. Cut a slit down the side of each portion, but not all the way through. Arrange the drained oysters in the pork and close the fillet. Season it with salt, pepper and salad herbs. Remove the rind from the bacon. Wrap the bacon spirally down each portion and secure it with toothpicks. Cook the fillets on the barbecue with the lid on, for 15-25 minutes. Serve them with vegetables or salad.

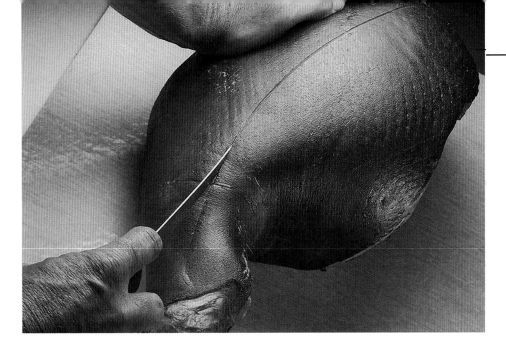

EASY BAKED GLAZED HAM

Normal fire, indirect, 1¼ hours, with lid on.
1½-2 drip trays required. Serves 10-12.

5-6kg cooked leg ham

MARMALADE GLAZE

1 cup orange marmalade

With a sharp knife, cut the rind around the ham and down the centre to free it on all sides. Ensure that you have cut right through the rind to the fat. Place the ham on the barbecue and cook it with the lid on for ¾ hour, or until the slit on top has widened to about 2.5 cm. Remove the skin from the ham and then score the fat with a knife to form 2.5cm diamonds. Warm the marmalade until it becomes a thick liquid. Brush this lavishly over the ham to glaze it. Be careful not to splash any marmalade on the coals. Cook with the lid on for 5 minutes. Re-glaze and cook for another 5 minutes. Place 1 piece of hickory on each side, on the coals and allow them to catch fire before replacing the lid. Finish cooking for 20 minutes with smoke. Serve the hot ham sliced with vegetables or a salad.

If you wish to dress the ham, pineapple rings, cloves and cherries may be added during the last 30 minutes of cooking. Hold them in place with toothpicks.

Easy Baked Glazed Ham

Home Made Baked Glazed Ham

HOME MADE BAKED GLAZED HAM

A Christmas Speciality!
Normal fire, indirect, 3¹/₂ hours, with lid on. 1¹/₂-2 drip trays required.

5-6kg pickled leg of pork, uncooked

440g can pineapple rings

6 glacé cherries

HAM GLAZE

2 cups soft brown sugar

¹/₂ cup canned pineapple syrup

2 teaspoons mustard powder

Well in advance, ask your butcher to pump and pickle a 5-6 kg raw leg of pork. With a sharp knife, cut the rind around the pork and down the centre to free it on all sides, ensuring that you have cut right through the rind to the fat. Place the prepared leg of pork on the barbecue and cook with the lid on for 2 hours to blister the skin. Remove the skin (see photograph). This skin is delicious to eat when broken up and served with drinks. Score the fat to form diamonds 2.5cm across and continue cooking with the lid on. To make the glaze combine all the glaze

ingredients and heat them until the sugar dissolves. ¹/₂ hour later decorate the ham with pineapple rings and glacé cherries, using toothpicks to secure them. Liberally glaze and continue cooking. Smoke with hickory wood chunks after the glaze has been added. Glaze 2-3 more times during the last hour of cooking. When ready, serve the hot meat sliced with salad or vegetables. Cold left-over ham makes beautiful sandwiches. The ham bone may be frozen to make pea and ham soup in the winter months.

79

MARINATED PORK CHOPS

Normal fire, indirect, 20-30 minutes, with lid on. Serves 4-6.

6 thick pork loin chops

MARINADE

2 tablespoons lemon juice

1 teaspoon French mustard

1 teaspoon chopped fresh herbs, e.g. thyme, parsley

1 teaspoon sesame oil

1 clove garlic, pressed

Score the edge of chops (see picture). Place the marinade ingredients in a shallow dish and coat each side of the chops. Allow the chops to stand, covered, in the marinade for 1 hour, or refrigerate them overnight. Remove the chops from the marinade and reserve the remaining marinade. Place the chops on the barbecue and cook with the lid on for 10-15 minutes on each side. Brush them with the marinade while cooking.

PORK CHOPS

Hot fire, indirect, 20-30 minutes, with lid on. Serves 4-6.

6 loin pork chops, 1-1.5cm thick

Oil

Salt to taste

When barbecuing pork chops, ask your butcher to cut the chops 1-1.5 cm

Pork Chops

thick and to leave the skin and fat on them. Score the fat with a sharp knife and oil the rind. Season them with salt. Place the pork chops on the barbecue with the rind as close to the coals as possible. This will cause the skin to crackle like roast pork. Cook them on the barbecue with the lid on, for 20-30 minutes. Turn the chops half way through the cooking time to ensure even crackling on each side.

SMOKED PORK CHOPS

Normal fire, indirect, 20-30 minutes, with lid on. Serves 4-6.

6 loin pork chops, 1-1.5cm thick

Salt to taste

For a change the chops may be glazed with pineapple glaze (recipe page 85) and then smoked by placing 1-2 chunks of smoking wood on the barbecue. They are also delicious smoked without the glaze.

SWEET AND SOUR PORK

Direct fire, lid off, wok on. Serves 6-8.

500g diced pork

1 tablespoon sherry

1 tablespoon soy sauce

1 egg white, beaten

¹/₂ cup cornflour

¹/₄ cup oil

2 red peppers, seeded and cut into squares

2 green peppers, seeded and cut into squares

4 slices fresh or canned pineapple, cut up

SAUCE

¹/₂ cup white vinegar

¹/₂ cup sugar

¹/₄ cup tomato sauce

¹/₄ cup Worcestershire sauce

2 tablespoons cornflour

¹/₄ cup water

Marinate the pork for 30 minutes in the sherry and soy sauce. Remove the pork, dip it in the egg white and roll it in the cornflour. Heat the wok and add the oil. Stir-fry the pork until it is golden. Remove the pork from the wok and set it aside. Stir-fry the peppers, then add the sauce ingredients to the wok. Cook, stirring until it is smooth and thickened. Add the pork and pineapple and heat them through. Serve the sweet and sour pork with rice.

PORK SATAY

Normal fire, indirect, 15-20 minutes, with lid on. Serves 6.

1kg boneless pork

MARINADE

1 tablespoon brown sugar

3 cloves garlic, pressed

2 tablespoons soy sauce

1 tablespoon oil

Cut the pork into 2.5cm cubes. Thread

Sweet and Sour Pork

the cubes on to skewers and place them in a dish. Combine the marinade ingredients and pour this mixture over the satays. Marinate them for 4-6 hours or overnight, turning the skewers occasionally. Cook the satays on the barbecue with the lid on, for 15-20 minutes. Serve them on a bed of boiled rice with peanut sauce. Grilled bananas and pineapple go really well with this dish.

PEANUT SAUCE

1 onion, finely chopped

3 cloves garlic, pressed

1 tablespoon oil

1 tablespoon malt vinegar

2 tablespoons soy sauce

2 tablespoons dry sherry

1 tablespoon brown sugar

3 tablespoons crunchy peanut butter

In a saucepan, gently fry the onion and garlic in oil until the onion has softened. Add the vinegar, soy sauce, sherry and brown sugar. Heat this mixture for 1 minute and then stir in the peanut butter. Cook the sauce over a low heat until it is well blended.

SMOKED BELLY SPARE RIBS WITH SWEET AND SOUR SAUCE

Normal fire, indirect, 25-30 minutes, with lid on. Serves 4.

10-12 lean pork belly spare ribs, cut 2.5cm wide

SWEET AND SOUR SAUCE

1 onion, finely chopped

1 tablespoon butter

1 cup tomato sauce

¹/₄ cup vinegar

¹/₄ cup sugar

Juice of 1 lemon

Salt and pepper to taste

1 teaspoon mustard powder

1 teaspoon Worcestershire sauce

Make the sweet and sour sauce by combining all the sauce ingredients in a saucepan and simmering them for 5-10 minutes. Add I hickory chunk to the coals on each side of the barbecue. Place the spare ribs on the barbecue, with the fat facing the coals. Cook them with the lid on for 25-30 minutes. Baste them occasionally with the sweet and sour sauce while cooking.

PORK PASTRY PACKETS

Normal fire, indirect, 20-30 minutes, with lid on. Serves 6.

¹/₄ **cup chopped, dried apricots**

¹/₄ **cup pitted, chopped prunes**

¹/₄ **cup chopped macadamia nuts or almonds**

¹/₄ **cup natural yogurt**

Pinch of thyme

Salt and pepper to taste

6 pork schnitzels, pounded thin

1 packet ready rolled puff pastry

1 egg, beaten

In a bowl combine the apricots, prunes, nuts, yogurt, thyme, salt and pepper. Spread this mixture over ¹/₂ of each pork schnitzel. Fold the pork in half to cover the filling. Wrap it in the pastry and glaze it with the egg. Use pastry trimmings to decorate each packet. Place them on buttered foil and cook them on the barbecue, with the lid on, for 20-30 minutes, or until the pastry is crisp and golden. Serve the packets with salad and creamy apple sauce.

CREAMY APPLE SAUCE

¹/₂ **cup apple sauce**

¹/₂ **cup sour cream**

2 teaspoons horseradish

Combine the apple sauce, sour cream and horseradish and heat them gently.

MANGO PORK RIBS

Normal fire, indirect, 20-25 minutes, with lid on. Serves 4.

4 slabs pork back ribs (American Style)

MARINADE

1 large ripe mango, peeled and sliced

4 cloves garlic, peeled

3cm piece green ginger

1 teaspoon Chinese five spice powder

2 tablespoons plum sauce

¹/₄ **cup dry sherry**

Salt and pepper to taste

To make the marinade, puree the mango, garlic and ginger in a food processor until they are smooth. Add the five spice powder, plum sauce, sherry, salt and pepper. Pour this marinade over the ribs, turning the ribs to coat them well. Cover and allow them to marinate overnight in the refrigerator. Place the ribs on the barbecue and cook them for 20-25 minutes, with the lid on. Baste them occasionally with the marinade. Serve the ribs with vegetables or salad.

PORK-A-HOUSE STEAKS

These steaks may be cooked either direct or indirect.

DIRECT METHOD

Direct fire, 3-4 minutes per side, with lid on. Serves 6.

6 pork-a-house steaks, well trimmed

Oil

Salt and pepper to taste

Brush the steaks with oil, season them with salt and pepper and place them on the barbecue. Cook them with the lid on, for 3-4 minutes on each side. Serve them with salad or vegetables.

INDIRECT METHOD

Normal fire, indirect, 15-20 minutes, with lid on. Serves 6.

6 pork-a-house steaks, untrimmed

Oil

Salt and pepper to taste

Brush the steaks with oil and season them with salt and pepper. Place the steaks on the barbecue over a drip tray with the fat facing the coals. Cook them with the lid on, for 8-10 minutes each side. 1 piece of hickory wood placed on the coals on each side during cooking gives a great flavour. The steaks may be marinated or glazed if desired. Serve them with salad or vegetables.

MARINATED SPICY SPARE RIBS

Normal fire, indirect, 20-25 minutes, with lid on. Serves 4.

4 slabs pork back ribs (American Style)

MARINADE

2 onions, chopped

1 clove garlic, pressed

¹/₂ **cup peanut butter**

1 teaspoon ground coriander

1 tablespoon brown sugar

2 tablespoons soy sauce

2 tablespoons oil

2 tablespoons lemon juice

Salt and cayenne pepper to taste

To make the marinade, combine all the marinade ingredients and mix them well. Marinate the ribs overnight, or at least for several hours. Cook them on the barbecue with the lid on, for 20-25 minutes. Baste them with the marinade once or twice during cooking. Serve the ribs with potatoes cooked in their jackets and a mixed salad. Finger lickin' good!

PORK AND BACON KEBABS

Normal fire, indirect, 15-20 minutes, with lid on. Serves 3-4.

500g pork, cut into 2.5cm cubes

¹/₂ **cup Worcestershire sauce**

2 rashers bacon

4 spring onions

3 bananas

Marinate the pork in the worcestershire sauce for several hours. Cut both the bacon and bananas into 12 pieces. Cut the spring onions into pieces 2 cm long. Thread the pork, bacon, spring onion and banana pieces on to 6 skewers. Cook them on the barbecue, with the lid on, for 15-20 minutes. Serve the kebabs on a bed of rice.

Smoked & Glazed Pork Back Spare Ribs

SMOKED & GLAZED PORK BACK SPARE RIBS

Normal fire, indirect, 20-25 minutes, with lid on. Serves 4.

4 slabs pork back ribs (American Style)

PINEAPPLE GLAZE

1 cup soft brown sugar

1 tablespoon vinegar

1 tablespoon mustard powder

1 tablespoon cornflour

440g can crushed pineapple

To make the glaze, place all the ingredients in a saucepan and cook them stirring constantly, until they are well reduced to a syrupy consistency.

Dip the ribs in the glaze and place them on the barbecue. Add 1 chunk of hickory wood to the coals on each side. Cook for 20-25 minutes with the lid on, adding further glaze while cooking. Serve with salad and provide finger bowls and plenty of serviettes. You may wish to have the ribs pickled in butcher's brine, this gives the ribs a ham-like colour and flavour. You will need to order these 2-3 days in advance. Ask your butcher not to pickle them for any longer than 2 hours, otherwise they will be extremely salty. Wash the pickled ribs with fresh water to remove any excess salt before glazing.

Fruity Pork with Fried Rice (see page 161)

FRUITY PORK

Direct fire, lid off, wok on. Serves 6.

300g pork fillet, thinly sliced

Cornflour

3 tablespoons oil

1 green or red pepper, thinly sliced

1 onion, peeled and cut into thin wedges

425g can pear halves, drained and chopped

425g can Chinese mixed vegetables, drained

1 chicken stock cube

2 tablespoons tomato paste

Salt and pepper to taste

¹/₂ cup water

Toss the pork in the cornflour and shake off any excess. Heat the wok and add the oil. Stir-fry the pork, peppers and onion for 5 minutes, or until the pork lightly browns. Add all the remaining ingredients and stir-fry to heat them through. Serve the fruity pork with boiled rice, fried rice, or noodles.

BAKED FRUIT TO SERVE WITH PORK

APPLES

Cored apples may be placed around the pork for the last 50-60 minutes of cooking time. These may be filled with dried fruits if desired.

PINEAPPLE

A whole pineapple may be cooked with the pork for the last 1¹/₂ hours of cooking time. To do this, select a whole ripe pineapple in its skin. Remove the green top and stand the pineapple upright on the barbecue. Serve the pineapple cut into slices. It is sweet, juicy and delicious.

CHINESE ROAST PORK

Normal fire, indirect, 20-30 minutes, with lid on. Serves 4.

1.5kg boned loin pork, skin and fat removed

MARINADE

1 cup teriyaki sauce

¹/₂ cup sweet sherry

2 cloves garlic, pressed

1 teaspoon ground ginger

GLAZE

1 teaspoon sesame oil

1 tablespoon honey

Cut the pork into long, thin strips 2.5cm wide down the full length of the meat. To make the marinade, mix together the teriyaki sauce, sherry, garlic and ginger. Marinate the pork for 3-4 hours, turning the meat occasionally. Place the pork on the barbecue and cook it for 15-20 minutes with the lid on. Brush it with the sesame oil and honey and cook for 5-10 minutes longer. Serve it sliced with salad. It may also be chopped and served in fried rice.

INDIAN SPICED PORK

Direct fire, lid off, wok on. Serves 6-8.

¹/₄ cup desiccated coconut

1 can evaporated milk

2 tablespoons oil

500g pork fillet, cut into thin slices

1 onion, peeled and sliced

1 tablespoon curry powder

1 teaspoon cumin

1 teaspoon paprika

Salt to taste

440g can pineapple pieces, drained

2 red dessert apples, cored and cut into slices

Combine the coconut and milk and set it aside. Heat the wok and add the oil. Cook the pork, onion, curry powder, cumin, paprika and salt, stirring all the time. Add the pineapple pieces, coconut milk and apples. Continue cooking until the apples are tender. Serve the spiced pork with boiled rice, fried pappadams, cashew nuts, chutney and sliced bananas tossed in lemon juice.

STIR-FRIED PORK IN LETTUCE LEAVES

Direct fire, lid off, wok on. Serves 8.

2 tablespoons oil

750g, pork, minced

1 small can water chestnuts, drained and chopped

4 slices fresh ginger, peeled and chopped

¹/₄ cup chilli sauce

2 tablespoons dry sherry

1 tablespoon soy sauce

1 teaspoon sugar

Salt and pepper to taste

2 tablespoons cornflour

¹/₂ cup chicken stock

Lettuce leaves

Heat the wok and add the oil. Stir-fry the pork, chestnuts and ginger in the oil until the meat is no longer pink. Stir in the chilli sauce, sherry, soy sauce, sugar, salt and pepper. In a small bowl blend the cornflour with the chicken stock and add this mixture to the wok. Cook for a further 1-2 minutes, stirring. Place 1-2 tablespoons of this mixture on the lettuce leaves. Roll up the leaves and serve.

PORK PARCELS

Normal fire, indirect, 30-40 minutes, with lid on. Serves 4.

4 bacon rashers, rind removed

1 pork fillet, cut into 4

1 onion, sliced

1 tomato, sliced

4 mushrooms, sliced

4 slices cheese

Cut each bacon rasher into 4 pieces. Take 4 pieces of foil and place two of the bacon pieces on each sheet of foil. Place one piece of the pork on top of the bacon and season it with salt and pepper. Add the onion, tomato, mushroom and cheese slices in layers on top of the pork. Place 2 more pieces of bacon on the top of each one. Wrap the foil around each one to make a parcel. Cook them on the barbecue, with the lid on, for 30-40 minutes. Serve the parcels with potatoes and salad.

OLD-STYLE SMOKEY BACON

Normal fire, indirect, 1 hour, with lid on. 2 drip trays required.

2 kg strip of pork belly, uncooked

Ask your butcher to pickle a 2kg uncooked strip of pork belly. Wash the pork belly to remove any excess salt and pat it dry. Wrap it in foil to prevent the rind from hardening. Place the foil-wrapped pork belly on the barbecue and cook it with the lid on, for 30 minutes. Add 2 hickory chunks to the coals on each side and remove the foil from the bacon. Smoke cook the bacon with the lid on for another 30 minutes. Cool the bacon and store it in the refrigerator. Ask your butcher or delicatessen to slice it for you, or slice it as you need it.

Old-Style Smokey Bacon

Poultry

Poultry cooked on barbecue kettles is golden, crisp and delicious on the outside, tender and moist on the inside, with the juices bubbling under the skin. Whether it be roasted, smoked, glazed, spiced, herbed or deep fried, nothing can cook poultry like the barbecue kettle.

In this chapter we will introduce you to some of our favourite recipes for duck, chicken and turkey. Recipes like Old McGregor's Smoked Lemon Chicken, you'll need to cook twice as much as normal. Tandoori-style Grilled Chicken, not real Indian, but you've just got to taste it. Honey Smoked Duck, perfect for the intimate dinner for 2. But the very best of all is the Pickled, Glazed Roast Turkey, the ultimate Christmas treat for your family.

As you can see, we're pretty excited about this chapter.

Contents

Roast Chicken and Vegetables

ROAST CHICKEN

Normal fire, indirect, 1-1¼ hours, with lid on. Serves 4.

1 medium chicken

Oil

Salt and pepper to taste

Wash the chicken thoroughly and pat it dry. Tuck the wings behind the back. Brush the chicken with oil and season it with salt and pepper.

Place the chicken on the barbecue and cook it, with the lid on, for 1-1¼ hours, depending on size. The chicken will be juicy and golden brown, with crispy skin. Serve it with vegetables or salad.

CHILLI CHICKEN WINGS

Normal fire, indirect, 20-30 minutes, with lid on.

1-2kg chicken wings

1 cup oil

Salt and pepper to taste

SAUCE

180g butter, melted

¼ cup cider vinegar

½ cup chilli sauce with ginger

Dip the chicken wings in the oil then drain them on paper towels. Season them with salt and pepper. Cook the wings on the barbecue, with the lid on, for 20-30 minutes. To make the sauce, combine the melted butter, vinegar and chilli sauce. Place the wings in a serving dish and pour the sauce over them. Serve them with crisp celery stalks and blue cheese dip.

BLUE CHEESE DIP

½ cup crumbled blue cheese

Salt and pepper to taste

1 tablespoon finely chopped onion

Few drops Worcestershire sauce

1 tablespoon lemon juice

1 cup sour cream

Combine all of these ingredients and chill them well.

91

Tandoori-Style Grilled Chicken

TANDOORI-STYLE GRILLED CHICKEN

Normal fire, indirect, 45-50 minutes, with lid on. Serves 4.

1kg chicken, cut into 4 pieces

MARINADE

1 cup natural yogurt

1/4 cup white vinegar

1 tablespoon lemon juice

1 clove garlic, pressed

1 teaspoon ground coriander

1 teaspoon mustard powder

1/2 teaspoon pepper

1/2 teaspoon ground ginger

1/8 teaspoon ground cloves

5 drops Tabasco sauce

Combine all the marinade ingredients in a large bowl, mixing them well. Add the chicken pieces, turning them to coat them. Marinate the chicken, covered, in the refrigerator for 1 1/2 hours. Remove the chicken pieces from the marinade and place them on the barbecue. Cook them with the lid on, for 45-50 minutes. Serve them with hot boiled rice and a spicy sauce.

CHICKEN PIECES

Normal fire, indirect, 45-60 minutes, with lid on. Serves 6.

6 chicken quarters

1 tablespoon oil

Salt and pepper to taste

Any portion of chicken may be cooked on the barbecue. Brush the quarters with oil. Season them with salt and pepper. Place them on the barbecue skin side up. Cook them with the lid on, for 45-60 minutes.

The chicken may be smoked by adding 1 hickory chunk to the coals on each side of the barbecue at the commencement of cooking.

BARBECUED CRUMBED CHICKEN

Normal fire, indirect, 45-50 minutes, with lid on. Serves 4.

4 chicken quarters

125g butter, melted

1 tablespoon lemon juice

1 teaspoon Worcestershire sauce

Salt to taste

1 clove garlic, pressed

1/2 teaspoon paprika

Breadcrumbs

Combine the butter, lemon juice, Worcestershire sauce, salt, garlic and paprika. Dip the chicken quarters in this mixture and roll them in the breadcrumbs. Cook the chicken quarters on the barbecue, with the lid on, for 45-50 minutes. Serve them with vegetables, or a tossed salad.

KOREAN CHICKEN SATAYS

Normal fire, indirect, 10-15 minutes, with lid on. Serves 6.

6 boneless chicken breasts, cut into thin strips

1/2 cup soy sauce

1/4 cup salad oil

2 cloves garlic, pressed

2 tablespoons brown sugar

1 onion, finely chopped

1 tablespoon lemon juice

2 teaspoons grated fresh ginger

Combine all the ingredients and allow the chicken to marinate for 1-2 hours, covered, in the refrigerator. Thread the chicken strips on to bamboo skewers. Cook them on the barbecue, with the lid on, for 10-15 minutes. Serve them hot with fried rice and salad.

SPICED FRIED CHICKEN

Direct fire, lid off, wok on. Serves 4-6.

1-2 litres oil for deep frying

1-2kg chicken pieces

3 tablespoons cornflour

MARINADE

$^1/_2$ cup chopped spring onions

$^1/_4$ cup dry sherry

$^1/_3$ cup soy sauce

1 teaspoon finely chopped fresh ginger

To make the marinade, combine the marinade ingredients and mix them well. Place the chicken pieces in the marinade and allow them to marinate for 30 minutes. Add the cornflour to the marinated chicken and mix it in thoroughly. Heat the wok and add the oil. Heat the oil until bubbles appear when tested with the handle of a wooden spoon. Cook the chicken, a few pieces at a time, turning the chicken in the oil once or twice. When cooked, remove the chicken and serve it with fried rice and salad.

ORANGE SPATCHCOCK

Normal fire, indirect, 40-50 minutes, with lid on. Serves 4.

4 spatchcocks

MARINADE

$^2/_3$ cup orange juice

$^1/_4$ cup olive oil

2 tablespoons lemon juice

4 cloves garlic, pressed

2 bay leaves, crushed

Grated rind of one orange

2 teaspoons sugar

$^1/_4$ teaspoon cinnamon

Pepper to taste

Combine the orange juice, oil, lemon juice, garlic, bay leaves, orange rind, sugar, cinnamon and pepper, mixing them well. Butterfly the chickens by cutting out the back bones and discarding them. Open the chicken, skin-side up, on a board. Push down on

Spiced Fried Chicken

the breast bone to flatten it, using the heel of your hand . Remove the breast and rib bones. Place the chickens in the marinade, coating them thoroughly. Cover and refrigerate them overnight. Remove the chickens from the marinade, reserving the liquid. Place them on the barbecue, skin-side up and cook them with the lid on, for 40-50 minutes, or until done. Baste them occasionally with the reserved marinade. Serve them with vegetables or a salad.

CHICKEN PACKETS

Normal fire, indirect, 40-50 minutes, with lid on. Serves 4.

4 meaty chicken pieces

4 tablespoons butter

1 packet French onion soup

1 teaspoon paprika

125g button mushrooms

$^1/_2$ cup cream

Wash and dry the chicken pieces and place each on a piece of foil. Top each with the butter, soup mix, paprika, mushrooms and cream. Bring the foil up around the chicken, sealing the edges well. Cook the packets on the barbecue, with the lid on, for 40-50 minutes. Serve them with fresh bread and salad.

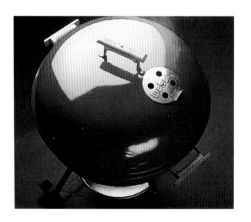

Boneless Chicken Roll

BONELESS CHICKEN ROLL

Normal fire, indirect, 1-1¼ hours, with lid on. Serves 6.

1 medium chicken, boned

1 tablespoon oil

Salt and pepper to taste

STUFFING

2 tablespoons butter

1 onion, chopped

¾ cup finely chopped ham

¾ cup minced pork, veal, or chicken

1 egg

2 tablespoons fresh breadcrumbs

1 tablespoon chopped fresh herbs

Salt and pepper to taste

Bone the chicken, or ask your butcher to bone it for you. To prepare the stuffing, melt the butter and cook the onion for 1-2 minutes. Then combine it with the meat, egg, breadcrumbs, herbs, salt and pepper. Allow this mixture to cool before using it.

Place the chicken, skin-side down and fill it with the stuffing. Roll the chicken up and secure the flesh with poultry pins and string. Brush it with oil and season it with salt and pepper. Cook it on the barbecue, with the lid on, for 1-1¼ hours. Serve it sliced, hot or cold, with salad or vegetables.

OLD MCGREGOR'S SMOKED LEMON CHICKEN

Normal fire, indirect, 1-1¼ hours, with lid on. Serves 4.

1 medium chicken

1 lemon, quartered, rind on

1 tablespoon oil

Salt and pepper to taste

Wash the chicken and pat it dry. Place the lemon quarters in the cavity. Tuck the wings behind the back, brush the chicken with oil and season it with salt and pepper. Add 2 hickory chunks to the coals on each side at the commencement of cooking. Cook it on the barbecue, with the lid on, for 1-1¼ hours. Served piping hot, this is the best chicken we have ever eaten.

PAELLA

Direct fire, lid off, wok on. Serves 6-8.

¼ cup oil

1 chicken, cut into serving pieces

2 tablespoons butter

1 clove garlic, pressed

2 cups rice, uncooked

¼ teaspoon saffron

4 cups chicken stock

Salt and pepper to taste

2 chorizo sausages, sliced

1 cup seeded and chopped red pepper

6 large green prawns, in shell

1 dozen mussels

Strips of red pepper to decorate

Heat the wok and add the oil. Wash and dry the chicken pieces. Place them in the wok with the butter and garlic. Cook them stirring occasionally until the chicken is golden brown. Remove the chicken and add the rice to the wok with the saffron and chicken stock. Bring this to the boil and season it with salt and pepper. Return the chicken to the wok with the sausages and red pepper. Cook with the barbecue lid on the wok for 30 minutes, adding extra stock from time to time. Add the seafood and continue cooking for 10-15 minutes longer. Garnish with the red pepper strips. Serve the paella with garlic bread and a tossed green salad.

CHICKEN KEBABS

Normal fire, indirect, 10-20 minutes, with lid on. Serves 4.

4 boneless chicken breasts, skin removed

1 red pepper, cut into squares

MARINADE

1 tablespoon soy sauce

1 tablespoon Dijon mustard

1 tablespoon brown sugar

1 tablespoon sherry

1 tablespoon oil

Cut the chicken breasts into 2 cm pieces. Marinate them in a mixture of the soy sauce, mustard, sugar, sherry and oil, covered, in the refrigerator, for at least 2 hours. Thread the chicken and pepper squares alternately on to 8 bamboo skewers. Cook the kebabs on the barbecue, with the lid on, for 10-20 minutes, or until they are cooked. Serve them with hot boiled rice and salad.

HONEY SMOKED DUCK

Normal fire, indirect, 1-1¼ hours, with lid on. Serves 2.

1 large duckling

¼ cup salt for brine

¼ cup oil

Freshly ground black pepper to taste

1 orange, unpeeled, cut into quarters

⅓ cup honey

Soak the duck in water with the salt overnight, or for several hours. Rinse the duck and pat it dry. Rub it with oil and sprinkle it with the pepper. Place the orange and honey in the cavity. Place 2 hickory chunks on the coals on each side of the barbecue and allow them to smoke. Smoke-cook the duck on the barbecue, with the lid on for 1-1¼ hours. Serve it with vegetables or a salad.

ORANGE GLAZED ROAST DUCK

Normal fire, indirect, 1-1¼ hours, with lid on. Serves 2.

1 large duckling

¼ cup salt for brine

Salt and pepper to taste

1 orange

1 onion

ORANGE GLAZE

1 cup marmalade

¼ cup brown sugar

¼ cup bourbon, sherry, brandy or orange juice

Soak the duck in enough water to cover it, add the salt and leave it in a cool place for 24 hours. Remove the duck from the water, pat it dry and sprinkle the cavity with salt and pepper. Cut the orange and onion into quarters and place them inside the duck. Cook it on the barbecue, with the lid on, for 1 hour. To make the glaze, combine the marmalade, brown sugar and bourbon and heat it to dissolve the sugar. Brush this over the duck 2-3 times during the

Orange Glazed Roast Duck

last 30 minutes of cooking time, A touch of hickory smoke during the last 15 minutes adds an exciting flavour. Vegetables may be cooked around the duck at the same time. However, they should be foil-wrapped if the duck is being smoked to prevent the smoke penetrating them.

DUCK WITH ORANGE

Normal fire, indirect, 1-1¼ hours, with lid on. Serves 2.

1 large duckling

¼ cup salt for brine

1 orange, cut into quarters

¼ cup oil

ORANGE SAUCE

2 tablespoons vinegar

½ cup brown sugar

125ml chicken stock

1 orange, peeled and sliced

¼ cup Grand Marnier

2 tablespoons Cointreau

Soak the duck in enough water to cover it, add the salt and leave it in a cool place for 24 hours. Rinse the duck and pat it dry. Place the orange quarters in the cavity. Brush the outside of the duck with oil. Cook the duck on the barbecue, with the lid on, for 1-1¼ hours, or until cooked.

To prepare the sauce, place the vinegar, sugar and stock in a pan. Simmer this for 5-10 minutes. Add the orange slices to the sauce and simmer gently. Add the Grand Marnier and Cointreau. Spoon this sauce over the duck when serving.

ROAST TURKEY

Normal fire, indirect, 2-2½ hours, with lid on. 2 drip trays required. Serves 8-10.

5-6kg turkey

¼ cup oil

Salt and pepper to taste

Wash and dry the turkey. Remove the giblets and neck. Set the giblets aside for the gravy. Tuck the wings behind the back. Oil the turkey well and season it with salt and pepper. Place the turkey on the barbecue, shielding the sides with foil. Cook it with the lid on for 2-2½ hours. If the bird has stuffing in its cavity, allow an additional 20-30 minutes cooking time. Carve and serve it hot with giblet gravy and vegetables.

GIBLET GRAVY

Turkey giblets

4 cups water

¼ cup flour

1 teaspoon prepared mustard

Salt and pepper to taste

2 tablespoons red wine or port wine

¼ cup cream

To make the giblet gravy, boil the giblets in the water for 30 minutes. Discard the giblets and measure 3 cups of the resulting stock for the gravy. Combine all the remaining ingredients with the stock, mixing them well. Bring this mixture to the boil, stirring constantly until it is smooth.

All over Australia thousands of kettle barbecue owners cook their turkeys this way. But we've found 3 other ways to serve a Christmas turkey fit for a King. They are glazed turkey,

smoked turkey and pickled turkey.

GLAZED TURKEY

Lavishly brush the turkey with a Redcurrant Glaze (Recipe page 203) 2-3 times during the last 20-25 minutes of cooking time.

SMOKED TURKEY

Add 2 chunks of hickory to the coals on each side of the barbecue at the commencement of the cooking time. Smoke cooked turkey - there is nothing like it!

PICKLED TURKEY

Ask your butcher to pump and pickle the turkey, using a low salt brine. It is advisable to order it several days before it is required. The pickled turkey may be cooked plain, or glazed and smoked. The beautiful, juicy, tender ham-like meat is unforgettable!

BONED STUFFED TURKEY ROLL

Normal fire, indirect, 1-1½ hours, with lid on. Serves 6-8.

3-4kg turkey, boned

Salt and pepper to taste

250g boneless chicken

250g sliced ham

1 egg white

¼ cup cream

½ teaspoon ground cardamom

1 bunch fresh asparagus, cooked

¼ cup oil

Chicken seasoning

SAUCE

2 tablespoons flour

1 cup chicken stock

1 cup sliced button mushrooms

½ cup dry sherry

¼ cup cream

1 tablespoon tomato paste

Salt and pepper to taste

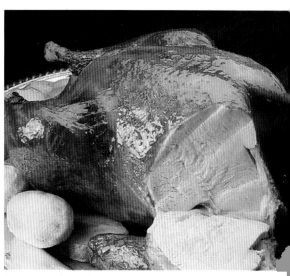

Ask your butcher to bone the turkey. Lay the turkey skin-side down and season it with salt and pepper. In a food processor puree the chicken and 100 g of the ham. Add the egg white, cream, salt, pepper and cardamom. Spread this mixture over the turkey. Arrange the cooked asparagus on top with the remaining ham. Roll up and secure the turkey with poultry pins and string. Brush the skin with oil and season it with the chicken seasoning. Cook it on the barbecue, with the lid on, for 1-1½ hours.

Make the sauce by combining all the ingredients and boiling the mixture for 2-3 minutes. Serve the meat sliced with the sauce.

PEPPERED TURKEY ROLL

Normal fire, indirect, 50-70 minutes, with lid on. Serves 6.

1 turkey roll

Oil

Prepared pepper steak mix

Rub the surface of the turkey all over with oil. Roll it in the pepper mix until it is black all over the surface. Cook it on the barbecue, with the lid on, for 50-70 minutes. Serve the meat sliced, hot or cold, with salad or vegetables.

Plain turkey rolls may be opened, filled with a stuffing, or dried fruits soaked in sherry and then re-tied. Strips of bacon may be placed on top of the roll during the last 20-25 minutes of cooking time for added flavour.

Pickled, Glazed and Smoked Roast Turkey

Fish and Shellfish

Australia has a vast variety of seafood readily available and there is no better way to cook all kinds of fish and shellfish than on the barbecue kettle.

Whole barbecued snapper, freshly boiled crayfish, smoked trout, baked barramundi and good old Aussie fish and chips with salt and vinegar. What a way to entertain friends!

The barbecue is bigger than most domestic ovens and quite large fish may easily be barbecued whole. The use of the indirect cooking method means the barbecued whole fish comes out tender, moist and delicious.

Many people don't realise that their barbecue is a great smoke oven. Fabulous smoke results come from hickory chunks, but dried wood from gum trees, mallee roots, and grapevines may be used to give good results. Placing the fish directly on the grill-bars gives them a beautiful golden smoke colour and sensational flavour.

The addition of a wok will open areas of kettle barbecue cooking that you will only have dreamed of. Imagine fresh yabbies, crabs or crayfish cooked in boiling water in the garden. The best fish and chips you've ever tasted. It sizzles deep fried in hot oil and cooks to perfection in gold crusty batter.

In the following recipes we tell you how it is all done. So pour yourself a glass of beer and sit back and let the barbecue do it all for you.

Contents

Baked Whole Snapper

BAKED WHOLE SNAPPER

Low fire, indirect, 40-50 minutes, with lid on.

1 whole Snapper, 46cm long - 2.5kg

Oil

Lemon

White wine

Salt and freshly ground black pepper

Wash and scale the fish. Place the fish upright on a sheet of oiled foil, formed into a tray, with its body curved and its fins used to prop it up. Brush it with oil and sprinkle lemon juice all over it. Splash it with wine and season with salt and pepper. (A little fresh mint and garlic tucked into the cavity adds extra flavour to the fish). Cook it on the barbecue with the lid on, for 40-50 minutes. Splash more wine over the fish occasionally and drink some too!

If desired, during the last 15 minutes of cooking time, 5-6 green gum leaves may be added to the coals on each side to add smoke flavour. Serve the snapper hot or cold, with tartare sauce and salad.

TOMMY RUFFS OR SEA HERRING VINAIGRETTE

Low fire, indirect, 15-20 minutes, with lid on. Serves 4-6.

4-6 tommy ruffs or sea herrings

Slices of rockmelon

Figs to garnish

Alfalfa sprouts

VINAIGRETTE DRESSING

1/2 cup oil

2 tablespoons lemon juice

1 tablespoon tarragon vinegar

Salt, pepper, mustard and sugar to taste

1 tablespoon chopped fresh herbs, (mint, parsley or tarragon)

1 teaspoon chopped capers

Clean the fish and pat them dry. Cook the fish-on the barbecue with the lid on for 15-20 minutes, or until the flesh flakes easily when tested.

Serve the fish on a platter decorated with melon, figs and alfalfa sprouts.

Make the dressing by combining all the ingredients and mixing them well. Spoon the dressing over the fish and serve.

WHOLE BREAM

Low fire, indirect, 15-20 minutes, with lid on. Serves 1-2.

1-2 whole bream - 300-400g each

1-2 tablespoons melted butter

Lemon juice

Salt and pepper to taste

Lightly butter the fish on both sides. Season them with salt and pepper. Cook them on the barbecue, with the lid on, for 15-20 minutes, or until the flesh flakes when tested with a fork. Serve the fish with a squeeze of lemon juice, tartare sauce and salad.

101

BONED SMOKED RAINBOW TROUT

Low smoke fire, indirect, 15-30 minutes, with lid on. Serves 4-6.

4-6 whole rainbow trout, about

20-25cm long

4kg cooking salt

BONING

Bone the rainbow trout by slitting the underside of the fish open from the gills to the tail. Using scissors, cut through the back bone just behind the head. Carefully lift the backbone and rib cage free. Cut through the back bone at the tail end. Check for any remaining rib bones and remove them. Salt the fish inside and out and allow them to stand covered in the salt, in the refrigerator for 4-6 hours. Wash off the salt and pat the fish dry.

Place 1 hickory chunk on the coals on each side of the barbecue. Smoke-cook the fish on the barbecue with the lid on for 15-30 minutes, or until the flesh flakes when tested. Serve this delicious fish hot or cold.

OUTDOOR BAKED FISH

Low fire, indirect, 25 minutes for first kg, 10 minutes each additional kg, with lid on.

Any whole fish, cleaned and scaled

Oil

Salt and pepper to taste

Lemon juice

Slices of tomato

Wash the fish and pat it dry. Brush it all over with oil. Place the fish on oiled foil. Season it with salt and pepper and sprinkle it with lemon juice. Arrange the slices of tomato along the top of the fish if desired and wrap the foil to make a package. Cook the fish on the barbecue with the lid on, for 25 minutes for first kg and a further 10 minutes for each additional kg.

Fish are cooked by thickness rather than weight. Most large fish should be completely cooked in 40-50 minutes. Always test the fish by cutting into the thickest part of the flesh. It should flake easily when tested. Serve the fish with salad, fresh bread and butter.

Boned Smoked Rainbow Trout

BARBECUED GOLDEN PERCH, CALLOP, YELLOW BELLY, OR MURRAY PERCH

Low fire, indirect, 25-30 minutes, with lid on. Serves 3-4.

2-3kg golden perch

Salt and pepper to taste

Oil

125g bacon rashers

Wash, scale and gut the fish. Place it in a salt solution (1 part salt to 4 parts water by volume) sufficient to cover the fish. Allow it to stand in a cool place for 1 -2 hours. Wash the fish, pat it dry, oil and season it with salt and pepper. Place the fish on oiled foil. Cook the fish on the barbecue, with the lid on, for 15 minutes. Add the bacon rashers to the top of the fish.

Add chunks of dried redgum or acacia wood to the coals to smoke it. Smoke cook on the barbecue for a further 15 minutes, or until the flesh flakes when tested. Serve the golden perch with fried potato slices, crusty bread and salad.

STUFFED FLOUNDER OR SOLE

(JOYFUL SOLE)

Low fire, indirect, 15-20 minutes, with lid on. Serves 2.

2 whole flounder or sole

$1/2$ cup prawns, chopped

1 clove garlic, pressed

1 tablespoon fresh coriander, chopped

Lemon juice

Salt and pepper to taste

Melted butter

Cut a slit down the centre of the top side of the fish. Run a sharp knife under the skin on each side, forming a pocket. In this pocket place the chopped prawns. Add the garlic, coriander, lemon juice, salt and pepper. Place the fish on buttered foil and brush it with butter. Season it with salt and pepper. Cook it on the barbecue with the lid on for 15-20 minutes, or until the flesh flakes when tested with a fork. Serve the fish with salad or vegetables in season.

Barbecued Golden Perch, Callop, Yellow Belly, or Murray Perch

WHOLE RAINBOW TROUT

Low fire, indirect, 15-30 minutes, with lid on. Serves 2-3.

2-3 rainbow trout, approx. 250g each

Oil

Salt and pepper to taste

Lemon juice or wine

Wash and dry the fish and place them on oiled foil. Brush the fish with oil. Season them inside and out with salt, pepper and lemon juice or wine. Cook them on the barbecue with the lid on for 15-30 minutes, or until the flesh flakes when tested with a fork. To retain extra moisture, wrap the fish completely in foil and cook them as above. Trout are even more delicious if you cook them stuffed, here are a few of our favourite fillings.

Fresh herbs, breadcrumbs, salt, pepper and lemon juice.

Chopped almonds, walnuts, macadamias or brazil nuts, salt, pepper and lemon juice.

Chopped fruit medley, lemon juice, salt and pepper.

Chopped cooked prawns, crab or other shellfish, cream, ground almonds or breadcrumbs, salt and pepper.

Tabouli: using chopped fresh parsley and mint, tomatoes, cracked Lebanese wheat, lemon juice, salt and pepper.

Fish and Chips

FISH AND CHIPS

Direct fire, lid off, wok on. Serves 4-6.

1½ litres oil for deep frying

6 fish fillets

Flour

1kg potatoes, peeled and cut into chips

Batter

½ cup self raising flour

½ cup water

Salt to taste

Prepare the chips and place them in cold water until required. Before frying the chips, pat them dry in paper towels or a cloth. Make the batter by combining the self raising flour, water and salt. Allow the batter to stand for 15 minutes.

Heat the wok and add the oil. Heat the oil until it bubbles when tested with the handle of a wooden spoon. Place the dry chips in the hot oil and cook until they are a pale gold colour. Coat the fish fillets with flour, then dip them in the batter. Place the fish in the hot oil with the chips. Turn the fish over when golden on one side and cook on the other side. When golden and crisp, remove and drain them on a paperlined tray. Serve them with tartare sauce and salad.

OCEAN TROUT OR ATLANTIC SALMON

Low fire, indirect, 30-40 minutes, with lid on.

2kg ocean trout or Atlantic salmon

Butter

Salt and pepper to taste

Fresh dill

1 small onion, sliced

White wine

Wash and dry the fish and place it on buttered foil. Pour melted butter over the fish. Season it with salt and pepper and sprinkle it with chopped dill. Add a few slices of onion and a little white wine. Seal the foil and cook the fish on the barbecue, with the lid on, for 30-40 minutes, or until the flesh flakes when tested. Serve the fish with Easy Mock Hollandaise sauce (recipe page 206) and new potatoes.

Ocean Trout or Atlantic Salmon

106

Rainbow Trout with Almonds and Grapes

Fish Cutlets

RAINBOW TROUT WITH ALMONDS AND GRAPES

Low fire, indirect, 20-30 minutes, with lid on. Serves 3-4.

3-4 rainbow trout, cleaned and back

bones removed (refer to page 103)

Salt and pepper to taste

Lemon and parsley to garnish

SAUCE

¼ cup slivered almonds

60g butter

2 tablespoons lemon juice

1 tablespoon chopped fresh herbs

¼ cup dry sherry

Salt and pepper to taste

1 cup sultana grapes

Prepare the fish, pat them dry and season them with salt and pepper.

Cook them on the barbecue with the lid on for 20-30 minutes.

Make the sauce by melting the butter in a pan, adding the almonds and cooking them until they are golden brown. Add the lemon juice, herbs, sherry, salt and pepper. Then add the grapes and heat them through. Spoon the sauce over the fish and serve them with peppered potatoes and snow peas.

WHOLE FLOUNDER OR SOLE

Low fire, indirect, 15-20 minutes, with lid on. Serves 1-2.

1 or 2 whole flounder or sole

Salt and pepper to taste

Lemon juice

Wash and dry the fish and brush it with oil. Season it with salt and pepper. Cook the fish on the barbecue with the lid on, for 15-20 minutes, or until the flesh flakes when tested.

FISH CUTLETS

Low fire, indirect, 15-20 minutes, with lid on.

4-6 blue-eye, snapper, or ocean trout

cutlets

60g butter

2 cloves garlic, pressed

3 tablespoons lemon juice

Salt and pepper to taste

2 teaspoons chopped, fresh basil

Paprika

Place the cutlets on buttered foil. Brush them with butter, then add the garlic, lemon juice, salt, pepper, basil and paprika. Seal the foil packages and place them on the barbecue. Cook the cutlets with the lid on, for 15-20 minutes, or until the flesh flakes when tested. Serve them with fresh bread, lemon wedges and salad.

Sweet and Sour Whole Fish

SWEET AND SOUR WHOLE FISH

Direct fire, lid off, wok on. Serves 2.

1-2 litres oil for deep frying

2 whole fish, about 500g each

2 tablespoons dry sherry

1/4 cup soy sauce

1 cup cornflour

SAUCE

1 tablespoon soy sauce

1/3 cup sugar

1/3 cup vinegar

2 tablespoons tomato sauce

1 green pepper, cut into fine shreds

1 red pepper, cut into fine shreds

1 cup bamboo shoots, cut into fine shreds

1 carrot, cut into fine shreds

1 tablespoon cornflour

1 cup water

Scale and clean the fish, leaving the head and tail intact. Wash and clean the fish, both inside and out. Pat the fish dry with paper towels. Make 2-3 diagonal cuts in the flesh on each side of the fish until the knife touches the bone. This allows the interior of the fish to cook.

Sprinkle the fish with sherry and soy sauce. Rub the cornflour all over the surface of the fish, inside and out. Heat the wok and add the oil. Heat the oil until it bubbles when tested with the handle of a wooden spoon. Cook the fish by turning it over until it is cooked through. The fish should be crisp and have a golden colour. Remove the fish and keep it warm. Make the sauce by placing the soy sauce, sugar, vinegar and tomato sauce in a saucepan. Stir until it is boiling, then add the prepared vegetables and cook for 1 minute. Thicken the sauce with cornflour and water. Pour the sauce over the fish and serve them hot.

Smoked Fish Fillets and Trout

BARRAMUNDI FILLETS

Low fire, indirect, 15-20 minutes, with lid on. Serves 3-4.

750g barramundi fillets

2 tablespoons melted butter

Juice of 1 lemon

Salt and pepper to taste

2 teaspoons finely chopped parsley

Pat the fillets dry with paper towels. Place them on foil and shape the foil to hold any juices. Brush the fish fillets with butter and squeeze lemon juice over them. Season them with salt and pepper. Cook the fish fillets on the barbecue, with the lid on, for 15-20 minutes, or until the flesh flakes when tested with a fork. Barramundi fillets are delicious cooked on the barbecue. Here are just a few more ways you can enjoy them.

SMOKED BARRA

Brush the fillets with melted butter and sprinkle them with paprika. Smoke-cook them with hickory chunks or your favourite smoking wood from the beginning of the cooking time.

BARRA WITH MELON

Use 2 fillets of barramundi, sandwich them together with slices of rockmelon and chopped coriander. Season them with salt and pepper then wrap them in foil. Cook them on the barbecue, with the lid on, for 30-40 minutes.

BARRA PACKAGE

Place 6 sheets of buttered filo pastry on top of each other. Place a fillet of barramundi in the centre of the pastry. Add chopped spring onions, chopped red pepper, sliced prawns, sliced hard boiled egg and season with salt and pepper. Sprinkle it with pernod, then wrap the filo pastry around it. Place it on a piece of oiled foil. Cook the package on the barbecue, with the lid on, for 30 minutes, or until the pastry is golden and crisp.

Whiting and Smoked Salmon Kebabs

WHITING AND SMOKED SALMON KEBABS

Low fire, indirect, 10-15 minutes, with lid on. Serves 3-4.

500g small whiting fillets

250g smoked salmon, sliced

1 tablespoon oil

1 tablespoon lemon juice

Salt and pepper to taste

Carefully remove the skin and bones from the whiting. Lay the whiting fillets out flat, then place a slice of smoked salmon on each fillet. Sprinkle them with the lemon juice, salt and pepper. Roll the layers up, Swiss-roll fashion, and thread them on to bamboo skewers. Brush the kebabs with oil. Cook them on the barbecue, with the lid on, for 10-15 minutes.

WHOLE TOMMY RUFF, SEA HERRING OR OTHER SMALL SALT WATER FISH

Low fire, indirect, 15-20 minutes, with lid on. Serves 4-8.

4-8 whole tommy ruffs or sea herrings

Oil

Salt and pepper to taste

Lemon juice

Wash, scale and clean the fish. Brush them with oil. Season them with salt, pepper and lemon juice. Cook them on the barbecue, with the lid on, for 15-20 minutes, or until the flesh flakes when tested with a fork. These small fish are delicious cooked on the barbecue. Here are a few of our favourite variations.

SMOKED TOMMYS

Place 2 hickory chunks on the coals on each side of the barbecue. Smoke-cook the fish on the barbecue, with the lid on, for 15-20 minutes, or until the flesh flakes when tested with a fork.

TOMMY CAPRICE

Remove the backbone from the fish from the inside, leaving the fish in one piece (refer photographs page 103). Place half a peeled banana, cut lengthways in the fish. Brush it with butter and season it with salt and pepper. Sprinkle the fish with chopped fresh herbs or parsley.

Cook it on the barbecue, with the lid on, for 15-20 minutes, or until the flesh flakes when tested with a fork.

HERBED TOMMYS

Bone the fish and fill their cavities with a mixture of fresh breadcrumbs, chopped fresh herbs, orange or lemon rind and juice. Add salt and pepper to taste. Cook them on the barbecue with the lid on, for 15-20 minutes, or until the flesh flakes when tested with a fork.

WHOLE BUTTERFISH, JEWFISH OR MULLOWAY

Low fire, indirect, 30 minutes, with lid on. Serves 6.

1.5kg butterfish (or other whole fish 45cm long)

Oil

Salt and pepper to taste

1 tablespoon pernod, or sherry

1/4 cup chopped bacon

Slices of orange or lemon

Fresh thyme sprigs

Take a large piece of foil and oil it well. Place the fish on the foil and turn up the edges of the foil to hold any liquid. Season it with salt and pepper. Add the pernod or sherry, bacon, orange, lemon and thyme. Cook the fish on the barbecue, with the lid on, for 30 minutes, or until the flesh flakes when tested with a fork. Baste the fish during cooking once or twice using its own juices. Serve the fish with salad or hot vegetables in season and crusty French bread.

The cavity of the fish may be filled with a mixture of onions, herbs and breadcrumbs, moistened well with wine or lemon juice.

Another favourite of ours is to insert 6 peeled cloves of garlic and 6 sprigs of mint into the cavity of the fish. Use some olive oil and lemon juice to baste the fish. Sit back and enjoy the aroma as it cooks.

A hint of smoke may be added during the last 15 minutes of cooking time by placing 2-3 chunks of hickory on the coals on each side of the barbecue.

Melbourne Cup Crayfish

MELBOURNE CUP CRAYFISH

Low fire, indirect, 15-25 minutes, with lid on. Serves 2-4.

2 whole crayfish, uncooked

Brush the crayfish all over with oil. Place the whole crayfish on the barbecue. Cook them with the lid on for 15-25 minutes, depending on their size.

Check them at regular periods to see if they are cooked (they will turn bright orange-red). Serve the crayfish hot with melted garlic butter and champagne.

GARLIC BUTTER FOR CRAYFISH
250g butter

2 tablespoons white vinegar

2 tablespoons chopped parsley

Few drops Tabasco

2 tablespoons chopped garlic

Blend all the ingredients together and serve melted with the crayfish.

111

MUSHROOM AND LOBSTER KEBABS

Normal fire, indirect, 8-10 minutes, with lid on. Serves 4.

1 lobster, uncooked

4 rashers bacon

8 button mushrooms

1/2 cup French dressing

Cut the lobster meat into 2.5cm cubes. Wrap the bacon around the lobster meat and thread them on to skewers alternating with the mushrooms. Marinate the kebabs in French dressing and cook them on the barbecue, for 8-10 minutes with the lid on.

CRAYFISH KEBABS

Low fire, indirect, 8-10 minutes, with lid on. Serves 3-4.

1 crayfish tail, uncooked

Cucumber

100g fresh button mushrooms

Cherry tomatoes

MARINADE

1 tablespoon capers, chopped

2 tablespoons fresh dill, chopped

1/4 cup olive oil

1/4 cup white wine

1 tablespoon lemon juice

Freshly ground black pepper to taste

Cut the crayfish meat into 2.5cm cubes. Peel the cucumber and cut it into cubes. Make the marinade by mixing all the marinade ingredients together. Marinate the crayfish meat, mushrooms and cucumber for 1-2 hours. Thread the cubes of crayfish on bamboo skewers alternately with the mushrooms, cucumber and tomatoes. Cook the kebabs on the barbecue, with the lid on, for 8-10 minutes. Serve them with herbed rice or salad.

DRUNKEN CRAYFISH WITH ORANGE

Low fire, indirect, 20-30 minutes, with lid on.

1/2 small crayfish tail per person, uncooked

Salt and pepper to taste

1 cup of white wine

1 tablespoon butter

Juice of 1/2 orange

1 tablespoon whisky, brandy or rum

1 tablespoon cream

Cook the crayfish tails on the barbecue in a Glad oven bag with the white wine, salt and pepper for 20-30 minutes. Remove the meat from the shells, reserving the shells. Place the crayfish meat in a pan with the butter and fresh orange juice. When heated through, add the spirit and flambé. When the flame dies down, season the tails with salt and pepper and stir in the cream. Place the crayfish tails back in their shells and serve them garnished with a twist of orange peel.

GARLIC PRAWN, YABBY, MORETON BAY BUG OR SCAMPI KEBABS

Low fire, indirect, 5-10 minutes, with lid on.

1-2kg shellfish

1 cup olive oil

4 cloves garlic, crushed

Freshly ground black pepper

Salt to taste

Juice of 1 lemon

1 tablespoon chopped, fresh coriander

Shell the yabbies, prawns, Moreton Bay bugs or scampi and place the meat with all the other ingredients in a bowl. Allow the meat to marinate, covered in a cool place for several hours. Thread the meat on bamboo skewers. Cook them on the barbecue, with the lid on, for 5-10 minutes. Serve the kebabs with slices of crusty French bread or Dinkum Damper. (Recipe page 199).

GARLIC LOBSTER RAMEKINS

Normal fire, indirect, 8-10 minutes, with lid on. Serves 4.

1 lobster, uncooked

1/2 cup olive oil

4 cloves garlic, pressed

1 teaspoon chopped fresh ginger

1 small red chilli, seeded and finely chopped

Salt and pepper to taste

Carefully remove the flesh from the lobster tail and cut it into 2.5 cm cubes. Place the cubes and other ingredients into 4 ramekins. Cook the lobster on the barbecue, with the lid on, for 8-10 minutes. Serve the steaming hot lobster in the ramekins as an entree.

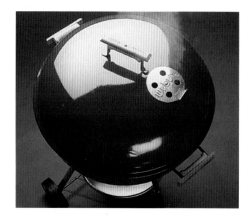

GINGER CHILLI PRAWNS

Direct fire, lid off, wok on. Serves 4.

2 tablespoons oil

750g large shelled prawns with the tails left on

2 cloves garlic, pressed

1 teaspoon chopped fresh ginger

1 teaspoon crushed chilli

1 tablespoon chopped fresh coriander

Heat the wok and add the oil. Fry the prawns with the garlic, ginger and chilli, tossing them well until the prawns turn pink and are cooked through. Add the coriander and serve the prawns as an entree.

Yabbies

BUGS OR YABBIES IN BLACK BEAN SAUCE

Direct fire, lid off, wok on. Serves 6.

2 cloves garlic

2 tablespoons black beans

4 spring onions

3 tablespoons oil

1kg bug or yabby tails, raw

2 tablespoons soy sauce

Salt to taste

Crush the garlic and black beans and blend them into a thick paste. Cut the spring onions into 3cm lengths. Heat the wok and add the oil. Stir-fry the thick paste for about 30 seconds. Add the tails and stir-fry them until they are pink. Add the soy sauce, salt and spring onions just before serving. Serve them with rice and salad.

CRABS, YABBIES, MORETON BAY BUGS AND CRAYFISH

Direct fire, lid off, wok on, 10-20 minutes. Serves 6-8.

3kg green shellfish

2-3 sprigs of parsley

1 onion, sliced

1 stick celery, sliced

4 litres sea water (or salted water)

The larger mud crabs of Queensland, the smaller blue swimmer crabs, the giant Tasmanian crabs, yabbies, Moreton Bay bugs and crayfish may be cooked on the barbecue with the help of the large wok. Drown the shellfish in fresh water and then bring the sea water (or salted water) to the boil in the wok. Add the parsley, onion, celery and simmer them for 5-10 minutes. Place the shellfish in the water and bring it to the boil. Cook them for 5-10 minutes, depending on the size of the shellfish. When cooked, the shellfish will turn red. Crack them open and serve them with herbed butter.

HERBED BUTTER

125g butter

½ cup white wine

3 tablespoons chopped parsley

1 teaspoon chopped, fresh thyme

¼ cup chopped spring onions

Melt the butter and combine all the ingredients. Serve this butter with the cooked shellfish as a dip. Have plenty of paper napkins and a large finger bowl at hand.

CHILLI CRABS

Direct fire, lid off, wok on. Serves 4-6.

1kg raw crabs

1 tablespoon lemon juice

3 teaspoons chilli sauce

1 tablespoon soy sauce

1 teaspoon sugar

$1/2$ teaspoon salt

$1/2$ cup oil

$1/4$ cup water

PASTE

1 red pepper

2 spring onions, chopped

2 cloves garlic, pressed

$1/4$ teaspoon cayenne pepper

4 thin slices fresh ginger, chopped

1 green chilli, sliced

Wash the crabs well and remove the hard top-shell, stomach bag and fibrous tissue. Cut the crabs into serving portions. To make the paste, puree the red pepper, spring onion, garlic and cayenne pepper. Add the chopped ginger and sliced chilli to the paste. In another bowl, combine the lemon juice, chilli sauce, soy sauce, sugar and salt. Heat the wok and add the oil. Fry the red pepper paste for 1-2 minutes. Add the lemon juice mixture and the crabs and mix well. Stir in the water and simmer, with the barbecue lid on the wok, for 5-10 minutes. Yabbies, bugs or prawns may be used instead of crabs.

MUSSELS WITH PERNOD

Direct fire, lid off, wok on, 5-6 minutes.

500g mussels per person

2-3 cups of water (or white wine)

$1/2$ cup cream

2 tablespoons Pernod

2 tablespoons chopped parsley

Wash the mussels well and thoroughly scrub them to remove any mud, seaweed and sand.

Soak them in water for 1-2 hours. Pull away the beard that clings around the edge of the shell and discard any mussel which is not tightly closed. Heat the wok and add 2-3 cups of water or white wine and bring to the boil. Place the mussels in the wok, stirring them occasionally. Cook them for 5-6 minutes, or until the shells open. Discard any unopen shells. Add the cream, Pernod and parsley to the wok, stirring well. Serve the mussels piping hot in individual bowls, with chunks of crusty French bread to soak up the juices.

SQUID SNAKES

Normal fire, indirect, 3-4 minutes, with lid on.

500g squid tubes, cut into long strips

MARINADE

$1/4$ cup olive oil

2 cloves garlic, pressed

1 tablespoon lemon juice

Salt and pepper to taste

A dash of chilli

Thread strips of squid, like a snake on to the skewer. Marinate them in a mixture of the oil, garlic, lemon juice, salt, pepper and a dash of chilli. Cook them on the barbecue with the lid on, for 3-4 minutes, or until the squid turns white. Squid is one of our seafood favourites. Here are a couple of other interesting ways to serve it to your family and friends.

SQUID KEBABS

Cut the squid into squares and alternate them on a bamboo skewer with squares of red pepper and onion petals. Brush them with the above marinade and cook them on the barbecue, with the lid on, for 3-4 minutes.

STUFFED SQUID

Wash the squid and fill the pockets with pressed garlic, chopped parsley, crumbled white bread, oil, wine, salt and pepper. Secure the pockets with toothpicks. Marinate the squid in oil and white wine before cooking. Cook it on the barbecue, with the lid on, for 16-15 minutes, or until the squid turns white. Serve it with salad or vegetables in season.

Tempura

TEMPURA

Direct fire, lid off, wok on. Serves 6.

1-2 litres oil, for deep-frying

6 prawns, shelled

6 squid rings

1 onion, sliced

1 green pepper, cut into squares

6 snow peas, with strings removed

6 button mushrooms

1 small egg plant, sliced

1 bunch asparagus

BATTER

1 egg yolk

$3/4$ cup cold water

$1/2$ teaspoon bi-carbonate of soda

$3/4$ cup plain flour

Combine all the batter ingredients and beat them until they are smooth. Set the batter aside for 30 minutes. Heat the wok and add the oil. Heat the oil until bubbles appear when tested with the handle of a wooden spoon. Dip the vegetables and seafood in the batter. Deep-fry them until they are golden and crisp. Drain them and serve them with a dipping sauce, such as chilli sauce or soy sauce.

Game

Traditionally game has been eaten in many parts of the world. For centuries Kings have eaten venison, quail, pheasant and wild duck. Recently Australian game has become increasingly popular. Kangaroo and buffalo meat have proved to be tender and tasty.

Cooking spectacular wild duck, pheasant or quail is as easy as cooking a chicken. Buffalo, goat or rabbit is no harder to cook than your favourite roast.

These meats tend to be fairly rich and there is nothing like a barbecue kettle to enhance their distinctive flavours.

So whether you get your game with a shotgun, or at a butcher, cook it in the great outdoors on your barbecue kettle.

Contents

Roast Pheasant

ROAST PHEASANT

Normal fire, indirect, 50-60 minutes, with lid on. Serves 3-4.

1 pheasant

1 apple, peeled, cored and sliced

4 rashers bacon

2 cups muscat grapes, seeds removed

2 slices bread

¹/₂ cup oil

MARINADE

¹/₂ cup oil

1 cup red wine

1 teaspoon mixed herbs

Salt and cracked pepper to taste

Small onion, cut into rings

Ask your butcher to prepare the pheasant by removing the head, neck, feet and entrails.

Prepare the marinade by combining all the ingredients and mixing them well. Allow the pheasant to marinate, covered, for 4 hours or overnight in the refrigerator. Remove the bird from the marinade and reserve the remaining marinade to make the sauce. Place the apple slices and 2 diced bacon rashers inside the cavity of the pheasant. Tie the legs together with string. Lay the remaining bacon rashers over the breast of the pheasant to protect the delicate meat. Cook it on the barbecue, with the lid on, for 50-60 minutes. Remove the bacon and discard it. To make the sauce, boil the left-over marinade for 5 minutes, adding the grapes at the last moment. Serve the pheasant with the sauce and croutons. Make the croutons by frying triangles of the sliced bread in the oil until they are golden and crisp.

ROAST PIGEON

Normal fire, indirect, 30-35 minutes, with lid on. Serves 4.

4 pigeons

1 tablespoon oil

Salt and pepper to taste

STUFFING

60g butter

1 rasher bacon

1 onion, chopped

¹/₄ cup pine nuts

1 cup breadcrumbs

2 teaspoons mixed herbs

Salt and pepper to taste

Wash the pigeons and pat them dry. To make the stuffing, melt the butter in a pan and sauté the bacon, onion and pine nuts. Combine this with the breadcrumbs, herbs, salt and pepper. Fill the pigeons with this mixture. Brush them with oil and season them with salt and pepper. Cook them on the barbecue with the lid on, for 30-35 minutes, or until they are golden brown. The pigeons may also be glazed and smoked.

119

Smoked Wild Duck

BARBECUED QUAIL

Normal fire, indirect, 25-30 minutes, with lid on. Serves 4.

6-8 quail

Salt and pepper to taste

1 lemon for garnish

MARINADE

$^1\!/_2$ cup olive oil

Juice of 1 lemon

1 tablespoon seeded, chopped red pepper

Salt and pepper to taste

Combine the marinade ingredients and mix them well. Wash and dry the quail. Place them in the marinade for at least 30 minutes, turning them occasionally. Remove the quail from the marinade and pat them dry. Cook them on the barbecue with the lid on, for 25-30 minutes, or until they are done. Serve them hot, garnished with lemon slices and accompanied with hot boiled rice and salad. The quail may be glazed in the last 15-20 minutes of cooking time with a marmalade or redcurrant glaze.

A hint of hickory smoke may be used to provide added flavour.

QUAIL WITH BLUEBERRIES

Normal fire, indirect, 25-30 minutes, lid on. Serves 4.

2 tablespoons butter

$^1\!/_3$ cup chopped spring onions

2 slices white bread, crumbled

$^1\!/_2$ teaspoon chicken seasoning

1 cup blueberries

8 quail

2 tablespoons butter, melted

Salt and pepper to taste

SAUCE

$^1\!/_2$ cup redcurrant jelly

$^1\!/_4$ cup port wine

1 tablespoon lemon juice

In a small saucepan melt the butter and add the onions. Cook them for 2 minutes. Add the bread, chicken seasonings and $^1\!/_2$ the blueberries.

Stuff each quail with this mixture and brush them with the butter. Season them with salt and pepper. Cook them on the barbecue with the lid on, for 25-30 minutes. To make the sauce, boil the jelly, port and lemon juice, then add the remaining blueberries. Serve the quail on a bed of noodles and coat them with the sauce.

SMOKED WILD DUCK

Normal fire, indirect, 50-60 minutes, with lid on. Serves 2-3.

1 kg dressed wild duck

2 tablespoons olive oil

Salt and pepper to taste

Wash the duck and soak it in salted water for 1 hour. Rinse the duck with fresh water and pat it dry. Rub it with olive oil and season it with salt and pepper. Add 1 hickory chunk to the coals on each side of the barbecue. Smoke-cook the duck on the barbecue for 50-60 minutes, with the lid on. Serve it with wholemeal bread and salad.

Buffalo Steak Mignons

BUFFALO KEBABS

Normal fire, indirect, 10-15 minutes, with lid on. Serves 4-6.

500g buffalo meat, cut into 2cm cubes

12 button mushrooms

12 squares bacon

2 tablespoons melted butter

MARINADE

¹/₂ cup beer

2 tablespoons oil

1 clove garlic, pressed

1 tablespoon lemon juice

1 teaspoon brown sugar

1 teaspoon prepared mustard

Pepper to taste

Place all the marinade ingredients in a bowl and mix them well. Add the meat and the mushrooms. Marinate them covered, overnight in the refrigerator.

Thread the meat, mushrooms and bacon pieces onto bamboo skewers. Brush them with the butter. Cook them on the barbecue with the lid on, for 10-15 minutes. Serve with hot boiled rice and salad.

BRAISED BUFFALO

Low fire, indirect, 40-50 minutes, with lid on. Serves 6.

750g buffalo fillet

425g can sweet and sour sauce

1 cup pineapple pieces

1 red pepper, cut into strips

Salt and pepper to taste

Place all the ingredients in a clay pot which has been soaked in water for ¹/₂ hour. Put the lid on the pot and cook on the barbecue with the lid on, for 40-50 minutes, or until the meat is cooked to your liking. Serve the meat sliced, with hot boiled rice and salad.

BUFFALO STEAK MIGNONS

Direct fire, 4-5 minutes per side, with lid on. Serves 4-6.

4-6 bacon rashers

4-6 buffalo steaks

1 tablespoon melted butter

Salt and black pepper to taste

Wrap the bacon rashers around the edge of the steaks and secure them with toothpicks. Brush the steaks with the butter and season them with salt and pepper. Pre-heat a cast iron cooking grill over the fire for 3-5 minutes. Place the steaks on the pre-heated grill. Cook them with the lid on, for 4-5 minutes each side. Serve the steaks with jacket potatoes and salad.

MARINATED BUFFALO FILLET

Normal fire, indirect, 40-50 minutes, with lid on. Serves 6.

4 bacon rashers

1.5kg buffalo fillet

MARINADE

¹/₂ cup oil

¹/₂ cup vinegar

¹/₂ cup red wine

¹/₄ cup port wine

1 teaspoon mixed herbs

1 carrot, sliced

1 onion, sliced

1 tablespoon soy sauce

1 tablespoon Worcestershire sauce

Salt and pepper to taste

Wrap the bacon rashers around the meat and tie them securely with string. Place the meat in a bowl. Add the marinade ingredients mixing them well. Allow the meat to marinate, covered, for at least 4 hours or overnight in the refrigerator. Remove the meat from the marinade and pat it dry. Place it on the barbecue and cook with the lid on, for 40-50 minutes, or until done. Remove the bacon and discard it. Serve the fillet sliced with vegetables in season and steamed wild rice.

Barbecued Leg of Goat

BARBECUED LEG OF GOAT

Normal fire, indirect, 1-1½ hours, with lid on. Serves 6-8.

2-3kg leg of goat

Strips of orange rind, finely shredded

BASTING SAUCE

1 teaspoon mustard powder

2 tablespoons brown sugar

½ cup orange juice

½ cup stock

½ cup vinegar

1 tablespoon honey

2 teaspoons soy sauce

Black pepper to taste

SERVING SAUCE

½ cup water

1 tablespoon arrowroot

To make the basting sauce, combine the mustard, sugar, orange juice, stock, vinegar, honey, soy sauce and pepper, mixing it well. Cook the meat on the barbecue with the lid on for 1½-2 hours, basting it once or twice during the last ½ hour. To make the serving sauce, heat the remaining basting sauce and thicken it with the blended arrowroot. Slice the meat and cover it with the sauce. Simmer the orange strips in water until they are tender and drain them well. Use these strips to garnish the meat. Serve with vegetables in season.

ROAST VENISON

Normal fire, indirect, 40-45 minutes, with lid on. Serves 4-6.

1kg piece venison fillet or rump

6 whole button mushrooms

4 rashers bacon

1 cup Italian dressing

Salt and pepper to taste

Cut a pocket along one side of the meat, but not all the way through it. Place the mushrooms in the pocket with 2 rashers of chopped bacon. Fold the meat over and tie it with string. Place the meat in a bowl and pour over the Italian dressing. Season it with salt and pepper. Allow it to marinate, covered, in the refrigerator for 2-4 hours. Remove the meat and pat it dry. Lay the remaining 2 bacon rashers over and around the meat. Secure them with string. Place the meat on the barbecue and cook it with the lid on, for 40-50 minutes. Remove the bacon and discard it. Serve the venison sliced with vegetables or salad.

VENISON KEBABS

Normal fire, indirect, 20-25 minutes, with lid on. Serves 6.

500g venison rump or fillet

12 squares bacon

12 wedges onion

12 button mushrooms

6 rosemary sprigs

MARINADE

1 onion, finely chopped

2 tablespoons oil

1 teaspoon salt

¼ teaspoon pepper

1 cup tomato puree

2 tablespoons tomato chutney

1 tablespoon Worcestershire sauce

1 tablespoon vinegar

Combine the marinade ingredients and mix them well. Cut the meat into 3cm cubes and place them in the marinade mixture for 1 hour. Thread the meat, bacon, onions and mushrooms on to skewers. Brush each kebab with a liberal amount of the marinade. Cook them on the barbecue with the lid on, for 20-25 minutes. Serve the kebabs with hot boiled rice and salad and decorate them with the rosemary.

Glazed Roast Rabbit

GLAZED ROAST RABBIT

(UNDERGROUND MUTTON)

Normal fire, indirect, 20-30 minutes, with lid on. Serves 2.

1 rabbit

6 dried apricots

6 prunes, pitted

1/2 cup port wine

1 cup redcurrant jelly

Wash the rabbit, remove the liver and lungs and soak it in salted water overnight. Remove the rabbit, wash it in fresh water and pat it dry. Soak the apricots and prunes in the port for 15 minutes. Place the apricots and prunes inside the rabbit. Secure it with poultry pins and string. Brush the rabbit with melted redcurrant jelly to glaze. Cook it on the barbecue with the lid on for 20-30 minutes. Glaze the rabbit an additional 2-3 times while cooking. To make the sauce, boil the port to reduce it and serve it with the rabbit.

SMOKED PICKLED RABBIT

(UNDERGROUND HAM)

Normal fire, indirect, 20-30 minutes, with lid on. Serves 2.

1 rabbit

2 tablespoons oil

Have your butcher pump and pickle the rabbit in brine. Wash the rabbit and pat it dry. Brush the rabbit with oil. Add a hickory chunk to the coals on each side of the barbecue. Smoke-cook the rabbit with the lid on, for 20-30 minutes. This hamcoloured meat is delicious served hot or cold with salad.

VENISON STEAKS

Direct fire, 4-5 minutes per side, with lid on. Serves 4-6.

4-6 venison steaks, cut 2.5cm thick

MARINADE

1 tablespoon soy sauce

1 tablespoon Worcestershire sauce

1 tablespoon brown sugar

1/4 cup port wine

1/4 cup vinegar

Salt and pepper to taste

1 clove garlic, pressed

Combine the marinade ingredients and mix them well. Place the meat in the marinade and allow it to stand, covered, in the refrigerator for 2-4 hours. Pat the steaks dry. Cook them on the barbecue with the lid on, for 4-5 minutes each side. Serve the steaks piping hot with potatoes or rice and salad.

Peppered Saddle of Kangaroo

PEPPERED SADDLE OF KANGAROO

Normal fire, indirect, 1¹/₂-2 hours, with lid on. Serves 6-8.

1 saddle of kangaroo, boned, 2-3kg

¹/₄ cup olive oil

1 cup black pepper mixture

MARINADE

1 onion, finely chopped

¹/₂ teaspoon peppercorns, crushed

1 bay leaf

1 teaspoon horseradish

1 teaspoon mustard

1 tablespoon basil

¹/₂ cup oil

¹/₂ cup red wine

1 tablespoon tomato sauce

Combine all the marinade ingredients in a bowl and mix them well. Allow the meat to marinate for 2-3 hours or overnight, covered, in the refrigerator. Remove the meat and reserve the remaining marinade to make a sauce. Roll the meat and tie it with string. Rub the meat with the oil and roll it in the pepper mixture. Cook it on the barbecue with the lid on, for 1¹/₂-2 hours, or until it is done. Boil the marinade to reduce it. Serve it spooned over the sliced meat. This roast is also delicious served with creamy mushroom sauce (Recipe page 207).

BRAISED ROO MEAT

Low fire, indirect, 50-60 minutes, with lid on. Serves 6.

1kg piece kangaroo meat, rump or fillet

2 cups tomato spaghetti sauce

6 black olives, halved

2 cloves garlic, pressed

Place the meat, sauce, olives and garlic in a casserole dish. Place the lid on the casserole dish and cook on the barbecue with the lid on, for 50-60 minutes. Serve the meat sliced, accompanied by the casserole sauce and vegetables in season.

Low Cost
Barbecue Delights

Money, money, money – thankfully, not all barbecue cooking requires the use of expensive cuts of meat. Delicious foods may be prepared using cheaper cuts of meat, vegetables, herbs and dairy products.

Quiche, pizza, sausage rolls, pies and pasties all fall into this category. You will see the surprised look on their faces when you lift the lid off the barbecue and reveal a magnificent cheese soufflé. Who would have thought you could make a soufflé on the barbecue?

Mincemeat comes to the fore in the form of casseroles and various hamburger mixtures, meatloafs and our speciality, pastry-wrapped Mince Wellington.

Shake off the budget day blues, and serve food that all your friends will think has cost a fortune.

Contents

PASTIES

Normal fire, indirect, 35-45 minutes, with lid on. Serves 4-6.

2, 375g packets puff pastry

Egg wash

FILLING

1 potato, finely chopped

1 onion, finely chopped

1 piece pumpkin, finely chopped

1 tablespoon chopped parsley

250g round steak, finely chopped

1 small turnip, peeled and finely chopped

Salt and pepper to taste

On a floured surface roll out the pastry to a very thin sheet. Cut the pastry into rounds using a bread and butter plate as a template. Prepare the filling ingredients and combine them well. Spoon 1-2 tablespoons of this filling on to the centre of the pastry circles. Brush the edges of the pastry with the egg wash. Shape them into pasty shapes and crimp the edges to seal them well. Place the pasties on a buttered tray and brush them with the egg wash. Cook them on the barbecue, with the lid on, for 35-45 minutes, or until the pastry is golden brown and crisp. Serve them hot with tomato sauce.

SAUSAGE ROLLS

Normal fire, indirect, 25-35 minutes, with lid on. Serves 6-8.

1 packet ready rolled puff pastry sheets

Egg wash

FILLING

3 slices bread

$\frac{1}{2}$ cup hot water

1kg sausage meat

1 onion, finely chopped

$\frac{1}{2}$ teaspoon mixed herbs

Salt and pepper to taste

In a bowl soak the bread in the hot water for 15 minutes. Mash the bread with a

Pasties and Sausage Rolls

fork and combine it with the sausage meat, onion, herbs, salt and pepper. Cut the sheets of pastry in half. Place the filling down the centre of each half. Brush the edges of the pastry with the egg wash. Roll the pastry into tubes and place them on buttered oven trays. Cut the rolls into regular sized portions, but not all the way through. Decorate the top of each portion with knife cuts and brush them with the egg wash. Continue making rolls until all the filling has been used. Cook them on the barbecue, with the lid on, for 25-35 minutes, or until they are golden brown and crisp. Serve them hot with tomato sauce.

SAUSAGES

Normal fire, indirect, 10-20 minutes, with lid on.

Sausages, thick or thin.

GLAZE (Optional)

1 cup brown sugar

1 teaspoon mustard powder

2 tablespoons stock

Place the sausages on the barbecue. It is not necessary to prick or turn them. Put the lid on the barbecue and cook thick sausages for 15-20 minutes. Thin sausages require 10-15 minutes cooking. If you wish to glaze the sausages, combine the brown sugar, mustard powder and stock. Heat this mixture in a saucepan until all of the sugar has dissolved. Brush the sausages with this glaze 2-3 times while they are cooking.

MUSHROOM QUICHE

Normal fire, indirect, 30-40 minutes, with lid on. Serves 4-6.

Shortcrust pastry

Paprika

FILLING

4 eggs, beaten

1 cup grated Cheddar cheese

Salt and pepper to taste

1 cup sliced mushrooms

¼ cup chopped spring onions

1 tablespoon chopped fresh herbs, (thyme or marjoram)

1 cup milk

Roll out the pastry on a floured surface until it is large enough to line a drip tray or lamington pan. Combine all the filling ingredients and spoon them into the pastry case. Sprinkle the paprika on the top. Cook the quiche on the barbecue, with the lid on, for 30-40 minutes, or until the filling has set. Serve it cut into squares with salad.

Mushroom Quiche

ALL-IN-ONE QUICHE

Normal fire, indirect, 30-40 minutes with lid on. Serves 4-6.

1½ cups milk

1 cup pastry mix

90g butter

3 eggs

1 cup diced ham, turkey, chicken or bacon

2 spring onions, chopped

½ cup sliced mushrooms

1 tomato, sliced

1 zucchini, sliced

1 cup grated Cheddar cheese

Combine the milk, pastry mix, butter and eggs in a food processor to mix them well. Pour this mixture into a buttered drip tray. Add the meat and place the onions, mushrooms, tomato, zucchini and cheese on top. Cook the quiche on the barbecue, with the lid on, for 30-40 minutes, or until the top is golden. Serve it hot or cold with salad.

Hamburgers and Heroic Hot Dogs

HAMBURGERS

Normal fire, indirect, 15-20 minutes, with lid on. Serves 6.

1kg minced beef

1 medium onion, finely chopped

1 cup dry breadcrumbs

2 eggs

Salt and pepper to taste

2 tablespoons oil

1 tablespoon finely chopped parsley

In a bowl combine all the ingredients and mix them well. Wet your hands and shape the mixture into 12 flat hamburger patties. Keep them covered in the refrigerator until required. Place the hamburgers on oiled foil and cook them on the barbecue, with the lid on, for 15-20 minutes, turning them once while cooking.

Serve them in hot buttered hamburger buns with your favourite hamburger filling. One of our favourite hamburger fillings is made by combining the following ingredients:

1 avocado, mashed

¹/₂ cup chopped tomato

¹/₄ cup chopped onion

1 tablespoon lemon juice

Salt and Tabasco to taste

ITALIAN HAMBURGERS

Normal fire, indirect, 15-20 minutes, with lid on. Serves 6.

1kg minced beef

1 medium onion, finely chopped

1 cup dry breadcrumbs

2 eggs

Salt and pepper to taste

2 tablespoons oil

1 tablespoon finely chopped parsley

125g grated Mozzarella cheese

¹/₄ cup tomato paste

1 clove garlic, pressed

¹/₄ cup red wine

In a bowl combine all of the ingredients and mix them well. Wet your hands and shape the mixture into 12 flat hamburger patties. Place the hamburgers on oiled foil and cook them on the barbecue, with the lid on, for 15-20 minutes, turning them once during cooking. Serve them in hot buttered hamburger buns, with your favourite filling.

HEROIC HOT DOGS

Low fire, indirect, 5-10 minutes, with lid on.

Frankfurts, Viennas or Saveloys

No water is required, just cook the hot dogs on the barbecue, with the lid on, for 5-10 minutes. You will be surprised at the magnificent flavour. Serve them in toasted hot dog rolls with your favourite sauce or mustard.

MINCE WELLINGTON

Normal fire, indirect, 35-45 minutes, with lid on. Serves 6.

375g packet puff pastry

Egg wash

FILLING

250g minced topside

125g sausage meat

1 bacon rasher, chopped

1 small onion, chopped

2 slices bread, crumbled

1 egg, beaten

1 tablespoon chopped parsley

1 can crushed pineapple, drained

Salt and pepper to taste

In a bowl combine all the filling ingredients and mix them well. Roll out the pastry to form a large rectangle. Place the filling down the centre of the pastry and wrap it like a parcel. Turn the parcel upside-down on a buttered drip tray, or a piece of foil. Decorate the parcel with strips of pastry. Brush it with the egg wash and cook it on the barbecue, with the lid on, for 35-45 minutes, or until the pastry is golden brown and crisp. Serve it sliced with salad.

DEVILLED BARBECUE MACARONI CHEESE

Low fire, indirect, 20-30 minutes, with lid on. Serves 6.

250g macaroni, cooked and drained

1 can cream of mushroom soup

¼ cup milk

125g grated Cheddar cheese

¼ cup chopped red pepper

2 teaspoons French mustard

Salt and pepper to taste

4 hard boiled eggs, sliced

¼ cup dry breadcrumbs

2 tablespoons melted butter

Mince Wellington

Combine the macaroni, soup, milk, cheese, red pepper, mustard, salt and pepper. Spoon half this mixture into a buttered drip tray. Add a layer of sliced eggs on top and spread the remaining mixture over the eggs. Mix the breadcrumbs with the butter and spread them over the top. Cook it on the barbecue, with the lid on for 20-30 minutes. Serve it hot with salad.

JINDABYNE BAKE

Normal fire, indirect, 35-45 minutes, with lid on. Serves 6-8.

1 cup brown rice, cooked

1 onion, sliced

1-2 cloves garlic, pressed

1 eggplant, sliced

2 tomatoes, sliced

6-8 mushrooms, sliced

½ teaspoon oregano

½ teaspoon basil

500g minced topside

250g cheese, grated

TOPPING

125g cream cheese

1 cup yoghurt

1 tablespoon chopped parsley

Place the rice in the base of a buttered drip tray. Top it with the onion, garlic, egg plant, tomato, mushrooms, oregano, basil, meat and cheese. Combine the cream cheese, yoghurt and parsley. Spread this mixture over the surface. Cook it on the barbecue, with the lid on, for 35-45 minutes, or until it is tender and golden brown. Serve it hot with salad.

135

Pizza

PIZZA

Normal fire, indirect, 20-30 minutes, with lid on. Serves 4-6.

BASE

1 tablespoon dry yeast

$^1/_2$ - $^3/_4$ cup warm water

1 tablespoon oil

2 cups plain flour

Salt to taste

TOPPING

$^1/_2$ cup tomato puree

$^1/_2$ teaspoon dry basil

$^1/_4$ teaspoon dry marjoram

Salt and pepper to taste

Sliced salami

Sliced mushrooms or peppers

Black olives or stuffed green olives

250g Mozzarella cheese

Dissolve the yeast in the water and mix it with the oil. To make the dough combine this mixture with the flour and salt in a food processor. Cover the dough and leave it in a warm place for 45 minutes. Knead the dough on a floured surface until it is smooth. Roll it out to fit an oven tray. Spread the dough with $^2/_3$ of the tomato puree, mixed with the basil, marjoram, salt and pepper. Top this with the salami, mushrooms or peppers, olives and cheese. Pour the remaining tomato puree on the top. Cook the pizza on the barbecue, with the lid on, for 20-30 minutes, or until the crust is cooked and the cheese is hot and bubbling.

SAUCY MEATLOAF

Low fire, indirect, 1-1$^1/_4$ hours, with lid on. Serves 6.

750g minced topside

$^1/_4$ cup fruit chutney

1 onion, grated

1 cup fresh breadcrumbs

1 green pepper, finely chopped

Salt and pepper to taste

SAUCE

2 tablespoons tomato sauce

1 tablespoon brown sugar

2 tablespoons vinegar

Mix the meatloaf ingredients together in a large bowl. Pack this mixture in a buttered loaf pan and cover it with foil. Cook it on the barbecue, with the lid on, for 50-60 minutes. Drain the liquid from the meatloaf into a saucepan and combine it with the sauce ingredients. Heat the sauce until it boils and pour it over the top of the meatloaf. Return the meatloaf to the barbecue and cook it for a further 10-15 minutes. Serve it hot or cold with vegetables or salad.

SAUERKRAUT AND SAUSAGE PIE

Normal fire, indirect, 25-30 minutes, with lid on. Serves 6.

1 tablespoon butter

1 onion, chopped

1 teaspoon dried thyme

300g cooked sausage, any variety, cut into 1cm cubes

2 cups sauerkraut, washed and squeezed dry

1/2 cup beer

1/2 cup brown sugar

Salt and pepper to taste

125g Swiss cheese, grated

375g packet puff pastry, cut in half

300g Swiss cheese, sliced

Egg wash

Melt the butter in a saucepan and add the onion and thyme. Cook this until the onion browns, stirring well. Add the sausage to the pan and set it aside to cool. In another pan, cook the sauerkraut, beer, brown sugar, salt and pepper until most of the moisture has evaporated. Stir in the grated cheese. Roll out 1/2 the pastry and use it to line a large drip tray or lamington pan. Spread the cold onion mixture on the base of the pie. Lay 1/2 the sliced Swiss cheese on top of the onion mixture. Now add all of the sauerkraut in a layer on top of the cheese. Top this with the remaining slices of cheese. Roll the remaining pastry and use it to cover the pie. Brush the pastry with the egg wash. Cook the pie on the barbecue, with the lid on, for 25-30 minutes, or until the pastry is golden brown and crisp. Serve the pie cut into squares with salad.

HAWAIIAN MEATLOAF

Low fire, indirect, 50-60 minutes, with lid on. Serves 6.

1 red pepper, seeded and cut into circles

425g can crushed pineapple, drained

1 tablespoon cornflour

1 small green pepper, finely chopped

750g minced pork or veal

1 1/2 cups soft, white breadcrumbs

1 large onion, chopped

1 egg

1 tablespoon vinegar

1 tablespoon soy sauce

2 teaspoons brown sugar

3/4 teaspoon ground ginger

Salt and pepper to taste

Butter a loaf pan and arrange some of the circles of red pepper over the base. Combine the pineapple and cornflour and spoon it over the pepper. Chop the remaining red pepper circles. In a bowl combine the chopped red and green peppers, meat, breadcrumbs, onion, egg, vinegar, soy sauce, brown sugar, ginger, salt and pepper. Mix this well. Firmly pack this meat mixture over the pineapple layer.

Cover it with foil and cook it on the barbecue, with the lid on, for 50-60 minutes. Drain off any excess liquid. Serve the meatloaf hot or cold with vegetables or salad.

LAMB BIRIANI

Low direct fire, lid off, wok on. Serves 10.

3 tablespoons oil

1kg boneless lamb shoulder, thinly sliced

1 large onion, chopped

2 cloves garlic, pressed

1 teaspoon grated fresh ginger

4 cloves

5cm piece cinnamon stick

5 cardamom pods

1 tablespoon curry powder

3 1/2 cups chicken stock

Salt to taste

2 cups raw long grain rice

2 tablespoons lemon juice

Heat the wok and add the oil. Add the lamb to the wok and brown it on all sides. After browning, push the lamb to one side. Add the onion, garlic, ginger, cloves, cinnamon, cardamom and curry powder to the wok. Then add 1 cup of the stock and salt to taste. Mix all the ingredients well. Cover the wok with the barbecue lid and simmer for 15-20 minutes. Add the remaining stock, bring it to the boil and stir in the rice and lemon juice. Cover the wok again and simmer for a further 15-20 minutes. This is great for larger groups.

CHEESE SOUFFLÉ

Low fire, indirect, 40-50 minutes, with lid on. Serves 4-6.

125g butter

1/3 cup plain flour

Salt to taste

1 teaspoon mustard powder

2 cups milk

1 tablespoon Worcestershire sauce

1/4 teaspoon cayenne pepper

6 eggs, separated

185g grated Cheddar cheese

Dash of paprika

Melt the butter in a saucepan and stir in the flour, salt, mustard and milk. Bring this to the boil, stirring the mixture until it is thick and smooth. Add the Worcestershire sauce, cayenne pepper, egg yolks, grated cheese and the stiffly beaten egg whites. Pile this mixture into a buttered 15 cm soufflé dish. Sprinkle the paprika on the top. Cook the soufflé on the barbecue, with the lid on, for 40-50 minutes, or until it has risen, turned golden brown and nearly set all the way through. Serve it immediately.

Chicken Pie

CHICKEN PIE

Normal fire, indirect, 25-35 minutes, with lid on. Serves 4.

4 boneless chicken breasts, cooked and chopped into 1cm cubes

1 onion, finely chopped

1 cup chopped, cooked carrot

¹/₂ cup frozen peas

1 cup sliced, fresh mushrooms

2 tablespoons flour

Dash Worcestershire sauce

¹/₂ cup chicken stock

2 tablespoons cream

Salt and pepper to taste

1 tablespoon chopped, fresh coriander

2 small chillies, seeds removed and chopped

375g packet puff pastry

Egg wash

In a bowl combine the chicken, onion, carrots, peas and mushrooms. Place the flour, Worcestershire sauce, chicken stock and cream in a small saucepan. Whisk this mixture until it is smooth. Bring it to the boil, then add the salt, pepper, coriander and chillies. Add this mixture to the chicken and vegetables, mixing them well. Pile this filling in a pie dish. Brush the edge of the dish with water. Top the pie dish with a sheet of rolled puff pastry. Trim the edges of the pastry and brush it with the egg wash. Decorate the pie as desired. Cook it on the barbecue, with the lid on, for 30 minutes, or until the pastry is golden brown and crisp. Serve with salad.

FRANKFURT AND POTATO BAKE

Low fire, indirect, 40-50 minutes, with lid on. Serves 4-6.

500g Frankfurts

2 potatoes, peeled and chopped

1 cup tomato puree

1 small green pepper, seeded and chopped

125g button mushrooms, sliced

Salt and pepper to taste

Cut the Frankfurts into 5 cm pieces. Boil the potatoes for 2 minutes. Drain the potatoes and place them in a drip tray. Add the Frankfurts, tomato puree, green pepper, mushrooms, salt and pepper. Mix them all together. Cover the drip tray with foil to make a lid. Cook it on the barbecue, with the lid on, for 40-50 minutes. Serve it hot with salad or vegetables.

STUFFED WINDSOR, DEVON OR FRITZ

Normal fire, indirect, 8-12 minutes, with lid on.

1 piece Windsor, Devon or Fritz

Slices Swiss cheese

Fruit chutney

Marmalade

Cut gashes in the sausage across the width, but not all the way through. Spread the slices of cheese with the chutney and place them in the gashes. Brush the sausage all over with the marmalade to glaze it. Cook it on the barbecue, with the lid on, for 8-12 minutes.

STUFFED FRANKFURTS

Low fire, indirect, 10-12 minutes, with lid on. Serves 5-6.

10 Frankfurts

Mustard to taste

¹/₂ cup Cheddar cheese, grated

10 rashers bacon

Slit the Frankfurts down the side to make a pocket. Open the pocket and brush the inside with mustard. Fill the pocket with cheese. Wrap a bacon rasher around each Frankfurt, spiral fashion and secure it with toothpicks. Cook them on the barbecue, with the lid on, for 10-12 minutes, or until the bacon is crisp and the cheese has melted. The Frankfurts may also be stuffed with chutney, dill pickle, fruit or baked beans.

STEAK AND KIDNEY PIE

Normal fire, indirect, 30-40 minutes, with lid on. Serves 4-6.

1kg chuck steak

250g lamb or beef kidney

3 tablespoons seasoned flour

3 tablespoons oil

1 onion, finely chopped

2 teaspoons Worcestershire sauce

1½ cups beef stock

2 tablespoons finely chopped parsley

Salt and pepper to taste

375g packet puff pastry

Egg wash

Trim and cut the meat into 1 cm cubes. Skin the kidneys, remove the fatty core and cut them into cubes. Toss the steak and kidney in the seasoned flour. Heat the oil in a saucepan, add the meat and brown it. Add the onion and cook for 2-3 minutes longer. Add the sauce, stock and parsley, stirring well. Cover and simmer it gently for 2 hours. Allow the steak and kidney mixture to cool. Place it in a pie dish and cover it with puff pastry. Trim and decorate the edges of the pastry. Brush the pie with the egg wash. Cook it on the barbecue, with the lid on, for 30-40 minutes, or until the pastry is golden brown and crisp.

SMOKED METWURST OR POLISH SAUSAGE

Low smoke fire, indirect, 10-15 minutes, with lid on.

1 fresh, soft metwurst or Polish sausage

Pineapple Glaze (Recipe page 85)

Peel the skin from the sausage to expose the meat. Removing the skin allows the smoke to penetrate the meat. Add one chunk of hickory to the coals on each side of the barbecue. Dip the sausage in the pineapple glaze and smokecook it with the lid on for 10-15 minutes. Brush the sausage with the pineapple glaze 2-3 times while cooking. Allow the sausage to cool and serve it sliced for snacks.

Shepherd's Pie

SHEPHERD'S PIE

Normal fire, indirect, 30-40 minutes, with lid on. Serves 3-4.

1 onion, chopped

¼ cup gravy powder

1 cup stock

Salt and pepper to taste

1 tablespoon Worcestershire sauce

1 tablespoon tomato sauce

500g cooked meat, finely chopped

2-3 cups mashed potato

Milk

Butter

Paprika

In a saucepan combine the onion, gravy powder, stock, salt, pepper, Worcestershire sauce and tomato sauce. Bring this mixture to the boil and simmer it gently for 3-5 minutes, or until the onions are tender. Add the meat and place the mixture in a drip tray or casserole dish. Pile the mashed potato on top. Brush the mashed potato with milk, dot it with the butter and sprinkle it with paprika. Cook the pie on the barbecue, with the lid on, for 30-40 minutes, or until the potato is golden brown. Serve with salad or vegetables of your choice.

139

Barbecue entertaining for vegetarian friends can be difficult.

When was the last time you asked a vegetarian friend to a barbecue?

It is a fallacy that barbecue cooking is only for people who eat meat.

So we thought we'd include a small chapter of superb vegetarian dishes like Vegetable Moussaka, Greek Spinach and Cheese Pie, Aussie Ratatouille, we even included a Vegetable Pizza. You'll probably find that your family like some of these just as much as they like meat.

Contents

VEGETABLE PIZZA

Normal fire, indirect, 20-30 minutes, with lid on. Serves 4.

YEAST BASE

1 tablespoon dry yeast

³/₄ cup warm water

2 cups plain flour

1 teaspoon salt

1 tablespoon oil

TOPPING

4 tablespoons tomato puree

1 teaspoon oregano

¹/₂ green pepper, chopped

1 small onion, chopped

1 cup pineapple pieces

1 cup sliced mushrooms

250g Mozzarella cheese, grated

Salt and pepper to taste

Combine all the ingredients for the yeast base in a food processor and beat them well to make a dough. Place the dough in a bowl, cover and allow it to rest for 30 minutes. Turn the dough out of the bowl on to a floured surface. Knead it well, then roll it out to fit a pizza tray. Spread the yeast base with the tomato puree and top it with oregano, green pepper, onion, pineapple, mushrooms and cheese. Season the pizza with salt and pepper and cook it on the barbecue, with the lid on, for 20-30 minutes. Mamma mia!

If you are short of time, you can use our scone base as a substitute for the yeast base.

SCONE BASE

125g self raising flour

30g butter

¹/₄ teaspoon oregano

Salt to taste

Milk to mix

Sift the flour, salt and oregano into a bowl. Rub in the butter and mix with milk to form a soft, but not sticky dough. Knead the dough lightly on a floured surface, then roll it out to fit a pizza tray. Cover this base with the topping as previously described.

GRILLED MIXED VEGETABLE PARCELS

Normal fire, indirect, 20-30 minutes, with lid on. Serves 4.

4 cabbage leaves

1 onion, thickly sliced

2 small potatoes

1 tomato, sliced

1 green pepper, sliced

1 zucchini, sliced

Salt and pepper to taste

Butter

For each serving, place a cabbage leaf on a large piece of foil. On top of each cabbage leaf, place a slice of onion. Next lay half an unpeeled potato. On top of the potato, add a slice of tomato, green pepper and zucchini. Add salt and pepper and dot with butter. Wrap the cabbage leaf around all of the vegetables and fasten it with toothpicks. Wrap the foil around the cabbage parcel and seal it carefully. Cook the parcel on the barbecue, with the lid on, for 20-30 minutes. Open the foil packages to test for tenderness. Reseal them for longer cooking if necessary.

VEGETABLE KEBABS

Normal fire, indirect, 10-15 minutes, with lid on. Serves 4-6.

1 small eggplant

3 small onions

3 zucchini

1 red pepper

MARINADE

¹/₄ cup olive oil

¹/₄ cup white wine

1 clove garlic, pressed

1 tablespoon chopped parsley

1 small red chilli, finely chopped

¹/₂ teaspoon dried mixed herbs

Cut the eggplant into cubes (about ice block size). Cut the top and tail off the onions and then cut them in half lengthways. Cut the zucchini and peppers into pieces. Place the vegetables and the marinade ingredients in a bowl and marinate the vegetables for 1 hour. Thread the vegetables on to skewers. Cook them on the barbecue, with the lid on, for 10-15 minutes, or until the vegetables are tender.

VEGETABLES WITH SPAGHETTI

Direct fire, lid off, wok on. Serves 6.

¹/₂ cup water

¹/₄ cup soy sauce

2 teaspoons sugar

3 teaspoons cornflour

Cayenne pepper to taste

150g spaghetti or soba noodles

2 teaspoons sesame oil

2 tablespoons oil

¹/₄ cup sliced spring onions

2 cloves garlic, pressed

180g snow peas, trimmed

1 cup chopped bok choy or spinach

1 cup bean sprouts

¹/₄ cup thinly sliced red pepper

Combine the water, soy sauce, sugar, cornflour, cayenne pepper and set it aside. Cook the noodles or spaghetti until it is tender in boiling salted water. Drain it well and toss it with the sesame oil. Heat the wok and add the oil. Stir-fry the onions, garlic, snow peas, bok choy, sprouts and red pepper for 2 minutes. Push them to one side of the wok. Stir the soy-sauce mixture and then add it to the wok, stirring constantly until it boils. Combine it with the vegetables and serve over the hot noodles or spaghetti.

Greek Spinach and Cheese Pie

GREEK SPINACH AND CHEESE PIE

Normal fire, indirect, 25-35 minutes, with lid on. Serves 8-10.

125g butter

¹/₂ cup chopped spring onions

3 packets frozen, chopped spinach, thawed and well drained

3 eggs

250g fetta cheese, crumbled

¹/₄ cup chopped parsley

1 tablespoon chopped fresh dill

Salt and pepper to taste

200g extra butter, melted

1 Packet filo pastry sheets

Melt the butter in a pan and sauté the onions. Add the spinach and stir to combine it with the onions. Remove them from the heat and set them aside. Beat the eggs and then add the cheese, parsley, dill, salt, pepper and spinach-onion mixture. Mix this well. Brush a drip tray with the melted butter. Lay 8 filo sheets over the base, one at a time, brushing extra butter over each sheet. Spread the spinach mixture evenly over the top. Cover it with 8 more sheets of filo pastry brushing each sheet with the extra butter. Trim the edges of the pastry. Cut through the top layers of pastry to form large diamonds. Cook the pie on the barbecue with the lid on, for 25-35 minutes, until the crust is puffy and golden brown.

144

VEGETABLE MOUSSAKA

Low fire, indirect, 50-60 minutes, with lid on. Serves 8.

500g potatoes, peeled and thinly sliced

500g zucchini

1 red pepper

2 cloves garlic, pressed

1/2 cup grated Parmesan cheese

CHEESE SAUCE

3 tablespoons butter

4 tablespoons flour

2 cups milk

3 tablespoons grated Parmesan cheese

Pinch nutmeg

Salt and cayenne pepper to taste

To make the cheese sauce, melt the butter in a saucepan, stir in the flour and add the milk. Bring this to the boil stirring constantly. Cook the sauce for a further 1-2 minutes. Then add the cheese and season with nutmeg, salt and pepper.

TOMATO SAUCE

1 large onion, finely chopped

1 tablespoon oil

440g can tomatoes, drained and chopped

2 tablespoons tomato paste

1/2 cup stock

2 tablespoons chopped parsley

1 teaspoon sugar

Salt and pepper to taste

To make the tomato sauce, fry the onions in oil until they are soft. Add the tomatoes, tomato paste, stock, parsley, sugar, salt and pepper. Bring this mixture to the boil and then cook it gently for 7-10 minutes. Set it aside.

To make the moussaka, place half the sliced potatoes on the base of a drip tray. Pour over half of the tomato sauce, then add the zucchini, red pepper and garlic. Pour over the remaining tomato sauce. Spread the cheese sauce over the top and sprinkle

it with the Parmesan cheese. Cook the moussaka on the barbecue, with the lid on, for 50-60 minutes, or until the vegetables are tender. Serve it with salad and crusty French bread.

VEGETABLE STRUDEL

Normal fire, indirect, 20-30 minutes, with lid on. Serves 6-8.

60g butter

500g carrots, peeled and grated

1 small onion, chopped

1 teaspoon sugar

1 teaspoon salt

1/2 teaspoon pepper

100g mushrooms, chopped

1/4 cup grated cheese

2 eggs

6 sheets filo pastry

Melted butter, extra

1/4 cup breadcrumbs

1/4 cup toasted coconut

Melt the butter in a pan and add the carrots, onion and sugar. Cook them until they are golden brown. Add the salt, pepper, mushrooms and cheese. Beat the eggs and add these to the carrot mixture then set it aside. Brush one sheet of filo pastry with melted butter and sprinkle it with breadcrumbs and toasted coconut. Lay another sheet of filo pastry on top and continue this process until all the sheets of filo, breadcrumbs and coconut are used. Place the carrot mixture along one end of the filo pastry, fold in the edges and roll it up. Place the strudel on a sheet of buttered foil. Cook it on the barbecue with the lid on, for 20-30 minutes. Serve it hot, sliced with salad.

VEGETABLE LASAGNE

Low fire, indirect, 30-40 minutes, with lid on. Serves 6-8.

1 packet instant lasagne pasta

2 cups tomato spaghetti sauce

2 cups mixed raw vegetables

250g Mozzarella cheese, sliced

Paprika

WHITE SAUCE

1 teaspoon butter

1 teaspoon flour

1 cup milk

Salt and pepper to taste

To prepare the white sauce, melt the butter in a small saucepan and stir in the flour. Then add the milk, salt and pepper. Bring this mixture to the boil while stirring and cook it for 1-2 minutes longer. In a large drip tray, make the lasagne by placing the tomato sauce, pasta, vegetables, cheese and white sauce in alternate layers. Repeat these layers, finishing with a layer of cheese on top. Sprinkle the lasagne with paprika and cook it on the barbecue, with the lid on, for 30-40 minutes, or until the pasta is tender.

DINNER IN A PUMPKIN

Normal fire, indirect, 3 hours, with lid on. Serves 10-12.

1 large pumpkin (Queensland Blue)

Oil

FILLING

Nutmeg, salt and cayenne pepper to taste

3 slices wholegrain bread, crumbed

2 cups cooked mixed beans

1 cup Lebanese cracked wheat, soaked in water and drained

1 large onion, chopped

2 cloves garlic, pressed

440g can tomatoes, chopped

1 teaspoon chopped ginger

1 teaspoon curry powder

Cut the top from the pumpkin to form a lid. Scoop out the seeds and pulp. Combine all the filling ingredients and mix them well. Place this mixture in the pumpkin and replace the lid. Rub the pumpkin skin completely with oil. Cook it on the barbecue, with the lid on, for 3 hours, or until it is tender when tested with a skewer.

Vegetable and Rice Stir-fry

VEGETABLE AND RICE STIR-FRY

Direct fire, lid off, wok on. Serves 6-8.

2 tablespoons oil

1 cup sliced celery

1 carrot, thinly sliced

1 onion, cut into rings

1 cup broccoli flowerets

1 red pepper, chopped

1 clove garlic, pressed

2 cups cooked brown rice

1 cup cherry tomatoes

1¹/₂ cups bean sprouts

Heat the wok and add the oil. Stir-fry the celery, carrot and onion and then add the broccoli, red pepper and garlic. Cook, stirring until they are barely tender. Add the rice, heat it thoroughly and finish by adding the cherry tomatoes and bean sprouts.

EASY VEGETABLE QUICHE

Normal fire, indirect, 20-25 minutes, with lid on. Serves 6.

3 eggs, beaten

³/₄ cup milk

³/₄ cup pastry mix

2 cups mixed raw vegetables, cut into pieces

Salt and pepper to taste

1 cup grated Cheddar cheese

Combine all the ingredients, mixing them well. Pour the mixture into a 20 cm pie dish. Cook the quiche on the barbecue, with the lid on, for 20-25 minutes, or until the egg mixture has set. Serve it with salad.

AUSSIE RATATOUILLE

Normal fire, indirect, 30-40 minutes, with lid on. Serves 8.

2 tablespoons oil

1 onion, chopped

2 cloves garlic, pressed

1 eggplant, chopped

125g mushrooms, sliced

1 cup tomato spaghetti sauce

1 red pepper, sliced

250g zucchini, thickly sliced

1 teaspoon honey

1 teaspoon soy sauce

¹/₄ teaspoon oregano

Salt and pepper to taste

Mix all the ingredients together in a large drip tray. Cover it loosely with foil. Cook the ratatouille on the barbecue, with the lid on, for 20-30 minutes, stirring it occasionally.

Vegetables

When planning a barbecue menu it's easy to include vegetables and they really do make the meal.

Large varieties of fresh vegetables are available all year round.

Many of our vegetables require no preparation, because they are cooked in their skins. People love them and all the natural goodness is sealed inside. The use of foil trays and oven bags makes cooking a selection of vegetables easy and there's no washing up.

We've covered all of the traditional vegetables and included some exciting new recipes ideal for a barbecue or a dinner party. Some of these have never been cooked on a barbecue by anybody but us.

Contents

TOMATOES

Normal fire, indirect, 10-15 minutes, with lid on.

Tomatoes

Salt and pepper to taste

Cut the tomatoes in halves and place them on foil or in a drip tray. Season with salt and pepper. Add any of the following toppings to them if desired:
- Chopped fresh herbs
- Sugar
- Chopped bacon or ham
- Chopped olives
- Butter
- Garlic
- Dry bread crumbs
- Grated cheese

Cook them on the barbecue, with the lid on, for 10-15 minutes, depending on size.

CHERRY TOMATOES

Normal fire, indirect, 5-10 minutes, with lid on.

1 punnet cherry tomatoes

1 tablespoon butter

2 tablespoons snipped chives or chopped parsley

1 tablespoon Parmesan cheese (optional)

Place the cherry tomatoes in a small drip tray with the butter. Cook them on the barbecue with the lid on, for 5-10 minutes or until they are just hot and the skin starts to wrinkle. Sprinkle them with chives or parsley and Parmesan cheese if desired. Be careful with cherry tomatoes as they may burst if they are over-cooked.

CRUMBED CHEESE TOMATOES

Normal fire, indirect, 10-15 minutes, with lid on. Serves 4.

2 tomatoes, halved

Salt and pepper to taste

1 slice bread, broken into crumbs

1/2 cup grated cheese

2 tablespoons butter, melted

Stuffed Tomato

Season each tomato half with salt and pepper. Combine the crumbs, cheese and butter. Sprinkle this mixture over the tomatoes. Wrap each tomato in foil. Place them on the barbecue and cook them with the lid on, for 10-15 minutes.

SCALLOPED TOMATO BAKE

Normal fire, indirect, 15-20 minutes, with lid on. Serves 4.

500g tomatoes, sliced

2 onions, peeled and sliced

Salt and pepper to taste

1 teaspoon mixed herbs

4-6 tablespoons breadcrumbs

1 tablespoon butter

Place a layer of sliced tomato in a drip tray. Top this with some of the sliced onions. Season with salt, pepper and herbs. Sprinkle with some of the breadcrumbs. Repeat this for further layers and finish with the breadcrumbs and butter. Cook it on the barbecue with the lid on, for 15-20 minutes, or until it is tender.

STUFFED TOMATOES

Normal fire, indirect, 10-15 minutes, with lid on. Serves 4.

4 tomatoes

Grated cheese

Breadcrumbs

FILLING

1 tablespoon butter

1 small onion, chopped

2 tablespoons chopped ham

3 tablespoons fresh breadcrumbs

Salt and pepper to taste

Cut a small round from the top of each tomato. Scoop out the pulp from the inside and turn the cases upside down for a short time to drain them. Melt the butter in a pan and fry the onion until it is cooked. Stir in the remaining filling ingredients. Fill the tomatoes with this filling. Sprinkle them with grated cheese and breadcrumbs. Place them in a small drip tray and cook them on the barbecue, with the lid on, for 10-15 minutes.

JACKET POTATOES

Normal fire, indirect, 50-60 minutes, with lid on.

Potatoes

Butter

Scrub the potatoes leaving their skins on. Place them on the barbecue and cook them with the lid on for 50-60 minutes, or until they are tender. There is no need to turn, oil or prick the potatoes. Cut a cross in the top of each potato and give it a squeeze to open the cross. Serve them with butter, or any of the following combinations:

- Sour cream, chopped parsley, salt and pepper.
- Cream cheese and sour cream.
- Sour cream and chopped chives.
- Crumbled crisp bacon.
- Sauteed sliced mushrooms.
- Grated cheese.
- Yogurt and chives.
- Yogurt and blue cheese.

SWEET POTATO

The sweet potato may be cooked in all the ways described for potatoes. The orange type of sweet potato is ideal, as it doesn't discolour when cut.

NEW POTATOES

Normal fire, indirect, 30-40 minutes, with lid on. Serves 4.

500g potatoes

¼ cup water

Sprig of mint

1 tablespoon melted butter

Salt and pepper to taste

Scrub the potatoes and leave the skins on. Place them in a small drip tray, or Glad oven bag, with the water and a sprig of mint. Cover the pan with foil or if using a bag, hold it together loosely with a twistie leaving a space for any steam to escape. Cook them on the barbecue with the lid on for 30-40 minutes, or until tender when tested. Serve them with melted butter, salt and pepper.

Roost Potatoes, Jacket Potatoes, Potato Chips, Hasselback Potatoes and Scalloped Potatoes

ROAST POTATOES

Normal fire, indirect, 50-60 minutes, with lid on.

Potatoes

Oil

Salt and pepper to taste

Peel the potatoes and cut them into halves, or quarters if they are large. Brush the potatoes with oil and place them on the grill around the meat with the lid on. Cook them with the lid on for 50-60 minutes, or until they are golden brown and tender when tested. Season them with salt and pepper and serve them with roast meat or poultry.

SWEET POTATOES WITH PINEAPPLE

Normal fire, indirect, 20-30 minutes, with lid on. Serves 4-6.

500g orange coloured sweet potatoes

2 rashers bacon, chopped

1/2 cup canned pineapple pieces

1/4 cup brown sugar

1-2 tablespoons pineapple syrup

1 tablespoon butter

Chopped parsley

Peel the potatoes and cut them into even sized pieces. Place them in a drip tray in alternate layers with the bacon and pineapple. Sprinkle them with the brown sugar. Dot them with the butter and pour over the pineapple syrup. Cover them with foil and cook on the barbecue, with the lid on, for 20-30 minutes, or until they are tender. Sprinkle them with parsley and serve.

DUCHESS POTATOES

Normal fire, indirect, 10-15 minutes, with lid on. Serves 6.

1kg jacket potatoes, cooked

1 cup sour cream

1 egg, beaten

1/2 cup finely chopped spring onions

Salt, pepper, nutmeg to taste

2 tablespoons butter, melted

2 tablespoons grated Parmesan cheese

1 teaspoon paprika

Peel and mash the potatoes until they are smooth adding the sour cream, egg, spring onions, salt, pepper and nutmeg. Spoon or pipe the mixture into a buttered drip tray. Brush the top with the melted butter and sprinkle it with the cheese and paprika. Place it on the barbecue and heat it through with the lid on for 10-15 minutes, or until it is tipped with gold.

POTATO CHIPS

Normal fire, indirect, 20-30 minutes, with lid on.

Potatoes

Oil

Wash and peel the potatoes. Cut them into chips 1cm wide. Dry them well and place them in a small drip tray with enough oil to cover them. Place the drip tray on the barbecue to one side of the cooking grill, over the coals. Cook the chips with the lid on, turning them occasionally for 20-30 minutes. They should be golden and crisp. Drain them well and serve.

If you wish to cook a large number of chips for a crowd, use the wok as described in the fish and chips recipe on page 106.

FROZEN CHIPS

Normal fire, indirect, 20-30 minutes, with lid on.

500g frozen chips

1 onion, finely chopped

Salt and pepper to taste

2 tablespoons butter, melted

Juice of 1/2 lemon

Place the potato chips in the centre of a large piece of foil and scatter the chopped onion over the top. Season them with salt and pepper and pour the butter over them. Close the foil package. Pierce a few holes in the top of the foil and cook it on the barbecue with the lid on for 20-30 minutes. Open up the foil, sprinkle with the lemon juice and serve.

SCALLOPED POTATOES

Normal fire, indirect, 50-60 minutes, with lid on. Serves 4.

4 medium potatoes

2 tablespoons flour

Milk

1 tablespoon butter

Salt and pepper to taste

1 onion, finely grated or

1 tablespoon snipped chives

Peel the potatoes and slice them fairly thinly. Dredge them well with flour and place them in layers in a buttered drip tray. Pour over sufficient milk to barely cover them. Dot them with the butter and season with salt and pepper. If you like, a little grated onion or snipped chives may be sprinkled between each layer. Cook them on the barbecue with the lid on, for 50-60 minutes, or until they are tender and golden brown.

POTATO SLICES

Normal fire, indirect, 15-20 minutes, with lid on.

Potatoes, peeled and thinly sliced

Oil

Salt and pepper to taste

Place the potato slices in a small oiled drip tray. Brush the potatoes with oil. Place the drip tray on the barbecue over the coals for 15-20 minutes, with the lid on. Turn the slices over after 8-10 minutes. The slices should be golden and crisp when cooked. This method allows you to cook a roast in the centre of the cooking grill while frying potatoes on the side.

HASSELBACK POTATOES

Normal fire, indirect, 40-50 minutes, with lid on.

Even sized, medium, round potatoes,

washed and peeled

Melted butter

Paprika

Slice the potatoes at even intervals, cutting them 3/4 of the way through. (Use a wooden spoon handle alongside the potato to stop the knife.) Place the potatoes in a drip tray, sliced slide up and brush with melted butter. Sprinkle them with paprika. Cook them on the barbecue with the lid on for 40-50 minutes, or until tender when tested.

153

ROAST PUMPKIN

Normal fire, indirect, 45-60 minutes, with lid on.

Pumpkin

Oil

Salt and pepper to taste

Peel and seed the pumpkin and cut it into serving pieces. Brush these lightly with oil and season with salt and pepper. Place them in cupped foil and cook them on the barbecue with the lid on, for 45-60 minutes.

BUTTERNUT PUMPKIN

Normal fire, indirect, 50-60 minutes, with lid on.

Butternut pumpkin

Butternut pumpkin may be cooked whole in its skin and then peeled and finished as desired. Alternatively, serving sized portions may be prepared, oiled and roasted in the same manner as pumpkin. Cooked on the barbecue with the lid on, whole butternut pumpkins take 50-60 minutes, pieces 30-40 minutes.

NUTTY BUTTERNUT

Normal fire, indirect, 55-70 minutes, with lid on. Serves 4-6.

1 butternut pumpkin

1 tablespoon butter

FILLING

2 apples, cored and chopped

1 stick celery, chopped

1/4 cup pecans, chopped

1 tablespoon onion, chopped

1 tablespoon honey

Cook the butternut on the barbecue with the lid on for 40-50 minutes, or until it is tender. Remove it from the barbecue and cut it in half lengthways. Scoop out the seeds and filaments. Combine all the filling ingredients and mix them well. Fill the cavities with this mixture and dot with butter. Return them to the barbecue and cook for a further 15-20 minutes, to heat through.

BUTTERNUT CASSEROLE

Normal fire, indirect, 55-65 minutes, with lid on.

1 whole butternut pumpkin

1/2 cup cream

1 cup grated Cheddar cheese

Salt, pepper and nutmeg to taste

Cook the whole butternut on the barbecue with the lid on, for 40-50 minutes, or until it is tender. Allow it to cool and cut it into slices, removing the skin. Arrange the slices in a drip tray. Top them with the remaining ingredients. Reheat it on the barbecue, with the lid on, for 15 minutes, or until it is hot and bubbling.

SCALLOPED PUMPKIN

Normal fire, indirect, 30-40 minutes, with lid on. Serves 4.

500g pumpkin, peeled and thinly sliced

1/2 cup cream

1 cup grated cheese

Salt, pepper and nutmeg to taste

Arrange the pumpkin slices in a drip tray. Top them with the remaining ingredients and cook them on the barbecue, with the lid on, for 30-40 minutes, or until the pumpkin is tender and the cheese has browned lightly.

MINTED BUTTON SQUASH

Normal fire, indirect, 15-20 minutes, with lid on. Serves 4.

500g yellow and green button squash

1 tablespoon oil

1 teaspoon butter

Salt and pepper to taste

Chopped fresh mint

Wash and trim the squash and place them in a small drip tray or Glad oven bag with oil, butter, salt and pepper. Cook them on the barbecue, with the lid on, for 15-20 minutes, or until they are tender. Dust them with chopped mint and serve.

ZUCCHINI CASSEROLE

Normal fire, indirect, 15-20 minutes, with lid on. Serves 4.

1 tablespoon oil

1 tablespoon butter

1 clove garlic, pressed

3-4 zucchini, sliced

1/2 cup grated Romano cheese

1 teaspoon chopped fresh basil

Salt and pepper to taste

GARNISH

1 tablespoon chopped parsley, or snipped chives

Combine all the ingredients and place them in a drip tray. Cook it on the barbecue with the lid on, for 15-20 minutes, or until it is tender. Garnish the casserole with parsley or chives.

SEASONED BUSH MARROW

Normal fire, indirect, 30-40 minutes, with lid on. Serves 6.

1 medium bush marrow, cut in half lengthways

2 tablespoons grated Parmesan cheese

FILLING

2 tablespoons butter

1 clove garlic, pressed

1 onion, chopped

1 cup peeled, chopped, fresh tomato

1 cup cooked rice

Salt and cayenne pepper to taste

1/2 teaspoon dried oregano

Scoop out the centre of each marrow half and chop the flesh finely. Combine all the filling ingredients with the chopped marrow. Mix them well. Fill the marrows with this mixture. Dust them with Parmesan cheese and place them in a drip tray. Cook them on the barbecue, with the lid, on for 30-40 minutes.

Dinner in a Pumpkin (page 145)

CHOKOS

Normal fire, indirect, 40-50 minutes (whole), 30-40 minutes (sliced), with lid on.

Chokos

Chokos may be peeled, oiled and roasted along with potatoes or pumpkin around a roast. They may also be peeled, sliced and cooked in a drip tray with tomatoes, or flavoured with butter, garlic, salt, pepper, chives, dill, mint or parsley. Cook them on the barbecue, with the lid on for 40-50 minutes, or until they are tender.

CHOKOS AND TOMATO

Normal fire, indirect, 30-40 minutes, with lid on. Serves 4.

2 chokos, peeled, seeded and sliced

1 small onion, sliced

440g can tomatoes, cut up

1 clove garlic, pressed

Salt, pepper and paprika to taste

Combine all the ingredients and place them in a drip tray. Cover the tray with foil and cook on the barbecue with the lid on for 30-40 minutes, or until the chokos are tender and the flavours are well blended.

ZUCCHINI WITH RED PEPPERS

Normal fire, indirect, 10-15 minutes, with lid on. Serves 4-6.

1 onion, cut into strips

500g zucchini, cut into serving pieces

1 red pepper, seeded and cut into strips

30g butter

1 teaspoon chopped fresh basil

1 clove garlic, pressed

1/4 cup chicken stock

Salt and pepper to taste

Combine all the ingredients in a drip tray and cover it with foil. Cook it on the barbecue, with the lid on, for 10-15 minutes, or until it is just tender.

RED AND GREEN PEPPERS

Normal fire, indirect, 5-10 minutes, with lid on.

Red or green peppers, seeded

Cut the peppers into serving portions. Brush them with oil and cook them on the barbecue, with the lid on, for 5-10 minutes.

STUFFED PEPPERS

Normal fire, indirect, 20-25 minutes, with lid on. Serves 4.

4 peppers

Oil

1/2 cup grated cheese

Paprika

1/4 cup pine nuts

2 tablespoons sultanas

1 cup cooked brown rice

1/4 cup yogurt

1/2 teaspoon ground cumin

Salt and pepper to taste

Cut the peppers in half and remove the seeds. Oil them well. Combine the filling ingredients and stuff the peppers. Top them with the grated cheese and sprinkle them with paprika. Cook them in a small drip tray on the barbecue with the lid on, for 20-25 minutes.

MUSHROOMS WITH PRAWN MEAT

Normal fire, indirect, 10-15 minutes, with lid on. Serves 6.

6 large mushroom caps

1/2 cup sour cream

1 small can prawns, strained

1/4 cup chopped spring onions

1 tablespoon sherry

2 teaspoons cornflour

1 tablespoon lemon juice

Salt and pepper to taste

1/2 cup grated tasty cheese

Paprika or parsley flakes

Remove the stems from the mushrooms. Combine the sour cream, prawns, onions, sherry, cornflour, lemon juice, salt and pepper and mix them well. Spoon this mixture into the mushroom caps. Sprinkle them with cheese and dust them with paprika or parsley flakes. Place them on foil, or in a drip tray and cook on the barbecue, with the lid on for 10-15 minutes. Serve as an entree or as an accompaniment to a roast.

PEA AND MUSHROOM PARCEL

Normal fire, indirect, 10-15 minutes, with lid on. Serves 4.

2 cups frozen peas

2 tablespoons butter

1 cup button mushrooms

Salt and pepper to taste

Place all the ingredients on a piece of foil. Wrap the foil around them loosely. Cook the parcel on the barbecue, with the lid on for 10-15 minutes. Unwrap the foil and serve immediately.

GARLIC MUSHROOMS

Normal fire, indirect, 10-15 minutes, with lid on. Serves 4.

250g button mushrooms

2 cloves garlic, pressed

2 tablespoons butter

2 tablespoons olive oil

Salt and pepper to taste

2 spring onions, chopped

Place all the ingredients in a drip tray and cook them on the barbecue, with the lid on, for 12-15 minutes. Serve the garlic mushrooms as an entree on toothpicks, or as a vegetable accompaniment.

Frozen Vegetables

FROZEN VEGETABLES

Normal fire, indirect, 10-15 minutes, with lid on.

Any frozen vegetable, or mixture of frozen vegetables may be cooked on the barbecue. Place them in foil packages, Glad oven bags or drip trays, with a little water, salt, pepper and dobs of butter.

Cook them on the barbecue with the lid on for 10-15 minutes, or until they are tender.

VEGETABLE PARCELS

Normal fire, indirect, 20-25 minutes, with lid on.

Most combinations of vegetables and flavourings may be placed in foil packets. Cook them on the barbecue with the lid on, for 20-25 minutes, or until they are tender. The advantage of this method is that it eliminates the need for washing up saucepans.

CAULIFLOWER OR BROCCOLI AU GRATIN

Normal fire, indirect, 15-20 minutes, with lid on. Serves 4.

Cauliflower or broccoli portions, (sufficient for 4)

1 tablespoon butter

1 tablespoon flour

1 cup yogurt

1 cup grated cheese

Salt and pepper to taste

Paprika

Place the vegetables in a drip tray. Heat the butter in a saucepan, add the flour and stir until it is smooth. Add the yogurt and continue cooking until the sauce thickens slightly. Add the cheese. Pour this mixture over the vegetables. Dust them with paprika. Cook them on the barbecue with the lid on, for 15-20 minutes, or until the vegetables are tender.

BEETROOT

Normal fire, indirect, 50-70 minutes with lid on. Serves 6.

1 bunch beetroot

2 cups water

Salt, pepper and sugar to taste

1 tablespoon vinegar

Wash the beetroot thoroughly being careful not to break or cut the skin. Leave about 4cm of the stems intact. Place them in a Glad oven bag with the water and salt. Seal the bag and make a hole for any steam to escape. Cook them on the barbecue with the lid on for 50-70 minutes. Remove the skin and pour over the vinegar. Sprinkle them with salt, pepper and sugar.

BROCCOLI & CAULIFLOWER

Normal fire, indirect, 15-20 minutes, with lid on. Serves 4.

Broccoli or cauliflower

Broccoli or cauliflower are delicious served hot with butter and seasonings, cheese, or hollandaise sauce. Herbs such as tarragon and oregano blend well with these vegetables. The addition of sesame seeds, poppy seeds, lemon juice, grated lemon rind, mustard or curry powder may create interesting variations. To cook broccoli or cauliflower, wash the vegetable and break it into portions. Place them in a Glad oven bag with herbs and seasonings of your choice and a small amount of stock or water. Cook them on the barbecue with the lid on for 15-20 minutes.

CABBAGE CASSEROLE

Normal fire, indirect, 30-40 minutes, with lid on. Serves 4.

500g cabbage, cored and shredded

2 cloves garlic, pressed

1 onion, finely sliced

Salt and pepper to taste

1 tablespoon oil

1/4 teaspoon turmeric

1 cup chicken stock

Place all the ingredients in a large drip tray, cover it with foil and place it on the barbecue. Cook with the lid on for 30-40 minutes, stirring once during the cooking.

CABBAGE ROLLS WITH MUSHROOMS

Normal fire, indirect, 15-20 minutes, with lid on. Serves 6.

1 tablespoon oil

30g butter

500g mushrooms, roughly chopped

1 clove garlic

1 can water chestnuts, drained and chopped

2 teaspoons chopped, fresh coriander

1 tablespoon dry sherry

2 teaspoons cornflour

1/3 cup water

6 cabbage leaves

1 cup tomato spaghetti sauce

Heat the oil and butter in a frying pan and add the mushrooms, garlic, water chestnuts, coriander, sherry and the cornflour blended with water. Stir these well over the heat to make a sauce. Continue stirring until the sauce thickens. Blanch the cabbage leaves in boiling water then rinse them in cold water. Place the mushroom sauce equally on the cabbage leaves. Roll them up firmly and place them in a drip tray. Pour over the tomato sauce and cover it with foil. Cook on the barbecue, with the lid on, for 15-20 minutes.

BRAISED RED CABBAGE

Normal fire, indirect, 60-80 minutes, with lid on. Serves 6-8.

60g butter, melted

1 red cabbage, shredded

1/2 cup chopped onion

Salt to taste

1 cup red wine

2 apples, sliced

1/2 cup redcurrant jelly

Combine the butter, cabbage, onion, salt and wine in a large drip tray. Cover it with foil and cook the cabbage on the barbecue, with the lid on, for 40-50 minutes. Stir well and add the apples and jelly. Continue cooking for 20-30 minutes longer. Serve the cabbage with beef, pork or game.

BRUSSELS SPROUTS

Normal fire, indirect, 15-20 minutes, with lid on.

Brussels sprouts

Remove the coarse stalks and any discoloured leaves. Cut a cross in the stalk ends. Place the sprouts in cold, salted water for a few minutes. Rinse them. Place them in a drip tray with a little water, butter, salt and pepper. Cover the drip tray with foil. Cook on the barbecue, with the lid on, for 15-20 minutes, or until they are tender.

BRUSSELS SPROUTS AND BACON

Normal fire, indirect, 20-30 minutes, with lid on. Serves 4-6.

125g bacon, trimmed and cut into strips

500g Brussels sprouts, trimmed

1 tablespoon oil

1 tablespoon vinegar

Salt and pepper to taste

1 cup white wine

Combine all the ingredients in a drip tray and cover it with foil. Cook the sprouts on the barbecue with the lid on for 20-30 minutes, or until they are tender.

VEGETABLE SPAGHETTI

Normal fire, indirect, 60-80 minutes, with lid on. Serves 6-8.

1 vegetable spaghetti

Place the vegetable spaghetti on the barbecue and cook it for 45-60 minutes, or until it is tender when tested with a skewer. Cut it in half lengthways, scoop out the seeds and remove the flesh from the skins. Toss the flesh with any of the following:

– Cream
– Butter
– Grated cheese
– Chopped ham
– Fresh chopped herbs
– Tomatoes
– Mushrooms
– Curry powder
– Onion

Return the flesh to the shells and reheat them on the barbecue with the lid on, for 15-20 minutes.

BUTTERED VEGETABLE SPAGHETTI

Normal fire, indirect, 60-80 minutes, with lid on.

1 vegetable spaghetti

125g butter, melted

1/2 cup sliced spring onions

1/2 cup grated Parmesan cheese

Salt and pepper to taste

Cook the vegetable spaghetti on the barbecue with the lid on for about 50-60 minutes, or until it is tender. Cut it in half lengthways and scoop out the seeds. Using a fork remove the long strands of flesh. Toss these with the butter, onions, cheese, salt and pepper. Reheat this in a foil drip tray, on the barbecue, with the lid on, for 15-20 minutes, or until it is hot and bubbly.

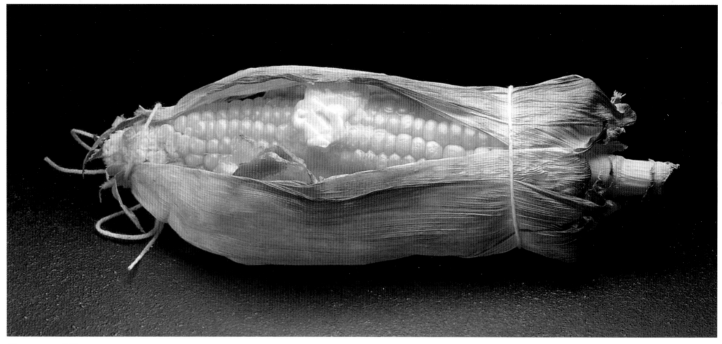

Bacon and Corn

CORN ON THE COB

Normal fire, indirect, 30-40 minutes, with lid on.

1 cob corn per person

Butter

Salt and pepper to taste

Turn back the husks and strip the silk. Return the husks back into position over the corn. Tie the ends of the husks with string. Place them on the barbecue and cook them, with the lid on, for 30-40 minutes. They are delicious with lots of melted butter, salt and pepper.

FOIL ROASTED CORN

Normal fire, indirect, 30-40 minutes, with lid on.

1 cob corn per person, husk and silk removed

Butter

Salt and pepper to taste

Spread the corn cobs with butter, sprinkle them with salt and pepper and wrap them individually in foil. Cook them on the barbecue, with the lid on for 30-40 minutes.

BACON AND CORN

Normal fire, indirect, 30-40 minutes, with lid on.

1 cob corn per person

Butter

Salt and pepper to taste

1 bacon rasher per person

Turn back the husks and strip the silk. Brush the corn with butter and season it with salt and pepper. Wrap the corn with the bacon rashers. Return the husks into position over the corn. Tie the ends of the husks with string. Place them on the barbecue and cook them with the lid on for 30-40 minutes.

CORN IN THE BAG

Normal fire, indirect, 30-40 minutes, with lid on. Serves 4.

4 cobs corn

4 tablespoons butter

1 clove garlic

1 tablespoon chopped fresh herbs

2 tablespoons water

Place the corn cobs in a Glad oven bag with the butter, garlic, herbs and water. Secure it with a twist tie, piercing a hole in the bag to allow any steam to escape. Cook them on the barbecue with the lid on for 30-40 minutes.

FIONA'S GOLDEN NUGGETS

Normal fire, indirect, 45-60 minutes, with lid on. Serves 4.

1 large or 4 individual golden nuggets

oil

FILLING

1 cup cooked brown rice

1 packet French onion soup

1 cup grated Mozzarella cheese

$^1/_2$ cup yogurt

Cut the top from each golden nugget to form a lid. Scoop out the seeds and pulp. Combine all the filling ingredients and mix them well. Place this filling in the nuggets. Replace the lids. Rub the nuggets completely with oil. Cook them on the barbecue, with the lid on, for 45-60 minutes according to size, or until they are tender when tested with a skewer.

PEAS

Normal fire, indirect, 10-15 minutes, with lid on. Serves 2-3.

500g peas in pod

1 sprig mint

1 teaspoon sugar

1 teaspoon butter

$^1/_2$ cup water

Shell the peas and reserve some of the pods. Place the peas and reserved pods in a Glad oven bag with the mint, sugar, butter and water. Cook them on the barbecue, with the lid on for 10-15 minutes.

PEAS IN FOIL

Normal fire, indirect, 15-20 minutes, with lid on. Serves 4.

6 lettuce leaves

2 cups frozen peas

1 teaspoon sugar

Salt and pepper to taste

1 tablespoon butter

On a double thickness of foil, arrange the lettuce leaves overlapping to form a circle. Place the peas on the lettuce. Sprinkle them with the sugar, salt, pepper and dot them with butter. Bring the ends of the foil together and fold them over to secure. Cook the parcel on the barbecue, with the lid on for 15-20 minutes. Serve the peas with the juices.

SNOW PEAS

Normal fire, indirect, 10-12 minutes, with lid on.

Snow peas

These tender pods may be eaten raw but are sensational when cooked whole. They combine well with any other vegetables and may be cooked in foil packages or Glad oven bags. They may be seasoned to taste with salt, pepper, sugar, garlic, ginger or chives.

BEANS

Normal fire, indirect, 10-15 minutes, with lid on. Serves 4.

500g green beans

1 clove garlic, pressed

1 sprig thyme

1 teaspoon butter

$^1/_2$ cup water

Combine all the ingredients in a small drip tray or Glad oven bag. Cook them on the barbecue, with the lid on for 10-15 minutes.

BEANS IN CASSEROLE

Normal fire, indirect, 15-20 minutes, with lid on. Serves 4-6.

500g fresh green beans, cut into suitable lengths

1 tablespoon butter

1 small onion, chopped

1 bacon rasher, chopped

1 clove garlic, pressed

Salt and pepper to taste

Place all the ingredients in a drip tray. Cook them on the barbecue, with the lid on, for 15-20 minutes, or until they are tender, stirring them once during cooking.

CARROTS

Normal fire, indirect, 20-25 minutes, with lid on.

Carrots

Carrots may be cooked in Glad oven bags, or drip trays with a small amount of water, orange juice and brown sugar for extra flavour. Carrots blend well with seasonings such as nutmeg, allspice, chives, dill and rosemary. Dot them with a knob of butter. Cook the carrots on the barbecue, with the lid on, in any of the above combinations, for 20-25 minutes.

CARROTS AND SULTANAS

Normal fire, indirect, 15-20 minutes, with lid on. Serves 4.

500g baby carrots

1 onion, peeled and sliced

1 tablespoon butter

60g sultanas

$^1/_4$ cup water

$^1/_4$ cup orange juice

Salt and pepper to taste

Combine all the ingredients in a drip tray. Cook them on the barbecue, with the lid on, for 15-20 minutes, or until the carrots are tender.

FRIED RICE

Direct fire, lid off, wok on. Serves 6.

1 tablespoon oil

2 eggs, beaten

1 tablespoon oil, extra

6 large shelled prawns, chopped

2$^1/_2$ cups cooked rice

2 tablespoons chopped spring onions

4 Chinese mushrooms, soaked

$^1/_2$ cup diced cooked ham

3 tablespoons peas

Salt and pepper to taste

Heat the wok for 20-30 seconds and add the oil, then pour in the beaten eggs. Stir gently until the eggs set. Remove the eggs and cut them into strips. Heat the extra oil and stir-fry the prawns. Push them to one side of the wok. Add the cooked rice and the remaining ingredients, tossing them together to heat them through. If the mixture is dry, add a few drops of water. Add the egg strips and serve.

ONIONS

Normal fire, indirect, 40-50 minutes, with lid on.

Whole onions, washed and unpeeled

Place the onions on the barbecue with the lid on and cook them for 40-50 minutes, or until they are tender. Remove the skin to serve. Onions cooked whole in their skin retain full flavour and a natural sweetness, which is a taste sensation.

CASSEROLE OF ONIONS WITH ROSEMARY

Normal fire, indirect, 20-30 minutes, with lid on. Serves 4.

500g onions, peeled and sliced

$\frac{1}{2}$ cup oil

1 teaspoon coarsely cracked black pepper

1 tablespoon paprika

2 teaspoons sugar

Fresh rosemary

Combine the oil, pepper, paprika, sugar and rosemary in a small drip tray. Add the onions and cook them on the barbecue, with the lid on, for 20-30 minutes, stirring once during cooking.

ONIONS IN RED WINE

Normal fire, indirect, 20-30 minutes, with lid on. Serves 4.

4 onions, peeled and halved

1 tablespoon butter

Salt and pepper to taste

Paprika

$\frac{1}{2}$ cup red wine

Place the halved onions in a buttered drip tray and top each one with a knob of butter. Season them with salt, pepper and paprika. Pour the red wine over the onions. Cook them on the barbecue for 20-30 minutes, with the lid on, basting once with the liquid during cooking.

STUFFED ONIONS

Normal fire, indirect, 20-30 minutes, with lid on. Serves 4.

4 onions, peeled

Water

Oil

2 tablespoons butter

$\frac{1}{2}$ teaspoon curry powder

$\frac{3}{4}$ cup soft, white breadcrumbs

$\frac{1}{2}$ cup grated Cheddar cheese

Chopped parsley

Salt to taste

Cut a slice from the top of each onion. Place the onions in a saucepan with enough water to barely cover and cook for 15-20 minutes. You may also cook them in the microwave for 5-10 minutes. Drain them well and cool them slightly. Remove the centres from the onions, leaving a thick shell. Place the onion shells in a small buttered drip tray and brush them with oil. Pour $\frac{1}{3}$ cup of water around the onion shells. Chop the onion centres finely and mix them well with the butter, curry, breadcrumbs, salt and grated cheese. Place this mixture in the onion shells. Cook them on the barbecue for 20-30 minutes, with the lid on. Sprinkle them with chopped parsley and serve.

EGGPLANT

Normal fire, indirect, 30-40 minutes, with lid on.

Eggplants

Cook them whole on the barbecue with the lid on for 30-40 minutes, or until they are tender. There is no need to prick or turn them. Eggplant may also be cooked by slicing it and placing it in a drip tray or Glad oven bag.
Suggested seasonings and flavours to top the eggplants are:
– Olive oil
– Butter
– Grated cheese
– Tomato sauce
– Onion
– Salt and pepper to taste
– Chopped thyme
– Marjoram

STUFFED EGGPLANT

Normal fire, indirect, 50-60 minutes, with lid on. Serves 2-4.

1 eggplant

1 onion, chopped

1 cup chopped ham or luncheon meat

440g can tomatoes, chopped

1 clove garlic, pressed

Salt and pepper to taste

$\frac{1}{4}$ cup grated Parmesan cheese

1 tablespoon chopped fresh basil

Parmesan cheese, extra

Cook the eggplant on the barbecue with the lid on, for 30-40 minutes or until it is tender. Cut the eggplant in half lengthways and scoop out the flesh, leaving a shell 1 cm thick. Chop the flesh and combine it with the remaining ingredients. Pile this mixture into the eggplant shells. Dust them with extra Parmesan cheese and cook them in a drip tray on the barbecue with the lid on for 20 minutes.

Salad Magic

What good is an Aussie barbecue without a salad?

If you're going to serve barbecue kettle food, a selection of salads is almost essential and everyone has their own favourite dressing. When your friends ask "what can I bring?", you'll have all the answers.

Three or four beautiful salads from this collection, served with your cold smoked trout, glazed ham and hot roast beef will create an unforgettable smorgasbord atmosphere.

Contents

Pork Parcels served with Fresh Garden Salad

FRESH MUSHROOM SALAD

Serves 8.

1kg small button mushrooms

¹/₂ cup oil

2 tablespoons white vinegar

1¹/₂ teaspoons dried tarragon

Salt and pepper to taste

1 tablespoon chopped fresh parsley

Remove the stems from the mushrooms. Place the mushrooms in a bowl with the oil, vinegar, tarragon, salt and pepper. Toss this well and allow it to stand for 1-2 hours. Serve the salad dusted with the chopped parsley.

APPLE AND PEAR SLAW

Serves 6.

1 red or golden delicious apple, sliced

1 pear, peeled and sliced

1 cup shredded cabbage

¹/₄ cup grated carrot

¹/₄ cup natural yogurt

¹/₂-1 teaspoon prepared cream-style horseradish

Combine all of the ingredients, tossing them until they are well mixed. Chill this mixture thoroughly. Serve it on lettuce lined salad plates.

BANANA SALAD

Serves 4-6.

4 medium bananas, peeled

Juice of 1 lemon

¹/₂ cup mayonnaise

¹/₂ cup cream

1 teaspoon horseradish sauce

2 tablespoons chopped nuts

Slice the bananas and coat them with the lemon juice. Combine the mayonnaise, cream and horseradish sauce. Mix them well. Coat the bananas well with this cream mixture and sprinkle them with the chopped nuts.

STRAWBERRY AND SPINACH SALAD

Strawberries and sweet and sour dressing with fresh chives makes this a winner! Serves 4-6.

250g tender young spinach

2 cups fresh strawberries, hulled and sliced

60g almonds, toasted

Chopped fresh chives

DRESSING

$1/4$ cup sugar

2 tablespoons sesame seeds

1 teaspoon finely chopped spring onion

$1/4$ teaspoon Worcestershire sauce

$1/4$ teaspoon paprika

$1/4$ cup cider vinegar

$1/2$ cup oil

Wash and dry the spinach. Arrange the spinach and strawberries on individual plates, or in a clear glass salad bowl. Place the sugar, sesame seeds, onion, Worcestershire sauce, paprika and vinegar in a blender. While blending, add the oil in a steady stream until the dressing is creamy and thick. Pour the dressing over the salad. Garnish it with toasted almonds and chopped chives.

WALDORF SALAD WITH PINEAPPLE

Serves 6.

2 cups chopped apples

1 tablespoon sugar

$1/2$ teaspoon lemon juice

2 cups chopped fresh pineapple

1 cup chopped celery

$1/2$ cup chopped walnuts

$1/3$ cup mayonnaise

Lettuce

Sprinkle the apples with the sugar and the lemon juice. Mix this with the pineapple. Add the celery, nuts and mayonnaise. Mix lightly and chill. Serve it in lettuce cups or in a lettuce-lined bowl.

ORANGE AND AVOCADO SALAD

Serves 6-8.

$1/4$ cup fresh lemon juice

2 avocados

3 oranges

$3/4$ cup mayonnaise

$1/4$ cup fresh orange juice

$1/2$ teaspoon paprika

Lettuce

Pour the lemon juice into a bowl. Peel the avocados and cut them lengthways into 5 mm slices. Dip the slices immediately in the lemon juice. Peel the oranges and remove any white pith. Cut them crossways into 5mm slices. Mix the mayonnaise, orange juice and paprika to make orange mayonnaise. Line a serving bowl with lettuce. Place alternating layers of orange slices and avocado slices on to the lettuce, finishing with avocado slices. Do not toss. Pour a little of the orange mayonnaise over the salad and serve the remaining sauce at the table.

KIWI SALAD

Serves 6.

1 lettuce

3 zucchini, thinly sliced

4 kiwi fruit, peeled and sliced

2 stalks celery, sliced

30g pistachio nuts

DRESSING

4 tablespoons oil

$1/4$ cup lemon juice

Salt and pepper to taste

A little sugar

A little fresh thyme

To make the dressing, combine the oil, lemon juice, sugar, salt, pepper and chopped thyme and mix them well. Toss the lettuce, zucchini, kiwi fruit and celery with the dressing. Top the salad with chopped pistachio nuts just before serving.

SNOW PEA AND POTATO SALAD

Serves 8-10.

750g small new potatoes, cooked

1 cup sunflower sprouts

175g snow peas, trimmed and blanched

1 red pepper, sliced

$1/2$ cup sliced celery

3 tablespoons thinly sliced spring onions

2 tablespoons chopped parsley

green pepper, sliced

DRESSING

$1/2$ cup oil

3 tablespoons white wine vinegar

2 tablespoons lemon juice

1 teaspoon dried oregano

Salt to taste

$1/2$ teaspoon pepper

Prepare the dressing by mixing all the ingredients together. Combine this with all the salad ingredients and toss them well before serving.

WITLOOF WALNUT AND SUNFLOWER SPROUTS SALAD

Serves 6-8.

2 tablespoons red wine vinegar

Salt and pepper to taste

$3/4$ cup oil

4 witloof

A little watercress (if available)

2 cups sunflower sprouts

$1/2$ cup walnut halves

Prepare the dressing by whisking together the vinegar, salt, pepper and oil. Cut the witloof into julienne strips (long thin match-like strips) and chill them in iced water. Remove the witloof and drain it well. Pour the dressing over the witloof and toss it with the watercress sprigs, sunflower sprouts and walnuts.

Fruity Pork with Fried Rice and Salad

CUCUMBER SALAD

Serves 8

3 long green cucumbers

1 bunch spring onions, chopped

$1/2$ cup white wine

Juice of $1/2$ lemon

$1/2$ cup French dressing

Peel the cucumbers and cut them into very thin slices. Add the spring onions, wine and lemon juice. Chill this well. Before serving, toss the salad with the French dressing and serve it in a lettuce lined bowl.

CUCUMBER AND TOMATO SALAD

Serves 4.

1 cucumber, peeled, seeded and chopped

2 tomatoes, seeded and chopped

2 spring onions, chopped

1 tablespoon chopped mint

3 tablespoons oil

3 tablespoons lemon juice

Salt and pepper to taste

In a salad bowl, combine the cucumber, tomatoes, onion and mint. In another bowl, mix together the oil, lemon juice, salt and pepper to make the dressing. Pour the dressing over the vegetables and mix them well.

ZUCCHINI SALAD

Serves 8.

3 tablespoons sour cream
or natural yogurt

3 tablespoons mayonnaise

1 tablespoon Dijon mustard

1 clove garlic, pressed

Salt to taste

1kg zucchini, grated

Lettuce leaves

Tomato wedges

Combine the sour cream or natural yogurt, mayonnaise, mustard, garlic and salt and mix them well. Add the zucchini, mixing it well. Chill the salad for 30 minutes. Serve it on a bed of lettuce and garnish it with the wedges of tomato.

TAMARILLO AND RED CABBAGE SLAW

Serves 8-10.

1 small red cabbage

1 large salad onion

2 apples

3 tamarillos

$1/2$ cup sugar

$1/2$ cup French dressing

Shred the cabbage and finely slice the onion. Grate the apples, then peel and chop the tamarillos. Toss them all together and sprinkle them with the sugar. Cover the bowl and chill the salad for 1 hour. Toss the salad well with French dressing. Drain off any excess liquid and serve.

COLESLAW

Serves 6-8.

3 cups shredded cabbage

1 cup grated apple

1 cup grated carrot

DRESSING

1/2 cup condensed milk

1 teaspoon mustard

1/2 cup vinegar

1 teaspoon salt

Combine the cabbage, apple and carrot in a large bowl. Mix the dressing ingredients and pour them over the cabbage, apple and carrot. Toss the salad well and serve it chilled.

POTATO AND NUT SALAD

Serves 6-8.

750g whole new potatoes, cooked

1 avocado, chopped (toss the avocado in lemon juice to prevent discolouration)

1/2 red pepper, cut into strips

1/2 cup chopped parsley

Mayonnaise

Cashew nuts

Combine the potatoes, avocado, pepper and 1/2 the parsley with sufficient mayonnaise to moisten the mixture. Garnish the salad with cashew nuts and the remainder of the parsley. Chill it before serving.

WITLOOF PECAN NUT AND ALMOND SALAD

Serves 6-8.

5 pieces witloof

100g pecan nuts

100g sliced almonds

1 cup mayonnaise

Green pepper, sliced

1 red pepper, sliced

Cut the witloof in half lengthways. Remove the core and separate the leaves. Roughly chop the pecan nuts into medium-sized chunks. Add the almonds and combine all with the mayonnaise. Garnish the salad with slices of the green and red peppers.

CELERY, APPLE AND WALNUT SALAD

Serves 8-10.

8 stalks celery

1 granny smith apple

1/2 cup sour cream

1/4 cup redcurrant jelly

1 cup seedless grapes

1 tablespoon lemon juice

1/3 cup walnuts

Trim the celery and cut it into slices. Peel and core the apple and cut it into 1cm cubes. Combine the sour cream and jelly, whisking it until it is smooth. Add the celery, apple, grapes and lemon juice. Chill it well. Add the walnuts and divide the mixture among salad plates lined with lettuce.

ZUCCHINI AND CORN SALAD

Serves 6-8.

750g zucchini, chopped

1/2 cup oil

300g corn kernels

1/2 cup red wine vinegar

Salt and pepper to taste

1/4 cup chopped parsley

1/4 cup chopped spring onions

Sauté the zucchini in hot oil for 1 minute. Add the corn and vinegar. Bring this to the boil. Transfer it to a bowl and season it with salt and pepper. Add the parsley and spring onions. Chill the salad before serving.

MACARONI SALAD

Serves 8.

250g cooked spiral macaroni

1 small salad onion, chopped

3/4 cup 1cm cubes Cheddar cheese

1 medium carrot, grated

1/2 cup chopped celery

1/2 tin crushed pineapple

1/2 cup sultanas

1/2 cup cashew nuts

1 teaspoon curry powder

1 red apple, chopped

1/2 cup mayonnaise

Combine all the ingredients. Mix them well and store the salad in the refrigerator until required.

APPLE, PEAR AND POTATO SALAD

Serves 6-8.

1 apple

1 pear

2 tablespoons lemon juice

3 potatoes

1 hard boiled egg, sliced

1/2 cup sour cream

1/4 teaspoon mustard powder

2 teaspoons snipped chives

Salt and pepper to taste

1 tablespoon coarsely chopped walnuts

Peel and core the fruit and cut it into 1 cm cubes. Sprinkle the cubes with the lemon juice. Boil the potatoes in their skins. Peel and chop them when they are cooked. Combine the fruit, potato and sliced egg. Mix the sour cream, mustard, chives, salt and pepper. Pour this mixture over the salad. Serve the salad topped with the walnuts.

Meatloaf with Salad

CREAM FRENCH DRESSING

For all types of tossed salad.

1/3 **cup cream**

2 **tablespoons lemon juice**

Salt to taste

In a bowl gently mix together the cream, lemon juice and salt. Toss this dressing with lettuce leaves and serve.

FRENCH DRESSING

For all types of tossed salad.

2 **tablespoons vinegar or lemon juice**

Salt and pepper to taste

1/3 **cup oil**

1/2 **teaspoon mustard powder**

Place all the ingredients in a blender or food processor and mix them well. Store the dressing in an airtight container in your refrigerator until required.

GARLIC FRENCH DRESSING

For all types of tossed salad.

1 **clove garlic, pressed**

Salt and pepper to taste

2 **tablespoons red wine vinegar**

1/3 **cup oil**

In a bowl combine the garlic, salt, pepper and vinegar. Pour in the oil, beating the mixture constantly. Store it in an airtight container in the refrigerator until required.

AMERICAN STYLE FRENCH DRESSING

For all types of tossed salad.

400g **can condensed tomato soup**

1 **teaspoon mustard powder**

1/4 **cup sugar**

Salt to taste

1 **teaspoon paprika**

3/4 **cup oil**

3/4 **cup vinegar**

1 **teaspoon Worcestershire sauce**

Place the ingredients in a jar. Put the lid on the jar and shake it until the mixture has thoroughly blended. Store it in the refrigerator until required.

BLUE CHEESE FRENCH DRESSING

For all types of tossed salad.

1/4 **cup vinegar**

Salt and pepper to taste

1/2 **cup oil**

2 **tablespoons cream**

1/4 **cup crumbled blue cheese**

Lemon juice

Place the vinegar in a bowl and add the salt and pepper, stirring the mixture well. Beat in the oil and the cream. Stir in the cheese and add a few drops of lemon juice. Store it in an airtight container in the refrigerator until required.

MUSTARD MAYONNAISE

For egg or potato salad.

3/4 **cup mayonnaise**

Juice of 1/2 **lemon**

1 **tablespoon Dijon mustard**

1/3 **cup cream, lightly whipped**

In a bowl combine the mayonnaise, lemon juice and mustard. Gently mix in the cream. Store it in an airtight container in the refrigerator until required.

THOUSAND ISLAND DRESSING

For any type of tossed salad.

1 **cup mayonnaise**

1 **tablespoon chilli sauce**

1 **tablespoon seeded and chopped green pepper**

1 **tablespoon seeded and chopped red pepper**

1/2 **teaspoon snipped chives**

Cream

To the mayonnaise add the chilli sauce, chopped peppers and chives. Add sufficient cream mixing it well until the dressing reaches the desired consistency. Store the dressing in an airtight container in the refrigerator until required.

Yogurt Dressing

For vegetable or potato salad.

2 **tablespoons chopped parsley**

1/2 **teaspoon dried dill**

Garlic salt to taste

1 **cup natural yogurt**

In a bowl combine the parsley, dill and garlic salt. Gently mix in the yogurt. Cover the yogurt dressing and chill it in the refrigerator until it is required.

Blender Mayonnaise

1 **egg**

1 **tablespoon lemon juice**

1 **teaspoon mustard powder**

Salt and white pepper to taste

1/2 **cup oil**

1 **tablespoon warm water (optional)**

In a blender or food processor combine the egg, lemon juice, mustard, salt and pepper. Blend them well. Add the oil in a thin stream, beating the mixture well. Add the warm water if the mayonnaise is too thick. Store it in the refrigerator, covered, until required.

Stuffed Flounder with Fresh Salad

BOILED SALAD DRESSING

For potato salad, Waldorf salad or egg salad.

$^1/_2$ **cup sugar**

2 teaspoons mustard powder

1 tablespoon plain flour

Salt to taste

1 cup water

$^1/_2$ **cup vinegar**

2 eggs

Mix the sugar, mustard, flour and salt together in a saucepan with $^1/_2$ a cup of the water. Add the remaining water, vinegar, eggs and beat the mixture well. Cook it until it has thickened. Store it in an airtight container in the refrigerator until required.

MAYONNAISE

2 egg yolks

1 teaspoon vinegar

Salt and pepper to taste

$^1/_2$ **teaspoon mustard powder**

1 cup oil

1 teaspoon vinegar, extra or lemon juice

Place the egg yolks in a bowl with the vinegar, salt, pepper and mustard. Beat the mixture vigorously with a whisk. Add the oil drop by drop, until about a $^1/_4$ of the oil has been used. Then add the remaining oil in a thin stream, beating constantly. Stop adding the oil from time to time to ensure that it is mixing in well. Finish the sauce by beating in the extra vinegar or lemon juice. Store it in an airtight container in the refrigerator until required.

GREEN GODDESS DRESSING

For any type of tossed salad.

2 tablespoons tarragon vinegar

2 tablespoons chopped parsley

2 teaspoons anchovy paste

2 teaspoons lemon juice

2 teaspoons chopped spring onion, or snipped chives

1 clove garlic, pressed

1 cup sour cream or natural yogurt

In a bowl combine the vinegar, parsley, anchovy paste, lemon juice, onion or chives and garlic. Gently mix in the sour cream or yogurt. Cover and chill the dressing until you require it.

Desserts on the Barbecue

After the meat and vegetables are cooked, the coals are usually at their best and ready to cook a beautiful dessert.

In this chapter you'll find a superb range of desserts that will provide a perfect ending for every meal.

For a formal dinner party, Pears in Red Wine are perfect, but what better way of ending a backyard barbecue than with Bread and Butter Pudding.

If you really want to show your talent, you'll probably choose our Pineapple Dream or Bombe Kosciusko.

Contents

Roll over Pavlova

ROLL OVER PAVLOVA

Low fire, indirect, 10-15 minutes, with lid on. Serves 6-8.

4 egg whites

1 teaspoon vinegar

1½ cups castor sugar

½ teaspoon vanilla

1 tablespoon cornflour

1 tablespoon desiccated coconut

1 kiwi fruit

1 banana

1 punnet strawberries

1 passionfruit

2 cups cream, whipped

Beat the egg whites with the vinegar until they are stiff. Gradually add the sugar and beat in the vanilla and cornflour. Pour this mixture into a foil lined Swiss roll tin. Sprinkle it with the coconut. Cook it on the barbecue with the lid on for 10-15 minutes. Turn it out on to sugar - sprinkled greaseproof paper. Spread it with the fresh fruit and whipped cream. Roll the pavlova up and serve with chilled passionfruit sauce.

PASSIONFRUIT SAUCE

½ cup castor sugar

2 teaspoons cornflour

½ cup orange juice

8 passionfruit

¼ cup orange flavoured liqueur

Combine the sugar, cornflour and orange juice in a saucepan. Bring it to the boil, stirring all the time. Add the pulp of the passionfruit and the liqueur and mix them well.

PAVLOVA

Low fire, indirect, 45-60 minutes, with lid on. Serves 8.

4 egg whites

1 teaspoon white vinegar

1 cup castor sugar

1 tablespoon cornflour

½ teaspoon vanilla

TOPPING

300ml thickened cream, whipped

3 bananas

3 passionfruit

1 punnet strawberries

Beat the egg whites and vinegar until stiff. Gradually beat in the sugar, cornflour and add the vanilla. Pile this mixture on a Gladbake lined tray. Shield the sides with foil. Cook on the barbecue with the lid on for 45-60 minutes, or until pale gold. Turn it upside down on to a serving plate. Remove the Gladbake. When it has cooled, top it with whipped cream, sliced bananas, passionfruit pulp and whole strawberries.

Grandpa Magor's Easy Apple Pie

GRANDPA MAGOR'S EASY APPLE PIE

Normal fire, indirect, 30-40 minutes, with lid on. Serves 6.

250g puff pastry

Milk to glaze

Icing sugar

FILLING

2 cans pie apples

Grated rind of 1 lemon

1/4 cup sugar

1 teaspoon cinnamon

1 tablespoon cornflour

Roll out the pastry and cut out 1 circle large enough to cover a 23cm pie dish. Toss all the filling ingredients together and place them in the pie dish. Top with the round of pastry. To get thicker edges, cut strips of left-over pastry and place them around the edge of the pie dish. Neatly trim the edge of the pastry and brush it with water to help the pastry stick. Flute the edges of the pastry with a knife. Cut a slit in the centre, decorate the pie and brush the top with milk. Cook the pie on the barbecue with the lid on, shielding the edges with foil, for 30-40 minutes or until the pastry is cooked and golden brown. Sprinkle it with icing sugar and serve hot with whipped cream.

PINEAPPLE DREAM

Normal fire, indirect, 5-10 minutes, with lid on. Serves 6-8.

1 pineapple

1 punnet strawberries

Grated rind of 1 orange

Cointreau to taste

MERINGUE

4 egg whites

1/2 cup sugar

Cherries to decorate

Cut the pineapple in half, lengthways, leaving the top intact. Remove the core, cut away the flesh and chop it into small pieces. Combine the chopped pineapple, strawberries, orange rind and Cointreau. Mix this well and use it to fill the pineapple shells.

Make the meringue by beating the eggwhites until stiff. Gradually add the sugar and continue beating. Pile this meringue on to pineapple halves and swirl to make it look attractive. Top them with the cherries and cook them on the barbecue with the lid on for 5-10 minutes. Shield the edges with foil to protect them. Turn the pineapples around halfway through cooking to colour them evenly. Serve them topped with passionfruit and strawberries on a platter with other tropical fruits.

178

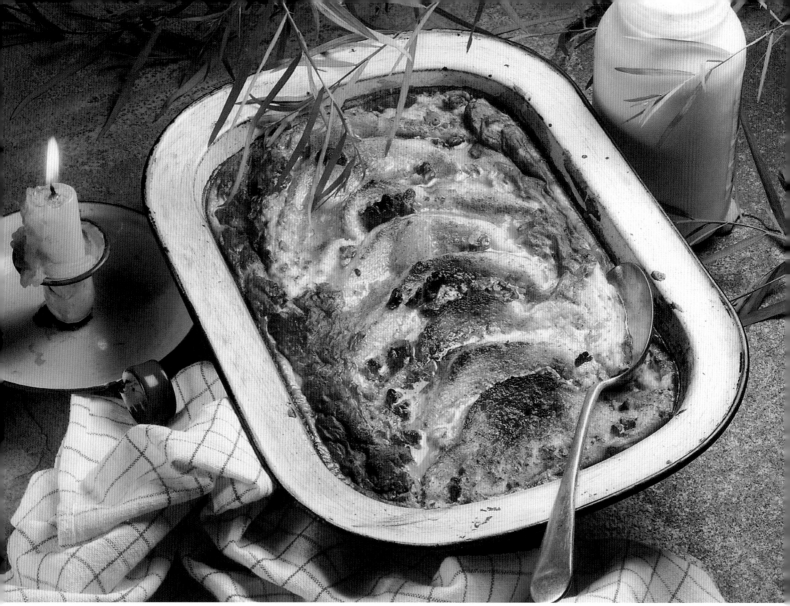

Bread and Butter Pudding

BREAD AND BUTTER PUDDING

Low fire, indirect, 30-40 minutes, with lid on. Serves 6.

4 eggs

1 tablespoon sugar

1 teaspoon vanilla essence

600ml milk

1 tablespoon sultanas

1 tablespoon chopped pineapple (optional)

1 tablespoon chopped walnuts (optional)

2-3 slices bread, crusts removed and buttered

1 teaspoon sugar, extra

1 teaspoon cinnamon

Beat the eggs with the sugar, vanilla and milk. Strain this into a lightly-buttered shallow casserole dish. Add the sultanas, pineapple and nuts.

Cut the bread into fingers or triangles and float them on top of the custard. Sprinkle the pudding with the extra sugar and cinnamon. Cook it on the barbecue with the lid on for 30-40 minutes, or until the custard has set. It should be golden brown and slightly crispy at the edges. Serve warm with whipped cream.

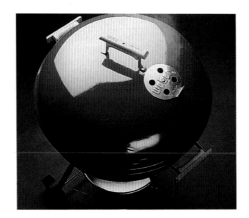

BAKED PINEAPPLE

Low fire, indirect, 40-50 minutes, with lid on. Serves 4.

1 pineapple

2 tablespoons castor sugar

2 tablespoons butter

2 tablespoons rum

Leaving the green top on the pineapple, set it on its side and cut a slice from the top to form a lid. Remove the flesh from the pineapple and cut away the core. Chop the flesh and mix it with the sugar, butter and rum. Place this mixture in the pineapple shell and place the pineapple lid on top, securing it with toothpicks. Wet the green top and wrap it in foil to protect it. Place the pineapple on the barbecue with the lid on and bake for 40-50 minutes until the pineapple is hot and tender. Serve this pineapple hot with icecream.

180

Apple Strudel

APPLE STRUDEL

Normal fire, indirect, 20-30 minutes, with lid on. Serves 8.

2 cans pie apples

¼ cup sultanas

¼ cup brown sugar

½ teaspoon cinnamon

¼ cup chopped almonds

2 teaspoons cornflour

6 sheets filo pastry

250g butter, melted

Combine the apples, sultanas, sugar, cinnamon, almonds and cornflour. Mix them well and set them aside. Layer six sheets of buttered filo pastry one upon the other. Sprinkle the filling over half the pastry. Roll the pastry up, folding the edges to hold the filling intact. Slide the strudel on to foil and brush it with melted butter. Cook it on the barbecue with the lid on, for 20-30 minutes, or until the strudel is golden brown. Sprinkle it with icing sugar and serve it hot or cold. Peaches, apricots, plums or cherries may be used as alternative fillings for the strudel.

SPICY PECAN PIE

Low fire, indirect, 20-30 minutes, with lid on. Serves 6.

PASTRY

¾ cup plain flour

½ cup self raising flour

2 tablespoons castor sugar

125g butter

1 egg yolk, beaten

2-3 tablespoons water

FILLING

3 eggs

½ cup sugar

½ cup golden syrup

60g butter, melted

1 cup pecan nuts

To make the pastry, sift the flour and sugar into a bowl and rub in the butter until the mixture resembles coarse breadcrumbs. Add the egg yolk and sufficient water to make a firm dough. Roll this out and use it to line a 23cm pie dish.

To make the filling beat the eggs lightly and add the sugar, golden syrup and butter. Place the pecan nuts in the pastry-lined pie dish and pour in the filling. Shield the side edges of the pie with foil. Cook it on the barbecue with the lid on for 20-30 minutes. Serve the pie hot or cold with cream or icecream.

PINEAPPLE APRICOT CRUMBLE

Low fire, indirect, 20-30 minutes, with lid on. Serves 6.

2 cans pie apricots

1 can pineapple pieces, drained

CRUMBLE TOPPING

¹/₃ cup brown sugar

1 cup wholemeal self raising flour

90g butter

¹/₂ teaspoon cinnamon

¹/₄ cup walnuts

¹/₂ cup oatmeal

¹/₄ cup cornflakes

Combine all the ingredients for the topping in a food processor until they are crumbly. Place the apricots and pineapple pieces in a shallow pie dish and cover them with the crumble topping. Cook it on the barbecue with the lid on for 20-30 minutes, or until it is golden brown and crisp. Serve it with cream or icecream.

BAKED STUFFED APPLES

Low fire, indirect, 40-50 minutes, with lid on. Serves 4.

4 apples

4 tablespoons brown sugar

2 tablespoons dried fruit and nuts

2 tablespoons butter

2 tablespoons maple syrup

¹/₄ cup sherry

Remove the cores from the apples using an apple-corer. Cut a slit in the skin around the circumference of the apples. Place the apples in a small drip tray. Fill the centres with a mixture of the sugar, fruit and butter. Pour the maple syrup over the apples and the sherry around them. Cook the apples on the barbecue, with the lid on, for 40-50 minutes, or until they are tender. Serve them hot with custard.

FROZEN FRUIT PIES

Low fire, indirect, 20-30 minutes, with lid on.

Leave the pies in their foil dishes. Cook them on the barbecue for 20-30 minutes with the lid on, or until the pastry is golden. Serve them with lashings of cream or icecream.

IRISH APPLECAKE

Low fire, indirect, 30-40 minutes, with lid on. Serves 6-8.

2 cups self raising flour

125g butter, softened

¹/₂ cup castor sugar

4 apples, peeled and roughly chopped

1 egg

Milk

Sugar

Cinnamon

Sift the flour into a bowl and add the butter, castor sugar and apples. Blend them with the beaten egg and sufficient milk to make a batter consistency. Place this in a buttered drip tray and cook on the barbecue with the lid on for 30-40 minutes. Sprinkle the applecake with sugar and cinnamon. Serve it warm with whipped cream.

CREAMED RICE

Low fire, indirect, 1-2 hours, with lid on. Serves 4.

4 tablespoons short grain rice

¹/₄ cup sugar

3¹/₂ cups milk

2 tablespoons cream

Place the rice, sugar and milk in a shallow casserole dish or drip tray. Cook on the barbecue with the lid on for 1-2 hours, stirring from time to time. The rice is ready when the milk is the consistency of thickened cream. Stir in the cream and serve it hot or cold with stewed fruit.

Frozen Fruit Pies

INDIVIDUAL CHOCOLATE SOUFFLÉS

Low fire, indirect, 15-20 minutes, with lid on. Serves 8.

125g butter

4 tablespoons plain flour

1 cup milk

180g chocolate

4 eggs

2 egg whites, extra

¹/₄ cup sugar

¹/₄ cup brandy

Melt the butter in a saucepan, add the flour and stir them until they are smooth. Pour on the milk and bring to the boil, stirring all the time. Add the chocolate and stir until it has melted. Separate the eggs and place all the egg whites in a large bowl. Beat the egg whites until they are stiff, add the sugar and continue beating. Add the egg yolks to the chocolate custard along with the brandy. Stir until it is smooth. Fold the egg whites into the chocolate custard base and spoon it in to individual dishes, filling them to the top. Place the soufflés on the barbecue and cook them with the lid on for 15-20 minutes. Serve them immediately with whipped cream.

Bombe Kosciusko

BOMBE KOSCIUSKO

Normal fire, indirect, 5-10 minutes, with lid on. Serves 8.

Sponge cake, cut in half

1-2 tablespoons liqueur (optional)

425g can of raspberries or other canned berries, drained

2 litres icecream

MERINGUE

6 egg whites

¼ cups castor sugar

TO FINISH

½ cup flaked almonds

2 tablespoons castor sugar

Brandy to flame (optional)

Line an oven tray with foil. Place one layer of the sponge cake on the tray, sprinkle it with half the liqueur and top it with the fruit. Place the icecream, cut to fit, on top of the cake and then finish with another layer of cake. Sprinkle the cake again with the remaining liqueur.

Make the meringue by beating the egg whites until they are stiff, then add the sugar, a little at a time, beating continuously. Coat the cake and the icecream completely with meringue. Sprinkle it with nuts and sugar. If prepared ahead of time, place the Bombe Kosciusko in the freezer until required. When ready to serve the dessert, cook the Bombe on the barbecue with the lid on for 5-10 minutes, or until it is tipped with gold. Flambé with hot brandy or decorate with sparklers.

FRUIT KEBABS

Normal fire, indirect, 5-10 minutes, with lid on. Serves 6-8.

2 bananas, peeled and quartered

2 red apples, skin on and quartered

1 pineapple, peeled, cored and cut into large cubes

½ cup orange juice

GLAZE

¼ cup honey, warmed

1 teaspoon grated orange rind

1 teaspoon lemon juice

60g butter, melted

2 tablespoons rum

¼ teaspoon cinnamon

Place the fruit in a bowl, and pour the orange juice over it. Toss well. Place the fruit alternately on bamboo skewers. Combine the glaze ingredients and brush the glaze over the fruit. Cook the kebabs on the barbecue, with the lid on for 5-8 minutes.

PEARS AND CHOCOLATE SAUCE

Low fire, indirect, 30-40 minutes, with lid on. Serves 4.

4 pears, peeled and cored, stems intact

1 cup water or sauternes

1/3 cup sugar

Strip lemon rind

CHOCOLATE SAUCE

200g cooking chocolate

1 cup cream

1 tablespoon sugar

2 tablespoons brandy

Place the pears in a foil drip tray. Add the water, sugar and lemon rind. Cover the tray with foil and cook it on the barbecue with the lid on, for 30-40 minutes or until the pears are tender. To make the chocolate sauce, place all the ingredients in a drip tray and place it on the barbecue. Cook with the lid on 5-10 minutes, stirring it occasionally until it is smooth.

Drain the pears and spoon over the chocolate sauce. Sprinkle them with toasted almonds and serve with whipped cream.

PLUM DESSERT CAKE

Low fire, indirect, 25-30 minutes, with lid on. Serves 8.

500g fresh or frozen plums, cut up, stones removed

1/4 cup ground almonds

1/2 cup castor sugar

2 teaspoons cornflour

CAKE

2 eggs

1/3 cup sugar

Grated rind of 1 lemon

1/2 cup cream

Self-saucing packet puddings

60g butter

1 1/2 cups self raising flour

Self-saucing Packet Puddings

Place the plums in a shallow casserole dish or buttered drip tray and sprinkle them with the almonds, sugar and cornflour. Combine all the cake ingredients in a food processor to mix them well. Pour this mixture evenly over the plums. Spread it smooth. Place it on the barbecue and cook with the lid on for 25-30 minutes or until the cake is cooked through and golden brown. Serve the cake hot with runny cream.

SELF-SAUCING PACKET PUDDINGS

Low fire, indirect, 20-30 minutes, with lid on. Serves 6.

There are many variations of self-saucing puddings on the market. Follow the instructions on the packet and prepare the dessert in a casserole dish or drip tray. Place it on the barbecue and cook it with the lid on for 20-30 minutes. Serve these puddings hot with cream or icecream.

Honey Bananas

HONEY BANANAS

Low fire, indirect, 15 minutes, with lid on. Serves 6.

125g butter

¹/₂ cup honey

6 bananas in skins, well washed

¹/₄ cup brandy or rum

Place the bananas (still in their skins) in a small drip tray. Add the honey and butter and place the tray on the barbecue. Cook them with the lid on for 15 minutes. When the bananas are tender, remove them and take off their skins. Replace the bananas in the butter and honey mixture, add the rum or brandy and reheat them. Serve them hot with icecream.

BAKED CUSTARD

Low fire, indirect, 30-40 minutes, with lid on. Serves 6.

3 cups milk

4 eggs

2 tablespoons sugar

¹/₂ teaspoon vanilla

¹/₂ teaspoon nutmeg

Beat the milk, eggs, sugar and vanilla until they are well mixed. Pour this mixture in to a lightly-buttered pie dish or drip tray. Sprinkle the top with nutmeg. Cook it on the barbecue with the lid on for 30-40 minutes, or until it has set. Serve the custard with stewed fruit in season. The top may be sprinkled with desiccated coconut if you wish.

SOUFFLE OMELETTE

Low fire, indirect, 8-10 minutes, with lid on. Serves 4.

6 egg whites

¹/₂ cup sugar

4 egg yolks

2-3 tablespoons rum

Icing sugar

Beat the egg whites until they are stiff and then beat in the sugar. Continue beating, adding the egg yolks and rum. Pour this mixture into a well-buttered drip tray. Place it on the barbecue and cook it with the lid on for 8-10 minutes or until it has set. Turn it out and dust it with the icing sugar. Serve the souffle with whipped cream.

BAROSSA PEARS

Low fire, indirect, 25-35 minutes, with lid on. Serves 6.

6 pears

1 cup red wine

¹/₂ cup sugar

Strip lemon rind

Stick cinnamon

1 tablespoon arrowroot

Whipped cream

Slivered almonds

Peel the pears, but leave them whole with their stems intact. Using a melonballer, scoop out the core from the base. Place the pears in a drip tray with the red wine, sugar, lemon rind and cinnamon and cover it loosely with foil. Cook them on the barbecue with the lid on for 25-35 minutes until they are tender, turning the pears halfway through cooking. Blend the arrowroot with a little water and add it to the liquid in the drip tray. Stir it well until the liquid has thickened. Serve the pears hot or cold with whipped cream and slivered almonds.

CHERRIES JUBILEE

Normal fire, indirect, 15 minutes, with lid off. Serves 6.

1 large can or jar pitted cherries

1 teaspoon arrowroot

2 tablespoons water

¹/₄ cup cherry brandy

¹/₄ cup brandy

Drain the cherries and place the juice in a small drip tray. Place the drip tray on the barbecue to one side of the cooking grill over the coals and bring this juice to the boil. Thicken it with the arrowroot blended with water. Add the cherries and stir them until they are heated through. Pour the heated cherry brandy and brandy over the cherries and set it alight. Serve with icecream.

Barossa Pears

Fruit dipped in Chocolate Sauce (sauce page 185)

Pears dipped in Brandy Custard

SWEET SAUCES

HOT CARAMEL SAUCE FOR ICECREAM

50g butter

¹/₂ cup brown sugar

¹/₂ cup water

1 tablespoon golden syrup

3 teaspoons cornflour

¹/₄ cup cream

Place the butter and sugar in a saucepan. Heat it gently until it is thick and syrupy. Combine the remaining ingredients and add them to the mixture. Bring the mixture to the boil and cook gently for 2 minutes. Remove it from the heat and stir in the cream. Pour it lavishly over icecream.

BRANDY CUSTARD

¹/₄ cup custard powder

¹/₃ cup sugar

2 cups milk

2 tablespoons brandy

2 egg yolks, beaten

In a saucepan blend the custard powder, sugar, milk and brandy. Heat the mixture, stirring it occasionally. Beat in the egg yolks and serve.

ALMOND BUTTER SAUCE

125g butter

¹/₂ cup icing sugar

¹/₄ cup ground almonds

¹/₄ cup brandy

Cream the butter and sugar and add the almonds and brandy. Beat the mixture well. Serve this sauce with hot chocolate slab cake, (Recipe page 193) or with your Christmas pudding.

BUTTERSCOTCH CUSTARD

¹/₂ cup brown sugar

2 tablespoons custard powder

¹/₂ cup milk

2 teaspoons butter

1 egg

Combine the brown sugar and custard powder in a bowl. Stir in the milk. Bring this mixture to the boil. Remove from the heat, then beat in the butter and egg until it is smooth. Serve it with your favourite dessert.

Cakes and Breads

The barbecue kettle is a complete baking oven. Breads and cakes baked in a barbecue kettle have the aroma and flavour we remember from the good old days. Imagine beautiful crusts on breads and prize-winning scones, with straight sides and good colour, top and bottom. You don't have to be a cooking genius to make beautiful rustic looking damper. Given some flour, butter, milk and half an hour, any bloke can make it. And if you're into tea parties, you'll need some pink roses, freshly brewed black tea and a delicate cake fork to do justice to our Raging Cream Puffs. What a way to entertain mum!

Quite often you don't have to light a special fire to cook these cakes and breads. If you've already cooked something and there's plenty of heat left in the barbecue, give one of them a try.

Contents

UPSIDE-DOWN CAKE

Low fire, indirect, 25-30 minutes, with lid on.

DECORATION

125g butter

1 cup brown sugar

440g can pineapple rings or pieces

Glacé cherries

CAKE

2 cups self raising flour

1 cup castor sugar

125g butter

2 eggs

1/2 cup milk

1 teaspoon vanilla

Combine the butter and the brown sugar for decoration and spread it over the base of 1 large or 2 small drip trays. Place the pineapple and cherries in a decorative manner on top. Make the cake by combining all the cake ingredients in a food processor and mix them until they are creamy. Pour this mixture over the pineapple decoration and spread it evenly. Place the cake on the barbecue and cook, with the lid on, for 25-30 minutes, or until golden brown. Turn it out upside down and serve hot or cold with cream or icecream.

SULTANA CAKE

Low fire, indirect, 45-60 minutes, with lid on.

500g sultanas

3/4 cup water

1/4 cup sherry

250g butter

1 cup sugar

1 tablespoon cornflour

3 eggs

1 cup self raising flour

1 cup plain flour

Place the sultanas, water and sherry in a saucepan. Boil until nearly all the liquid has evaporated. Allow it to cool slightly.

Upside-down Cake

Cream the butter and sugar until they are well mixed. Add the cornflour, eggs and sultanas and beat them well. Sift the self raising and plain flours. Add them to the mixture and mix them well. Spoon this mixture into a buttered and lined 23cm cake pan. Cook the cake on the barbecue with the lid on, for 45-60 minutes, or until it is cooked and golden brown.

FRUIT MUFFINS

Low fire, indirect, 10-15 minutes, with lid on.

2 cups self raising flour

1 cup castor sugar

1 teaspoon baking powder

90g butter

3/4 cup milk

1 egg, beaten

1 cup blueberries, raspberries or blackberries

Place the flour, sugar, baking powder and butter in a food processor and mix them well. Add the milk and egg and mix to combine. Gently mix in the fruit of your choice. Spoon this mixture into buttered muffin pans. Place them on the barbecue and cook them with the lid on, for 10-15 minutes, or until golden brown. Serve them warm with butter.

CHOCOLATE SLAB CAKE

Low fire, indirect, 30-40 minutes, with lid on.

1 cup cocoa

1½ cups hot water

3 cups self raising flour

250g soft butter

1½ cups castor sugar

4 large eggs

Place the cocoa in the hot water and mix it well. Set it aside to cool slightly. Place all the ingredients in a food processor or mixing bowl and beat them until they are smooth. Pour the mixture into a buttered large drip tray or roasting pan. Cook it on the barbecue with the lid on for 30-40 minutes. The cake is cooked when it begins to shrink from the edges and is springy to touch. Ice it with chocolate icing when cold.

CHOCOLATE ICING

2 cups icing sugar

¼ cup Cocoa

1 egg

60g butter

½ teaspoon vanilla

Combine all the ingredients and mix them well until they are smooth.

BEER CAKE

Low fire, indirect, 30-40 minutes, with lid on.

60g butter, softened

2 cups self raising flour

½ cup sugar

1 egg, beaten

1 cup beer

1 cup mixed dried fruit

½ teaspoon mixed spice

TOPPING

45g butter

½ cup sugar

½ cup plain flour

To make the cake, rub the butter into the flour and then add the sugar, egg, beer, fruit and spice.

Beer Cake

Spoon this mixture into a buttered drip tray or cake pan. Prepare the topping by mixing the butter into the sugar and flour. Sprinkle the topping over the cake. Cook the cake on the barbecue, with the lid on, for 30-40 minutes, or until done. Serve warm and buttered, with coffee.

BEER BREAD

Low fire, indirect, 30-40 minutes, with lid on.

3¼ cups self raising flour

1 teaspoon salt

2 teaspoons sugar

375ml beer

Sift the flour and salt into a bowl. Add the sugar and beer, mixing it into a sticky dough. Knead the dough lightly on a floured surface until it is smooth. Divide the mixture in half and place it in 2 buttered loaf pans or drip trays. Cook them on the barbecue with the lid on, for 30-40 minutes. Serve the bread warm, sliced and spread with butter.

Scones with jam and cream

SCONES

Normal fire, indirect, 15-20 minutes, with lid on.

4 cups self raising flour

1 teaspoon baking powder

1 teaspoon salt

2 tablespoons butter

1½ cups milk

Combine the flour, baking powder and salt in a food processor. Add the butter and process until it is well mixed. Add the milk and mix to form a soft, sticky dough. Turn it out on a floured surface and lightly knead it until it is smooth. Roll the dough out to a 1.5cm thickness. Cut out the scones using a scone cutter. Place the scones on some foil or in a

large drip tray, spacing them evenly. Some scones may be cooked in a drip tray on the charcoal grill. Another layer may be placed on the cooking grill using foil. Cook them on the barbecue-with the lid on, for 15-20 minutes. Serve them hot, either buttered or with jam and cream. Makes approximately 20 scones.

RAGING CREAM PUFFS

Normal fire, indirect, 20-30 minutes, with lid on.

¾ cup water

3 tablespoons butter

¾ cup plain flour

3 eggs

Place the water and butter in a saucepan and bring it to the boil. Remove from the heat, add the flour and beat this well. Allow it to cool slightly and then beat in the eggs one at a time, until the mixture is smooth. Make each cream puff by placing a tablespoon of this mixture on buttered foil. Cook them on the barbecue with the lid on for 20-30 minutes, or until they are well puffed and firm to touch. Do not lift the lid from the barbecue during the first 15 minutes of the cooking time. Immediately the cream puffs are cooked, pierce them with a

skewer to allow the steam to escape. Allow them to cool and serve them filled with sweetened and flavoured whipped cream. Sprinkle them with icing sugar. These puffs can also be filled with icecream and served with chocolate sauce, or used as containers for savoury fillings.

BLUEBERRY CREAM CHEESE STREUSEL CAKE

Low fire, indirect, 30-40 minutes, with lid on.

2½ cups self raising flour

1 cup castor sugar

180g butter

¾ cup milk

2 eggs

1 teaspoon vanilla

FILLING

1 cup ricotta cheese

1 egg

1 tablespoon sugar

Grated rind of 1 lemon

1 cup fresh or frozen blueberries

TOPPING

1 cup reserved cake mixture

½ cup chopped nuts

⅓ cup brown sugar

1 teaspoon cinnamon

Place the flour, sugar and butter in a food processor. Mix it until it is crumbly. Remove 1 cup of this mixture to be used for the topping. To the remainder, add the milk, eggs and vanilla. Beat this mixture well. Pour it into a buttered drip tray and spread it evenly.

To make the filling, blend the ricotta cheese, egg, sugar and lemon until it is smooth. Sprinkle the berries over the cake. Spoon the cheese mixture over the berries spreading it as gently and evenly as possible.

For the topping, mix the reserved cake mixture, nuts, brown-sugar and cinnamon. Sprinkle this over the cheese layer. Cook the cake on the barbecue, with the lid on, for 30-40 minutes, or until it is done when tested with a skewer.

HERBED FRENCH STICK

Normal fire, indirect, 10-15 minutes, with lid on.

French stick

125g butter, softened

1/2 packet French onion soup

1 teaspoon mixed dried herbs

2 tablespoons chopped fresh parsley

Cut the bread into slices from the top but not all the way through. Mix all the remaining ingredients. Spread the mixture on to the slices. Wrap the bread in foil. Cook it on the barbecue with the lid on, for 10-15 minutes, to heat it through. If a crusty exterior is required, leave the foil wrapping open at the top.

GARLIC BREAD

Normal fire, indirect, 10-15 minutes, with lid on.

French stick

125g butter

2 cloves garlic, pressed

Cut the bread into slices from the top, but not all the way through. Mix the butter and garlic. Spread the garlic butter on the bread slices. Wrap the bread in foil. Cook it on the barbecue with the lid on, for 10-15 minutes, to heat it through. If a crusty exterior is required, leave the foil wrapping open at the top.

FRENCH STICKS

Normal fire, indirect, 25-30 minutes, with lid on.

1 tablespoon dry yeast

1 1/2 cups warm water

4 1/2 cups plain or bread flour

2 tablespoons castor sugar

1 teaspoon salt

3 tablespoons soft butter

1 egg white

2 tablespoons milk

Sesame or poppy seeds

Combine the dry yeast with 1/2 cup of the warm water. Mix this well and it let stand while the other ingredients are being prepared. Place 2 cups of the flour in a food processor. Add the sugar, salt, butter, egg white and the remaining water. Mix them well. Then pour in the yeast and water mixture and beat it well until it is smooth. Place 2 cups of flour in another bowl, pour the batter onto this flour and mix it well. Cover the bowl and place the mixture in a warm place. Allow the dough to rise until it doubles in size (about 1 hour). Turn it out onto a floured surface and knead it well. Form the dough into 2 French sticks and place them in bread tins, or on a foil-lined tray. Cut slits in the top of them and allow them to rise in a warm place until double in size. Brush the tops with milk and sprinkle with sesame or poppy seeds. Place the bread on the barbecue and cook, with the lid on, for 25-30 minutes. The bread should have a good crust and be coloured underneath. Tap the base and it should give a hollow sound when cooked. Serve the bread sliced, with butter and wait for the sounds of appreciation from your guests.

DATE AND CHOCOLATE CHIP CAKE

Low fire, indirect, 30-40 minutes, with lid on.

CAKE

1 cup chopped dates

1 teaspoon bi-carbonate of soda

1 cup boiling water

180g butter, softened

3/4 cup castor sugar

2 eggs, well beaten

1 1/2 cups self raising flour

TOPPING

1/2 cup chopped nuts

1/4 cup castor sugar

180g choc bits

Place the dates in a bowl and sprinkle the soda over them. Pour the boiling water over them. Allow the mixture to stand for 15 minutes.

Mix the remaining ingredients together and add the date mixture to this. Pour it into a buttered drip tray and sprinkle it with the topping.

Make the topping by mixing all the ingredients. Cook the cake on the barbecue, with the lid on for 30-40 minutes, or until the cake is done when tested with a skewer.

CHOCOLATE APPLE CAKE

Low fire, indirect, 30-40 minutes, with lid on.

3 eggs

1 1/2 cups castor sugar

250g butter, softened

1/2 cup water or apple cider

2 1/2 cups self raising flour

2 tablespoons cocoa

1 teaspoon bi-carbonate of soda

1 teaspoon cinnamon

1 teaspoon allspice

1 cup chopped nuts

100g choc bits

2 cups chopped, peeled apples

1 tablespoon vanilla essence

To make the cake, beat the eggs, sugar, butter and water until it is fluffy. Sift the flour, cocoa, soda, cinnamon and allspice together. Add this to the egg mixture and beat it until it is thoroughly combined. Fold in the nuts, choc bits, apples and vanilla. Pour the mixture into a buttered drip tray. Cook it on the barbecue, with the lid on, for 30-40 minutes. Cool, then ice it with chocolate icing. (Recipe page 193).

PACKET CAKES

Low fire, indirect, 20-25 minutes, with lid on.

Any variety of packet cake

Follow the instructions on the packet and prepare it as directed. Cook it on the barbecue, with the lid on, for 20-25 minutes, or until cooked. Decorate it as desired.

Freshly baked bread

FRUITY WHOLEMEAL LOAF

Low fire, indirect, 45-60 minutes, with lid on.

1 cup plain wholemeal flour

1 cup self raising flour

1 teaspoon baking powder

1/2 teaspoon nutmeg

1/2 teaspoon cinnamon

185g butter

1 cup soft brown sugar

3 eggs, beaten

1/2 cup chopped, dried apricots

1/2 cup chopped raisins

1/2 cup sultanas

1/2 cup chopped mixed nuts

3 tablespoons milk

Sift together the flours, baking powder, nutmeg and cinnamon. Place the butter and sugar in a food processor and mix them until they are light. Add the eggs to the mixture and beat them in one at a time. Now combine the flour mixture, egg mixture and the fruit, nuts and milk, mixing them well. Place this in a buttered loaf pan. Cook the loaf on the barbecue with the lid on, for 45-60 minutes. Serve the loaf sliced and buttered.

CHEESE AND WALNUT LOAF

Normal fire, indirect, 30-40 minutes, with lid on.

1 tablespoon dry yeast

1 teaspoon sugar

1/2 cup warm water

2 eggs, beaten

1/3 cup oil

2 3/4 cups plain flour

1 teaspoon salt

1 cup grated cheese

1 cup chopped walnuts

Combine the yeast, sugar and warm water. Allow it to stand for a few minutes. Place the yeast mixture, eggs, oil, 1 cup of the flour and salt in a food processor and mix them well. Add the remaining flour. Allow it to rise, covered, in a warm place until it has doubled in size (about 1 hour). Turn it out on to a floured surface and roll it out to a large round. Place the cheese and nuts in the centre and encase them with the dough. Knead well to incorporate the filling. Shape it into a loaf and place it in a buttered bread pan. Press it well into the corners. Allow it to rise in a warm place until it has doubled in size. Cook it on the barbecue with the lid on, for 30-40 minutes, or until it is golden

brown and sounds hollow when tapped. Serve the loaf sliced and buttered.

IRISH SODA BREAD

Normal fire, indirect, 25-30 minutes, with lid on.

2 cups wholewheat plain flour

1 1/2 cups self raising flour

1/2 cup quick cooking oats

1 tablespoon sugar

1 teaspoon salt

1 teaspoon bi-carbonate of soda

3 tablespoons butter

1 1/2 cups buttermilk or sour milk

1 large egg, beaten

Combine the plain flour, self raising flour, oats, sugar, salt and soda in a large bowl. Rub in the butter. Combine the buttermilk and egg in a separate bowl. Add this to the flour mixture and mix it to form a dough. Knead the dough lightly on a floured surface until it is smooth. Place the dough on buttered foil. Cut a deep cross in the centre of the loaf with a sharp knife dipped in flour. Cook the loaf on the barbecue for 25-30 minutes with the lid on. The bread is cooked if it sounds hollow when the bottom is tapped. Serve the loaf sliced, with butter.

BREAD ROLLS USING BREAD MIX

Normal fire, indirect, 25-30 minutes, with lid on.

1kg packet bread mix

2 tablespoons milk

1 tablespoon poppy seeds, or sesame seeds

Follow the directions on the packet and divide the mixture into 20 pieces. Roll the pieces into balls and place them on buttered foil. Allow them to rise until they have doubled in size (about 45 minutes). Brush them with the milk and sprinkle them with the poppy or sesame seeds. Cook them on the barbecue, with the lid on, for 25-30 minutes, or until they are golden brown. If you have any difficulty in obtaining the bread mix, use the recipe for French sticks on page 197.

Dinkum Damper

DINKUM DAMPER

Normal fire, indirect, 20-30 minutes, with lid on.

3 cups self raising flour

1 teaspoon salt

3 tablespoons butter, softened

¹/₂ cup milk

¹/₂ cup water

Combine all the ingredients and mix them to form a sticky dough. Knead it lightly on a floured surface. Place it in a small buttered drip tray. With a sharp knife, cut slits across the top 1cm deep. Brush the top with milk and sprinkle it with a little sifted flour. Cook the damper on the barbecue, with the lid on, for 20-30 minutes, or until golden brown. Serve it sliced and buttered.

WHOLEWHEAT BREAD

Normal fire, indirect, 30-40 minutes, with lid on.

1 tablespoon dry yeast

1 cup milk, warmed

1 cup water, warmed

5 cups wholewheat plain flour

2 cups plain flour

1 teaspoon salt

1 tablespoon sesame or poppy seeds

1 egg to glaze

Dissolve the yeast in the milk and water. Add the flours and salt. Mix them in well. Knead the dough until it is smooth. Allow it to rise in a warm place for 1 hour. Knead and shape it into 2 loaves and place them in buttered loaf pans. Brush the top of each with the egg glaze and sprinkle them with the seeds. Set them in a warm place to rise again for 30-40 minutes. Cook on the barbecue with the lid on, for 30-40 minutes, or until they are golden brown and sound hollow when tapped.

Glazes, Stuffings and Sauces

Contents

APRICOT CURRY GLAZE

For ribs or pork chops.

2 tablespoons oil

1 medium onion, chopped

1 clove garlic, pressed

3 teaspoons curry powder

1 cup apricot nectar

1 cup brown sugar

2 tablespoons cider vinegar

$1/2$ teaspoon Tabasco sauce

In a medium saucepan, heat the oil and cook the onion and garlic until they are golden. Stir in the curry powder and cook for 1 minute longer. Stir in the apricot nectar, brown sugar, vinegar and Tabasco. Simmer for 5-10 minutes, stirring frequently, until the sugar has dissolved.

APRICOT GLAZE

For lamb, pork or poultry.

1 cup apricot jam

$1/2$ teaspoon crushed rosemary

Salt and pepper to taste

1 clove garlic, pressed

1 tablespoon vinegar

1 teaspoon Dijon mustard

In a saucepan, combine all of the ingredients and heat them gently until the jam has become thin and runny.

ORANGE GLAZE

For ham, duck or chicken.

$2/3$ cup orange juice

1 cup brown sugar

$1/2$ teaspoon ground ginger

In a small saucepan, combine the orange juice, sugar and ginger. Heat the mixture, stirring, until it becomes thick and bubbly.

PINEAPPLE RUM GLAZE

For pork, chicken, turkey or duck.

1 cup pineapple jam

2 tablespoons rum

$1/8$ teaspoon ground cloves

$1/8$ teaspoon ground nutmeg

In a saucepan, combine all the ingredients. Gently heat them, stirring constantly to mix them well.

CRANBERRY GLAZE

For turkey, lamb, beef or venison.

1 jar cranberry sauce

$1/2$ cup red wine

2 tablespoons brown sugar

1 tablespoon tarragon vinegar

2 teaspoons cornflour

Place all the ingredients in a saucepan and mix them well. Heat the mixture until it becomes bubbly and thick.

CITRUS GLAZE

For lamb, pork, chicken or duck.

1 cup orange marmalade

1 tablespoon lemon juice

2 tablespoons brown sugar

Place all the ingredients in a saucepan and heat, stirring, until they are hot and well blended.

PEACH GLAZE

For chicken, quail, turkey or fish.

1 cup peach jam

2 tablespoons teriyaki sauce

1 teaspoon grated fresh ginger

Place all the ingredients in a saucepan and heat, stirring, until they are hot and well blended.

REDCURRANT GLAZE

For beef, poultry or game.

1 cup redcurrant jelly

2 tablespoons port wine

$1/2$ cup brown sugar

Place all the ingredients in a saucepan and heat, stirring, until they are hot and well blended.

BROWN SUGAR GLAZE

For salmon, ham or poultry.

1 cup brown sugar

60g butter

2 tablespoons lemon juice

Place all the ingredients in a saucepan and heat, stirring, until they are hot and well blended.

MINT GLAZE

For lamb.

1 jar mint jelly

$1/2$ cup brown sugar

Place the jelly and sugar in a saucepan and heat, stirring, until they are hot and well blended.

BEER GLAZE

For lamb shanks, pork ribs or beef.

$1/2$ cup beer

1 cup brown sugar

2 teaspoons hot pepper sauce

2 teaspoons prepared mustard

In a saucepan, combine all the ingredients and mix them well. Heat the mixture gently until the sugar has dissolved.

HERB STUFFING

For poultry, fish or meat.

3 cups white breadcrumbs

1/2 cup chopped parsley

1/4 cup pine nuts, toasted

4 spring onions, chopped

Grated rind of 1 lemon

1 1/2 tablespoons fresh chopped marjoram

1 1/2 tablespoons fresh chopped thyme

Pinch nutmeg

30g butter, cut into cubes

2 eggs, beaten

Salt and pepper to taste

1/3 cup milk

In a large bowl, combine all the ingredients except the milk. Then mix this with the milk to form a soft, but not soggy, stuffing for use with poultry, fish, or meat.

HAM AND NUT STUFFING

For poultry.

1 cup chopped ham

I onion, chopped

2 cups fresh breadcrumbs

1/2 cup pine nuts

2 tablespoons mixed herbs

1/2 teaspoon salt

2 tablespoons chopped parsley

1/4 teaspoon nutmeg

1/4 teaspoon black pepper

Grated rind of 1 lemon

2 tablespoons softened butter

1 egg

Combine all the ingredients and mix them well. Use this stuffing to fill a turkey or chicken.

WALNUT STUFFING

For poultry.

1 tablespoon butter

1 chicken or turkey liver (optional)

1 onion, chopped

1/2 cup chopped mushrooms

1/2 cup fresh breadcrumbs

1/2 cup chopped walnuts

1 hard boiled egg, chopped

1 teaspoon grated nutmeg

1 teaspoon mace

1/2 teaspoon thyme

1 tablespoon chopped parsley

1/4 teaspoon celery salt

1/4 teaspoon pepper

1 tablespoon brandy

Melt the butter and cook the liver. Remove the liver and chop it into small pieces. Add the onion and mushrooms to the pan and sauté them until they are tender. Add the remaining ingredients and use the mixture to fill a chicken or turkey. It may also be cooked in a Glad oven bag alongside the poultry.

RICE STUFFING

For poultry.

60g butter

125g mushrooms, sliced

1 onion, chopped

2 cups cooked brown rice

1 tablespoon pine nuts

Salt and pepper to taste

1 egg, beaten

Melt the butter in a saucepan. Add the onion and mushrooms and cook for 2-3 minutes. Add the rice, pine nuts, salt and pepper. Cool this mixture and bind it with the egg. Use it to fill chicken, turkey, or duck. It may also be cooked in a Glad oven bag alongside the bird.

MANGO STUFFING

For poultry.

1 tablespoon butter

1 onion, finely chopped

425g can mango slices

2 cups wholemeal breadcrumbs

1 stalk celery, finely chopped

1/4 cup chopped walnuts

Salt and pepper to taste

1/2 teaspoon oregano

Melt the butter and sauté the onion until it is tender. Chop 1/2 the mango slices and reserve the remainder. Combine the chopped mango, breadcrumbs, celery, walnuts, salt, pepper, oregano and onion. Use this mixture to fill a chicken or turkey. Garnish it with the reserved mango slices.

CASHEW STUFFING

For poultry.

1 onion, chopped

1 clove garlic, pressed

1 cup chopped celery

2 tablespoons butter

1 cup chopped salted cashews

2 cups cooked brown rice

1 1/2 tablespoons dry sherry

2 teaspoons chopped parsley

1 teaspoon mixed herbs

Pinch thyme

1 teaspoon salt

1/2 teaspoon black pepper

1/2 teaspoon ground ginger

1/2 teaspoon grated nutmeg

Sauté the onion, garlic and celery in the butter. Combine this with all the remaining ingredients. Use this stuffing to fill a chicken or turkey.

WAIST WATCHER'S CAPER SAUCE

For fish.

1¹/₂ tablespoons flour

Salt and white pepper to taste

²/₃ cup undiluted evaporated low-fat milk

¹/₃ cup water

¹/₂ teaspoon onion powder

2 tablespoons capers, chopped

Whisk the flour, salt, pepper and a small amount of the low-fat milk in a saucepan. Stir in the remaining milk, water, onion powder and capers. Cook over a medium heat, stirring constantly until the mixture comes to the boil and thickens.

WAIST WATCHER'S MUSTARD TARRAGON SAUCE

For fish.

1¹/₂ tablespoons flour

Salt and pepper to taste

²/₃ cup undiluted evaporated low-fat milk

¹/₃ cup water

¹/₄ teaspoon crushed tarragon leaves

1 tablespoon prepared mustard

Whisk the flour, salt, pepper and a small amount of the low-fat milk in a saucepan. Stir in the remaining milk, water, tarragon leaves and mustard. Cook over a medium heat, stirring constantly until the mixture boils and thickens. Serve this sauce over barbecued fish.

WAIST WATCHER'S DILL SAUCE

For fish.

1¹/₂ tablespoons flour

Salt and pepper to taste

²/₃ cup undiluted evaporated low-fat milk

¹/₃ cup water

1 clove garlic, pressed

¹/₈ teaspoon mustard powder

¹/₂ teaspoon dill

Whisk the flour, salt, pepper and a small amount of the low-fat milk in a saucepan. Stir in the remaining milk, water, garlic, mustard powder and dill. Cook this over a medium heat, stirring constantly until the mixture boils and thickens. Serve this sauce over barbecued fish.

AVOCADO BEARNAISE SAUCE

For steak, vegetables or fish.

4 tablespoons white vinegar

1 small onion, finely chopped

6 peppercorns

4 egg yolks

250g butter

1 tablespoon lemon Juice

Salt and pepper to taste

1 ripe avocado, stoned, peeled and chopped

In a pan combine the vinegar, onion and peppercorns and bring them to the boil. Reduce the heat and simmer very gently, uncovered, until the mixture is reduced by half. Strain the mixture, reserve the liquid and allow it to cool. Place the egg yolks in a small saucepan, with the reserved liquid and mix this over a very gentle heat. (This may best be achieved by placing the small saucepan in a large saucepan containing gently boiling water.) Mix this well. Melt the butter, cool it and then gradually add it to the mixture. Stir constantly until the mixture is thick and creamy, then remove it from the heat immediately. Add the lemon juice and season with salt and pepper. Put the sauce in a blender, add the avocado and mix it in until it is smooth. Serve it with steak, vegetables or fish.

SAUCE VERONIQUE

For chicken or fish.

¹/₂ cup chicken stock

¹/₂ cup cream

2 tablespoons butter

2 tablespoons plain flour

2 egg yolks

1 tablespoon lemon juice

³/₄ cup peeled, halved, seedless, green grapes

Nutmeg

Salt and pepper to taste

In a saucepan heat the stock and the cream to make a cream mixture. In another pan melt the butter, add the flour and cook it over a gentle heat for 2-3 minutes, stirring. Remove this pan from the heat and whisk in the cream mixture. Cook this over a moderate heat for 5 minutes, stirring occasionally to make a sauce. In a bowl beat the egg yolks lightly with the lemon juice and beat in three tablespoons of the sauce. Add this mixture to the remaining sauce. Cook the sauce over a low heat, stirring until it is thick, but do not let it boil. Add the grapes, nutmeg, salt and pepper. Serve it with fish or chicken.

FLAMINGO SAUCE

For meat or poultry.

2 onions

2 tablespoons oil

2 tomatoes

1 red pepper

1 teaspoon paprika

Salt and pepper to taste

Lightly fry the onions in the oil. Peel the tomatoes and cut them into thin slices. Remove the seeds from the red pepper and cut its flesh into thin strips. Add the tomatoes and red pepper strips to the onions with the paprika, salt and pepper. Stir the mixture and simmer it until it is ready to be used.

CUCUMBER SAUCE

For fish.

1 cucumber, peeled and chopped

1 small onion

1 clove garlic, pressed

1 teaspoon lemon juice

3 tablespoons sour cream

2 tablespoons Worcestershire sauce

1 teaspoon mayonnaise

Salt and pepper to taste

Combine the cucumber with the chopped onion and garlic. Mash them together and pour off any excess liquid. Combine this mixture with the remaining ingredients and chill them well.

SEAFOOD COCKTAIL SAUCE

For barbecued fish.

2 egg yolks

90g butter

2 teaspoons lemon juice

$^1/_2$ teaspoon Tabasco

2 teaspoons tomato paste

2 tablespoons cream

Combine the egg yolks, butter and lemon juice in a small saucepan and mix over a very gentle heat (this may best be achieved by placing the small saucepan inside a larger saucepan containing gently boiling water). Stir until the sauce has thickened. Remove the sauce from the heat. Stir in the Tabasco and tomato paste, mixing it well. Stir in the cream. Pour the sauce in to a bowl. Cover it and allow it to cool.

HEARTY PRAWN SAUCE

For fish, vegetables or steak.

500g green prawns in their shells

2 cups water

$^1/_3$ cup cream

1 egg yolk

Salt and pepper to taste

Shell and de-vein the prawns, saving the shells. Place the shells in water in a pan and bring it to the boil. Reduce the heat and simmer for 15 minutes. Strain the stock through a fine sieve to remove the shells. Return the stock to the pan, bring it to the boil and add the prawn meat. Cook them until they are just tender - about 2 minutes. Drain them immediately, reserving $^1/_2$ cup of the stock. Place the reserved stock, cream and egg yolk in a pan. Stir this over a low heat until the sauce thickens. Do not allow it to boil. Add the prawns and mix everything well. Season the sauce with salt and pepper.

SOUR CREAM DILL SAUCE

For fish.

1 cup sour cream

2 tablespoons white vinegar

1 tablespoon lemon juice

1 teaspoon Dijon mustard

Salt and pepper to taste

$^1/_2$ cup oil

$^1/_4$ cup chopped fresh dill

Combine the sour cream, vinegar, lemon juice, mustard, salt and pepper. While beating, add the oil in a stream. Beat in the dill and serve this sauce with your favourite fish.

TARTARE SAUCE

For fish.

$1^1/_2$ cups mayonnaise

1 tablespoon chopped sweet gherkin

1 teaspoon Dijon mustard

1 teaspoon chopped capers

1 teaspoon chopped parsley

1 teaspoon chopped fresh chervil, or $^1/_4$ teaspoon dried chervil

1 teaspoon chopped fresh tarragon, or $^1/_4$ teaspoon dried tarragon

$^1/_2$ teaspoon anchovy paste

To the mayonnaise add all the remaining ingredients and mix them well. Serve this sauce with your favourite fish.

EASY MOCK HOLLANDAISE

Serve with fish and vegetables.

1 can cream celery soup

1 tablespoon lemon juice

$^1/_4$ cup mayonnaise

Blend the ingredients and heat them slowly, stirring frequently. Pour this sauce over fish or vegetables.

ALMOND AND SESAME SAUCE

For fish.

$^2/_3$ cup blanched almonds

2 tablespoons sesame seeds, toasted

60g butter

$1^1/_2$ tablespoons chopped parsley

Salt and pepper to taste

Using a food processor, grind the almonds and sesame seeds until the mixture is smooth. Add the butter and the parsley and soften them by mixing. Puree the mixture until it is light and fluffy. Add salt and pepper to taste.

BOURBON BARBECUE SAUCE

For meat.

1 cup tomato sauce

$^1/_3$ cup Bourbon

$^1/_4$ cup treacle

$^1/_4$ cup vinegar

1 tablespoon worcestershire sauce

2 teaspoons soy sauce

$^1/_2$ teaspoon mustard powder

$^1/_4$ teaspoon pepper

2 cloves garlic, pressed

1 tablespoon lemon juice

Mix all the ingredients together and allow them to stand for several hours. Use this mixture as a marinade, or basting sauce for hamburgers, steaks, sausages and all other meats.

CREAMY MUSHROOM SAUCE

For steaks, veal and chicken.

60g butter

1 onion, chopped

100g button mushrooms, sliced

1 teaspoon Dijon mustard

1 cup cream

Salt and pepper to taste

Melt the butter and saute the onion and mushrooms. Add the mustard and cream and boil this mixture rapidly. Season it with salt and pepper and reduce it to a suitable consistency. Serve this mushroom sauce with the meat of your choice.

GREEN PEPPERCORN SAUCE

For steak.

30g butter

1 tablespoon flour

$^1/_2$ cup dry white wine

2 teaspoons dry sherry

$^1/_2$ cup water

1 beef stock cube

$^1/_2$ teaspoon sugar

2 tablespoons canned green peppercorns

2 tablespoons cream

Melt the butter and add the flour, stirring it well. Stir in the wine, sherry, water, stock cube, sugar and green peppercorns. Bring this mixture to the boil and then reduce the heat and simmer it for 3 minutes. Add the cream and pour this sauce over the steak.

BARBECUE SAUCE

For meat.

1 onion, finely chopped

2 tablespoons oil

Salt and pepper to taste

1 cup tomato sauce

2 tablespoons tomato chutney

1 tablespoon Worcestershire sauce

1 tablespoon vinegar

Cook the chopped onion in heated oil until it has softened. Add all the other ingredients and bring the mixture to the boil, stirring it constantly. Lower the heat and simmer for 15-20 minutes. Use this sauce hot or cold at your next barbecue.

SATAY STEAK SAUCE

1 onion, finely chopped

2 tablespoons oil

Salt and pepper to taste

1 cup tomato sauce

1 tablespoon Worcestershire sauce

1 tablespoon vinegar

2 tablespoons peanut butter

1 clove garlic, pressed

$^1/_2$ teaspoon chilli powder

Cook the chopped onion in heated oil until it has softened. Add all the remaining ingredients and bring them to the boil, stirring constantly. Lower the heat and simmer for 15-20 minutes. Serve this sauce hot or cold.

SWEET AND SOUR SAUCE

For chicken and fish.

1 onion, sliced

1 green pepper, sliced

2 tablespoons oil

1 can pineapple pieces with syrup

1 tablespoon tomato paste

1 tablespoon brown sugar

2-3 tablespoons vinegar

1 small can mixed Chinese pickles, sliced

Salt and pepper to taste

Cook the onion and the green pepper in heated oil until they have softened. Add the remaining ingredients. Simmer for 7-10 minutes and serve hot.

EGG AND CUCUMBER SAUCE

For chicken or fish.

1$^1/_2$ cups mayonnaise

2 hard boiled eggs, chopped

3 tablespoons chopped cucumber

Dash Tabasco sauce

3 tablespoons cream

Salt and pepper to taste

Combine all the ingredients and serve warm or chilled.

SPICY ONION SAUCE

For steaks.

3 tablespoons French onion soup mix

1 tablespoon sugar

Salt and pepper to taste

1 tablespoon prepared mustard

$^3/_4$ cup water

$^1/_2$ cup tomato sauce

$^1/_4$ cup cider vinegar

1 tablespoon lemon juice

Combine all the ingredients in a saucepan. Simmer them, covered, for 10 minutes. Brush this sauce over your steaks while cooking them and then serve it with them.

SAUCE AURORA

For meatloaf, veal, chops or chicken.

1 can condensed tomato soup

$^1/_4$ cup cream

1 tablespoon chopped parsley

1 tablespoon snipped chives

1 teaspoon Worcestershire sauce

1 tablespoon sweet sherry

In a saucepan combine all the ingredients and simmer them until they are boiling. Spoon the sauce over the meatloaf, veal, chops or chicken.

MOCK SAUCE BECHAMEL

For vegetables.

¹/₄ **cup chopped onions**

60g butter

1 can cream of chicken soup

2 egg yolks

³/₄ **cup cream**

Saute the onions in the butter until they are a pale golden brown. Stir in the soup, egg yolks and cream. Cook this mixture over a low heat, stirring constantly until it bubbles and thickens. Serve this chunky sauce whenever a white sauce is required.

CHILLI SPICE SAUCE

For meat or poultry.

1 onion, chopped

1 clove garlic, pressed

1-2 teaspoons chilli powder

¹/₄ **cup red wine**

¹/₄ **cup spicy plum sauce**

2 tablespoons brown sugar

¹/₂ **teaspoon oregano leaves**

Combine all the ingredients and simmer them for 10 minutes. Serve this sauce with meat or poultry.

SPICY TOMATO SAUCE

For beef, lamb or chicken.

2 cups spaghetti tomato sauce

1 tablespoon Worcestershire sauce

3 tablespoons cider vinegar

2 cloves garlic, pressed

Salt and pepper to taste

Place the spaghetti sauce, Worcestershire sauce, vinegar and garlic in a saucepan. Mix them well and bring it to the boil. Simmer for 8-10 minutes and then season it with salt and pepper. This sauce is delicious served with beef, lamb or chicken.

BARBECUE SWEET AND SOUR SAUCE

For fish, chicken or pork.

³/₄ **cup unsweetened pineapple juice**

¹/₄ **cup cider vinegar**

3 teaspoons soy sauce

1¹/₂ **tablespoons sugar**

¹/₄ **cup thin strips red pepper**

¹/₂ **cup chicken stock**

2 teaspoons finely chopped fresh ginger

1¹/₂ **tablespoons cornflour**

¹/₃ **cup water**

Combine all the ingredients and heat them, stirring until the mixture boils. Simmer for 2-3 minutes. Serve this sauce hot with fish, chicken or pork.

LEMON SAUCE

For fish, chicken and vegetables.

125g butter

2 tablespoons lemon juice

2 teaspoons Worcestershire sauce

Salt and pepper to taste

2 tablespoons chopped parsley

Melt the butter in a saucepan, add the remaining ingredients except the parsley and mix them well. Stir in the parsley just before serving.

FRUITY SAUCE

For chicken, fish or pork.

2 tablespoons finely chopped onion

30g butter

¹/₂ **cup apricot nectar**

¹/₄ **cup cider vinegar**

¹/₄ **cup spicy plum sauce**

1 tablespoon Worcestershire sauce

1 tablespoon brown sugar

Combine all the ingredients and bring them to the boil. Boil for 1-2 minutes and serve with chicken, fish or pork.

SPICY WINE SAUCE

For pork, beef, lamb and chicken.

2 cups red wine

1 onion, finely chopped

2 cloves

2 whole allspice

Small piece cinnamon stick

2 tablespoons spicy plum sauce

¹/₄ **cup honey**

2 tablespoons flour

Salt and pepper to taste

Combine all the ingredients and mix them well. Bring them to the boil over a gentle heat, stirring all the time. Simmer for 5-10 minutes and then serve.

CHERRY SAUCE

For ham, duck or pheasant.

440g can pitted dark cherries

¹/₂ **cup port wine**

Grated rind of 1 orange

Juice of 1 lemon

2 tablespoons arrowroot

In a saucepan combine all the ingredients and bring them to the boil. Simmer for 2-3 minutes. Serve the sauce hot over sliced ham, duck or pheasant.

TOMATO ONION SAUCE

For chicken, beef or lamb.

30g butter

1 clove garlic, pressed

1 onion, finely chopped

440g can tomatoes

¹/₂ **cup water**

In a pan, melt the butter and saute the garlic and onion. Add the mashed, undrained tomatoes and water. Bring this mixture to the boil. Reduce the heat and simmer it, uncovered for 15 minutes. Serve this sauce with chicken, beef, or lamb.

ORANGE & LEMON SAUCE

For duck, ham, pork, chicken or veal.

1 lemon

1 cup marmalade

2 tablespoons port wine

$^1/_2$ teaspoon mustard powder

$^1/_2$ teaspoon French mustard

$^1/_4$ cup water

Remove the rind from the lemon using a vegetable peeler. Cut the rind into thin strips 5 cm in length. Place the rind in a pan of boiling water. Simmer it for 2-3 minutes, then strain it. Heat the marmalade in a pan until it has melted. Add the port, mustards, 1 tablespoon of juice from the lemon, water and lemon rind. Cook gently for 3-5 minutes. Serve over duck, ham, pork, chicken or veal.

AVOCADO SAUCE

For chicken, fish or vegetables.

2 large avocados

1 tablespoon lemon juice

Salt and pepper to taste

2 tablespoons oil

2 cloves garlic, pressed

2 tablespoons cream

Peel, stone and mash the avocados, but do not puree them. Mix in the lemon juice and add the salt and pepper. Heat the oil in a pan, add the garlic, then the avocado mixture. Heat this without boiling and stir in the cream. Serve it hot over chicken, fish or vegetables.

ONION SAUCE

For chicken, fish, lamb, beef or vegetables.

60g butter

1 onion, sliced

440g can tomatoes

1 packet French onion soup mix

1 tablespoon soy sauce

1 cup water

3 teaspoons cornflour

1 tablespoon water, extra

Melt the butter in a pan and add the onion. Cook until the onion is tender. Add the undrained mashed tomatoes, soup mix, soy sauce and water. Bring this mixture to the boil and simmer it for 5-10 minutes. Blend the cornflour with the extra water and then add it to the mixture. Continue stirring until the sauce boils. Serve it with chicken, fish, lamb, beef or vegetables.

CURRY SAUCE

For pork, chicken, fish or vegetables.

2 tablespoons oil

1 onion, chopped

2 tablespoons sultanas

1 teaspoon curry powder

$^3/_4$ cup water

1 teaspoon cornflour

1 teaspoon water, extra

Heat the oil in a pan and add the onion. Cook until the onion is transparent. Add the sultanas, curry powder and water. Blend the cornflour with the extra water, then gradually stir it in to the mixture. Stir until the sauce boils and thickens. Serve it with pork, chicken, fish or vegetables.

APPLE SAUCE WITH NUTMEG

For pork or ham.

2kg apples

1 cup soft brown sugar

1 cup apple cider

2 tablespoons lemon juice

$^1/_2$ teaspoon nutmeg

Peel and core the apples, slice them into eighths and set them aside in a drip tray. Place the sugar and cider in a pan and heat, stirring, until the sugar dissolves. Remove the mixture from the heat and add the lemon juice and nutmeg. Pour this over the apples.

Cover the drip tray and bake them on the barbecue with the lid on, for 45 minutes, or until the apples are soft. Mash them to a desired consistency. Serve this sauce with pork or ham.

CHIVE SAUCE

For chicken, fish or vegetables.

30g butter

$^3/_4$ cup water

1 chicken stock cube

1 tablespoon lemon juice

2 teaspoons cornflour

1 tablespoon cream

Salt and pepper to taste

2 tablespoons snipped chives

Melt the butter in a pan and add the water and stock cube. Mix them well. Add the lemon juice, cornflour and cream to make a sauce. Heat and stir until the sauce boils and thickens. Reduce the heat and simmer for 2 minutes. Add the salt and pepper and stir in the chives. Serve it with chicken, fish or vegetables.

PORT AND MUSHROOM SAUCE

For beef, lamb or chicken.

60g butter

1 onion, chopped

100g mushrooms, sliced

$^3/_4$ cup chicken stock

$^1/_4$ cup red wine

1 tablespoon port wine

Salt and pepper to taste

1 tablespoon cornflour

1 tablespoon chopped parsley

Heat the butter in a pan. Add the onion and cook it until it is tender. Add the mushrooms and cook for a further 2-3 minutes. Add the stock, wine, port, salt, pepper and cornflour to the pan. Stir these in well and bring them to the boil. Continue stirring until the sauce thickens. Add the parsley and serve with beef, lamb or chicken.

MOCK BEARNAISE SAUCE

For steak, lamb, vegetables or fish.

1 clove garlic, pressed

Salt and pepper to taste

1 can cream of chicken soup

60g butter, melted

2 teaspoons lemon juice

2 teaspoons tarragon vinegar

2 tablespoons capers

1/4 cup finely chopped parsley

Combine all the ingredients and heat them until they are bubbling. Serve the sauce hot over steak, lamb, vegetables or fish.

MUSTARD SAUCE

For chicken, fish, veal or pork.

1 cup chicken stock

2 teaspoons lemon juice

2 teaspoons French mustard

2 tablespoons cream

2 teaspoons cornflour

2 teaspoons water

Salt and pepper to taste

Combine all the ingredients, except the salt and pepper in a saucepan. Heat and stir until the sauce boils and thickens. Reduce the heat and simmer gently for 3 minutes. Add the salt and pepper and serve with chicken, fish, veal or pork.

RICH CURRY SAUCE

For chicken, turkey, fish or vegetables.

60g butter

2 tablespoons plain flour

2 teaspoons curry powder

2 cups water

2 chicken stock cubes

1/2 cup cream

1 tablespoon mango chutney

Salt and pepper to taste

Heat the butter in a pan. Add the flour and cook for I minute, stirring constantly.

Add the curry powder and cook for a further minute. Add the water and stock cubes. Stir this mixture until the sauce boils and thickens. Reduce the heat, add the cream, chutney, salt and pepper and simmer the mixture uncovered for 5 minutes. Serve with chicken, turkey, fish or vegetables.

TAMARILLO HOLLANDAISE

For fish or vegetables.

3 egg yolks

1/2 cup dry white wine

1 tablespoon vinegar

250g butter, melted

Pepper to taste

Lemon juice

2 tamarillos, pureed

Place the egg yolks, wine and vinegar in a small saucepan. Whisk them over a very gentle heat. (This may best be achieved by placing the small saucepan inside a larger saucepan containing gently boiling water.) Cool the mixture slightly, then gradually add the melted butter. Season this with the pepper and add the lemon juice and the tamarillo puree.

CHEESE SAUCE

For fish, shellfish, vegetables, veal or lamb.

30g butter

1 tablespoon plain flour

1 cup milk

Salt and pepper to taste

1/4 cup cream

1/4 teaspoon mustard powder

2 tablespoons grated Cheddar cheese

Melt the butter in a pan, add the flour and cook for 1 minute. Add the milk, stirring until the mixture boils and thickens. Remove the mixture from the heat and season it with salt and pepper. Add the cream, mustard and cheese. Mix them thoroughly until smooth. Serve by pouring the sauce over fish, shellfish, vegetables, veal or lamb.

CUMBERLAND SAUCE

For ham, lamb or venison.

3 tablespoons redcurrant jelly

1 orange

1 lemon

1 cup red wine

2 tablespoons arrowroot or 2 teaspoons cornflour

Place the redcurrant jelly in a saucepan. Grate the rind from the orange and lemon and add this to the jelly. Add the juice from the orange and lemon together with the wine. Boil the mixture well and simmer for 5-7 minutes. Mix the arrowroot with a small amount of water and add it to the sauce, beating it well. Serve this sauce with ham, lamb or venison.

MINT JELLY

For lamb.
(Makes approximately 2 cups)

1/2 cup finely chopped mint

1 cup white vinegar

3 tablespoons sugar

1/2 packet lime jelly

1/2 cup sweet sherry

Wash, dry and finely chop the mint. Place the vinegar and sugar in a saucepan and bring it slowly to the boil. Simmer it for 3 minutes. Remove the saucepan from the heat and add the mint and lime jelly. Mix well and allow it to cool. Stir in the sherry. Store the jelly in small glass jars.

ASIAN PLUM SAUCE

For pork, ham, chicken, beef or lamb.

1/4 cup plum sauce

3/4 cup water

1 teaspoon chilli sauce

2 teaspoons tomato sauce

2 teaspoons soy sauce

2 teaspoons cornflour

Place the plum sauce, water, chilli sauce, tomato sauce, soy sauce and cornflour in a small saucepan. Heat and stir until the sauce boils. Serve it with pork, ham, chicken, beef or lamb.

Index

212

216